Stitched Up

www.penguin.co.uk

Stitched Up

Stories of Life and Death
from a Prison Doctor

SHAHED YOUSAF

BANTAM PRESS

TRANSWORLD PUBLISHERS
Penguin Random House, One Embassy Gardens,
8 Viaduct Gardens, London SW11 7BW
www.penguin.co.uk

Transworld is part of the Penguin Random House group of companies
whose addresses can be found at global.penguinrandomhouse.com

First published in Great Britain in 2022 by Bantam Press
an imprint of Transworld Publishers

A CIP catalogue record for this book
is available from the British Library.

ISBN 9781787635951

Typeset in 12/14.5 pt Bembo Std by Jouve (UK), Milton Keynes
Printed and bound in Great Britain by Clays Ltd, Elcograf S.p.A.

The authorized representative in the EEA is Penguin Random House Ireland,
Morrison Chambers, 32 Nassau Street, Dublin D02 YH68.

Penguin Random House is committed to a sustainable
future for our business, our readers and our planet. This book
is made from Forest Stewardship Council® certified paper.

This book is dedicated to the countless offender healthcare staff and Her Majesty's Prison and Probation Services staff and their families who work tirelessly to keep us all safe.

Contents

Introduction: A Broken System

Why would anyone want to work with thieves, murderers and rapists? It's a question I've been asking myself for a decade. The year 2022 marks ten years of my working as a prison GP. I can't say it was a lifelong dream to end up behind bars, but it would also be an oversimplification to say it happened by chance. I had attained a degree in Biomedical Science and subsequently attended Warwick Medical School on a graduate entry programme in 2001. I wanted to help people on the margins of society, where the need was greatest. I am from a working-class background myself and grew up in a particularly deprived part of inner-city Birmingham. I was at medical school when I learned about the inverse care law, whereby those who have the greatest need for help are the least likely to receive it. I wanted to do something about it but I wasn't yet sure what form that would take.

The last year of medical school culminated in comprehensive examinations that covered all the learning over the past four or five years, depending on the length of the course. To fail these examinations would mean leaving without a medical degree. I was terrified of failure because there were no doctors in my family and I couldn't take success for granted. This was in 2006 and all of these years later I still have nightmares in which it's the night before my final examinations and I haven't prepared enough. It is a terror that many doctors will be familiar with. To make the situation even worse, unfortunately my father passed away unexpectedly on the night before my finals. In shock from seeing his dead body and having spent a sleepless night mourning with my mother and sister, I still drove to medical school the following morning with tears streaming down my face to sit my exams. It was a horrendous period in my life and one which has left a deep impression on me. I dealt with the bereavement in my own way – by not talking about it and trying to block it out. In retrospect it seems clear to me that I was trying to come to terms with my own trauma by choosing to work with people whose suffering outweighed my own.

As soon as I completed my GP training in 2012 I began to work in a homeless GP practice in the West Midlands. The vast majority of service users I work with are of no fixed abode or vulnerably housed and sleep on the streets, in homeless shelters, or they sofa-surf. Many have substance-misuse issues and inject heroin and smoke crack cocaine or inject a cocktail of both, which they call 'snowballing' or 'speedballing'. The homeless practice offers a needle exchange programme where dirty needles can be disposed of safely and clean needles given to prevent the spread of blood-borne viruses such as HIV and hepatitis. We work closely with the Community Drug Team, who prescribe safer opioid substitution therapies to heroin users, such as methadone and Subutex. The term opioid is used to describe naturally occurring opiates derived from the opium poppy and also synthetic products such as methadone. Long-term studies have shown that treatment works and people are less likely to be involved in crime and violence if they are stabilized on opioid substitution therapies.

A disproportionately large group of our patients have mental-health issues. Many of the female patients, and some of the men, are sex workers and sleep on our doorstep at the practice when they have finished for the night. Our service works closely with SWISH, or Sex Workers into Sexual Health, which is run through the Terrence Higgins Trust. Our SWISH van is unofficially known as the sex bus and one or two evenings a week our nurses drive to where the sex workers are located to offer STI (sexually transmitted infection) testing and free contraception. They also work with nationwide charities and the police to end violence against sex workers and support victims of human trafficking.

Most importantly to me the homeless practice humanizes people. They are our patients rather than 'problems' that need to be dealt with. During cold weather we give them our spare clothes so they can stay warm and dry. We have a partnership with a local cafe and food banks. There are booked appointments but also a drop-in service so the patients can come and see us when it is convenient for them. The practice was originally established by a group of socially minded Christian doctors and although I am a Muslim I feel a sense of pride in continuing their work. Some of our clients are highly educated professionals and former members of the armed forces who have become dependent on alcohol, drugs or gambling and have lost everything. They just need to get back on their feet and we hold out a helping hand.

The homeless practice also accepts violent and aggressive patients who have been removed from other GP lists under the Special Allocation Scheme. Under the scheme we are recognized as a secure environment and have a security guard posted outside our clinic door and a panic button hidden discreetly under the desk in case we are threatened. We're trying to help our patients, yet our front door always smells of the ammonia we use to clean up after some of them urinate against it when intoxicated or angry. Sometimes people aren't willing to accept the help on offer, or they aren't good at appreciating it. Some of the homeless patients will commit petty crimes in the hope that they can spend winter off the streets and in jail where they will be warm, have food and some company.

One of the doctors who worked in the homeless practice mentioned that they also did shifts in prisons and said I might enjoy it. That comment, made in passing, changed my life. Up until that point I was unaware GPs worked inside prisons. I had assumed, without giving it due thought, that prisoners would be taken to a community GP if they needed medical help or that they'd be sent to the outside hospital. I didn't know that offender healthcare was a sub-speciality of primary care and GP services. The terms prison medicine, prison GP, health in justice, healthcare in secure environments and offender healthcare are often used interchangeably, but I use the latter in this book to avoid confusion.

Since 2012 I have worked in women's prisons, with young offenders, and in men's prisons of all categories. Over the past ten years prisons in the United Kingdom have opened and closed but they currently hover around the 120 mark. That's over 88,000 men, women and children being cared for by the healthcare departments of a variety of prisons. Prisons in the UK are categorized from A to D, with A being maximum security and D being open prisons reserved for prisoners due to be released within a few months. Prisoners are sorted into these categories based on the risk they pose to the public if they were to escape. There is a further categorization into remand and non-remand prisons. Remand prisons see people fresh off the streets – sometimes before they have been sentenced. Non-remand prisons only accept sentenced prisoners who are already known to the prison system and are being transferred between sites.

I have heard people say the Covid lockdown has felt like being in prison. Deprivation of liberty and social isolation take a severe mental and physical toll on our well-being. But it is *not* like being in prison. My colleagues and I have been working inside prisons, seeing patients face to face, throughout the lockdown – through extraordinarily difficult circumstances for us and more acutely for the prisoners themselves. Imagine as a prisoner being confined to an eight-foot by ten-foot cell with a fellow inmate, a stranger from whom you have no privacy. This stranger might have issues with their physical health, mental health, substance misuse, antisocial behaviour, or all of the above. There are bars on the window and it might be nailed shut. There is a cell bell which can be used in case of emergencies – but it may not be working or responded to in a timely manner. The ventilation panels are blocked with paint and grime. There is no telephone or shower in the cell. Your thin mattress is on a wooden board which constitutes your bed. Clean sheets and laundry are a luxury. Beside your bed is a toilet which may not be screened off to allow for basic decency and hygiene. You will have no control of the temperature in this airless room, which might fluctuate from freezing to boiling. A kettle and a television will be considered privileges. The water taps, lights and electricity may be faulty. There might be rats and cockroaches. Basic nutrition will be provided to you and you will eat it in your cell – whether it is palatable or of sufficient quantity is another matter. During lockdown tens of thousands of prisoners have been subjected to these degrading conditions for almost twenty-four hours a day. There has been limited time outside of the cells to collect meals, wash, exercise, and contact loved ones. The impact of this appalling sense of isolation will be felt for years to come.

Why do we send people to prison? We send them there as a means of punishment, for rehabilitation, in the interests of public safety and as a deterrence. If you know anything about the prison system in the UK you'll understand why I say prisons mostly seem to look almost identical. Prison architecture resembles a smudged Escher-like drawing of concrete blocks, endless locked gates and staircases. But their greatest similarities lie in the problems they have in common: lack of resources, overcrowding and understaffing.

The Ministry of Justice controls prisons in England and Wales. Her Majesty's Prison and Probation Service (HMPPS) carries out the sentences handed down by the courts. The justice secretary has overall responsibility. When Liz Truss was justice secretary in 2016–17 she admitted that prisons were under 'serious and sustained pressure'. The prison population has risen by almost 70 per cent over the past thirty years. Scotland, England and Wales have the highest imprisonment rates in Western Europe, which means we are facing the worst crisis in the prison system in decades.

Each of the political parties wants to prove they take a tough stance on law and order. Many people, including some of my friends and family, think prisons are 'too soft'. When he was justice secretary for the Conservative Party in 2012 Chris Grayling said he would stop our jails being like holiday camps. This false narrative still prevails and must be challenged. There is a 'them' and 'us' mentality when it comes to prisoners. Many of us think of 'them' as monsters who deserve to be hidden away and fed nothing much better than gruel. This is nonsense – each and every one of us is just one bad decision away from being incarcerated. We could be serving a sentence next week if we were to knock somebody over when driving at forty in a thirty-mile-an-hour zone. Many of my patients in the prison are no different from my patients in the community. If I ignore the bars on the windows, and perhaps the noise, I could imagine I am working outside. However, if you systematically brutalize people, subject them to the indignities of helplessness, boredom and frustration, you will not see them at their best, let alone rehabilitate them. Prisons are a breeding ground for crime, radicalization, substance misuse, mental-health issues, self-harm, rape, suicide and murder.

The prison population continues to grow at an alarming rate and many individuals are forced to cohabit cells, or pads, designed for one. The most common request I get from a prisoner, other than for medications, is to not share a cell with another prisoner. It's not a request that in my position I can grant. Prisons have become cramped environments where bunk beds are the norm and single cells a rarity. There are no double beds or orthopaedic mattresses. No provision for people with claustrophobia, obesity, or for the very tall whose legs overshoot the small beds. The risk assessment of cell-sharing is undertaken by the prison staff and not by healthcare workers. Often prisoners will promise to attack anyone they are 'padded up' with – this is entirely plausible. And it happens. Zahid Mubarek, a British Pakistani teenager, was murdered by his racist cellmate in March 2000. A delayed public inquiry listed a catalogue of prison failings that led to eighty-eight recommendations. This is a sickening statistic indicating, in my opinion, that all cells should be single occupancy.

I am not a criminologist, sociologist or politician, but I am a doctor who works in prisons and I am a taxpayer. It costs the taxpayer an estimated £44,000 a year per prisoner. This cost would be worthwhile if prison sentences were rehabilitative, broke the cycle of crime, and cut down rates of reoffending. But the reoffending rate in England and Wales stands at 48 per cent within twelve months of release. The economic and social cost of reoffending, or recidivism, is estimated to set UK taxpayers back by £15 billion a year. By comparison the annual prison budget is just over £5 billion. Despite sending more people to prison the violent crime rate in England and Wales has risen every year since 2013. For every person we do not send to prison we could employ two prison officers, whose starting salary in England and Wales is a paltry £22,843 for working a gruelling thirty-nine-hour week.

The hard-earned money of UK taxpayers is being wasted on a broken system. There are better solutions and other developed nations are showing us the way. We could compare our system with the rehabilitative programme they have in Norway, which costs more in initial investment per prisoner but leads to vastly lower rates of reoffending, a safer society, and is much cheaper in the long run. Building more prisons and handing down longer sentences are short-sighted solutions – they will further exacerbate the problems we already have. We should review our sentencing policy to keep the prison population down, which can be done sensibly and safely. The staff would then have time to concentrate on helping those who really need it. Locking people behind their cell doors, without any meaningful activity or training, limiting family contacts and visits, with no job opportunities or housing on release, all lead to difficulties reintegrating into society and increase the likelihood of reoffending. There is worrying evidence that children with a parent in prison are twice as likely to become prisoners themselves.

The start of my career in offender healthcare coincided with the coalition government cutting the already stretched prison budget by a quarter. Staffing formed the bulk of the budget. Over the course of five years from 2010 the number of prison officers was cut by 10,000 – an astonishing third of the full-time staff. Officers were responsible for security, supervision, training and rehabilitation of prisoners, and these areas were now even more severely impacted. Moreover, a policy known as 'benchmarking' was rolled out in 2013 in which seasoned officers were encouraged into taking voluntary redundancy. New prison officers were recruited through a fast-track process and given less training and support, so retaining them in the long run became a predominant issue. All this led to a huge amount of instability in prisons across the UK, despite the best intentions of the people working on the front line. After discussions with the government broke down, members of the Prison Officers' Association (POA) staged mass walkouts in 2016 and 2018 to highlight staff shortages and unprecedented levels of violence. The disputes over junior doctor contracts also led to healthcare strikes throughout the NHS in 2016. Front-line staff expressed their concerns in the strongest possible ways to protect those in their care and were subsequently threatened with legal action by policymakers.

There are great disparities in who is sent to prison, for how long and why. Black and ethnic minority men are more likely to be remanded in custody at the Crown

Court than white men. Approximately 10 per cent of people in prison are on remand, the majority of them are awaiting trial, guilty until proven innocent, and many will not receive a custodial sentence when they do go to court. Almost 70 per cent of those currently in prison are there for non-violent crimes, such as possessing drugs. Yet in 2009 the government's 'drug tsar', Professor David Nutt, was forced to resign when he cited evidence that cannabis, ecstasy and LSD were less harmful to individual health and society in general than alcohol and tobacco. Indeed, approximately 40 per cent of those convicted of violent crimes do so while under the influence of alcohol. The consumption of alcohol leads to much more harm, physically, socially and economically, than cannabis. We desperately need to re-evaluate our attitude to drugs and alcohol as a society – and reform our laws in line with the facts.

In 2014 the then Chief Inspector of Prisons, Nick Hardwick, said 'political and policy failure' was behind our prison crisis. Another former Chief Inspector of Prisons, Lord Ramsbotham, was even more scathing when he stated, 'The failure of the prison system is a lack of dedicated, knowledgeable and experienced leadership ... chief executives of the Justice Ministry are politicians who have no working knowledge of the prison service, no management experience of leading large complex organisations.' Maybe a more radical solution is required – one spearheaded by the electorate – who, let's face it, are the only people whose views politicians take into consideration. Anybody applying for a senior role in the Ministry of Justice, Home Office, or to be governor of a prison should really have to spend at least a week living in a prison as a prerequisite for the job. I wouldn't take advice from a doctor who has never seen the inside of a hospital and the same standards should apply to those who seek to lead us by creating policies without the benefit of considerable insight.

I am passionate about literature and medicine and the intersection of the two. The illiteracy rates in prisons are shameful – the reading age of approximately 50 per cent of inmates in England and Wales is less than an eleven-year-old's. Chris Grayling tried to ban books being sent into prison, which was strongly opposed by the Howard League for Penal Reform and the writing community. We know what works in prisons – teaching literacy and numeracy. The excellent Shannon Trust prison literacy charity has taught an estimated 50,000 men and women to read – yet it receives no government funding.

Beyond literacy and numeracy, there are over a hundred different courses taught in UK prisons but scant evidence that they actually work in rehabilitation. Indeed, some might do more harm than good. For example, the Sex Offender Treatment Programme was abandoned after it was shown to increase further sex crimes. What does cut reoffending rates is education, which can release people into employment and stable accommodation.

I hope this book starts a conversation about penal reform, offender healthcare and prisoner welfare. I have been working through a perfect storm of challenges for both the NHS and the prison service, but I love working in offender healthcare – it is a privilege I do not take lightly. It has been both the most fun and the most frustrating work. The most exciting and anxiety-provoking experience. If you speak to anyone who works in prisons, they will have stories galore and the most shocking anecdotes, but underneath it all is a very real concern to protect those in our charge.

I have changed all names unless I have been given express permission to allow someone to be identified. I have merged or altered scenarios, changed dates and personal details for patient confidentiality. I have also used witness experiences from different prisons to form this account. There have been victories but there have also been near misses and disasters. I am aware of my own privilege – I work in prisons and can leave at the end of my shift. The experience of being a prisoner is far more brutal.

1

Offender Healthcare

Let me tell you about offender healthcare, starting with my very first working day in this men's prison. It was Valentine's Day, 2013, and I was made to feel like a criminal as soon as I arrived. My passport was examined closely, my pockets were unceremoniously emptied, and each item subjected to intense scrutiny by the prison officers. Nicotine gum was discovered and held up suspiciously.

'I gave up smoking recently,' I explained.

'Chewing gum is contraband in prisons,' one officer replied gruffly. He pointed to a sign on the wall which listed prohibited items including all recording equipment, cameras, batteries, smart watches, any metal objects, mobile telephones and large amounts of money. The officer yanked apart my doctor's bag and pulled out my blood-pressure machine and electronic thermometer. He said they would need to be confiscated because they contained batteries. I could collect them on my way out.

'What is this?' he asked as he extracted my stethoscope.

'I'm a GP and I need it to listen to hearts,' I said.

'It's got metal tubes that could be used as a weapon,' he replied.

'I need it to do my job,' I said with a little more force.

He relented and after an intrusive pat-down I was waved through and told to sit in the waiting area to be collected by a member of the healthcare team. I was given a visitor's badge and told to display it at all times. I sat in front of a board that identified the prison governor hierarchy with smiling photographs of each member of staff. The number one governor was at the top followed by the deputy governor and then a series of governors for different areas such as Safer Custody or the Offender Management Unit. Below them was a list of operational managers and custodial managers. A lot of managers, I noted. I had no idea what any of their roles or duties entailed and I looked forward to finding out. I was joining the prison as a GP, a relatively senior role, one would have thought, and expected that I would have some basic training in how a prison was run. That did not transpire. A decade later, I still have only a very rudimentary knowledge of how a prison operates outside of the healthcare department – I am sure most prisoners will understand the process better than I do. It turned out that the closest I got to physically seeing the number one governor was his smiling face in that photograph. Within a few months he was replaced and the photos on the board changed like a game of Guess Who? This quick turnover has been matched by the justice secretaries – over the past ten years there have been eight.

I had agreed to work in the prison on Wednesdays, Thursdays and Fridays. I was still employed at the homeless GP practice on Mondays and Tuesdays. Variety, I had concluded, would be the spice of life. My security clearance had finally been approved after a three-month vetting process. My personal, financial and employment history for the past ten years had been investigated thoroughly. If I had been born outside the UK, like many staff in the NHS, the vetting process would have taken much longer. While waiting for my security clearance to come through I was still able to work as a locum through an agency in prisons across the UK – it made no sense to me. The whole process, like my induction, was chaotic. That first day I was kept waiting like an unwanted Valentine's gift. Finally, after forty-five minutes, a woman called Helly from the administration team came to collect me. She apologized for the delay and revealed that no one had been expecting me. This prompted more than a raised eyebrow. I was already frustrated and insisted on showing her my paperwork which indicated my start date had been finalized weeks ago. I was in the right place at the right time, I needed her to know.

'I know. Shit, isn't it? I can only apologize to you, Doc,' Helly replied and shrugged her shoulders. It was a gesture I'd see a lot from various members of staff.

My first day, an hour in and I already had misgivings about offender healthcare and hadn't met any of the prisoners yet. From the off it was clear the prison was

not a well-oiled machine – and, as if to illustrate the
point, I was next led through a series of seemingly endless locked doors and gates and each one creaked
jarringly. With each door that was slammed and locked
behind me I felt my freedom ebb away a little further. I
felt as though I was entering the body of a gigantic
dystopian machine: thunderously loud, with men
shouting and, beneath it all, the unwelcome stench of
overflowing bins. We crossed quadrangles and I saw
men throwing their rubbish out of their windows on
to the quads below, which were also used as the exercise yards. They openly passed items to each other on
the end of long strips of torn bedding that they swung
deftly from window to window.

When we finally arrived in the healthcare department Helly introduced me to the two doctors who
were leaving and who I would be replacing. They had
both been working in prisons for years and had decided
to move abroad after growing disillusioned with
offender healthcare. It was perhaps not what I needed
to hear. Dr A was moving to Dubai and Dr S to Aus-
tralia. They were very gracious and allowed me to
shadow them in their clinics for the day. The first thing
I noticed was that each doctor would see a prisoner in
the clinic room alone – without an officer present. I
hadn't expected that. In the homeless practice there
was always security nearby. The second thing I picked
up was that the doctors didn't shy away from saying no
to patients. In fact they said no a lot and sometimes
would end a consultation abruptly by pointing to the
door and asking the prisoner to leave. I was shocked by
this lack of courtesy. If a prisoner shouted or made

threats against one of the doctors, they appeared not to notice and would simply continue typing their notes. Seasoned pros, they had some advice for me.

'You're a new face and will be popular to start with. They will come to you with lists of problems and will flatter, cajole and bully you. It's important to set clear boundaries or you will get yourself into all sorts of trouble. Believe me; it's not worth it,' Dr S said in a tone of resignation.

I would have liked to spend more time with these doctors and to have been given a more structured induction process. But time was in short supply. They clearly wished me well and, had I delved a little deeper, maybe they would have dissuaded me from working there, which wasn't exactly the outcome the prison was hoping for. And by the end of the week they had gone. So I needed to find my feet quickly. There were supposed to be two doctors working daily. Most of the GPs worked in the community and came into the prison once a week – like my colleague from the homeless practice – but I would be working Wednesdays to Fridays. They all helped me as much as they could but were already struggling with a huge backlog of work in a notoriously hectic prison, one of the largest and busiest category B remand prisons in the UK with approximately twenty men coming in and twenty released on a daily basis. This was referred to as 'the churn' and it was a battle to stay on top of it.

The prison healthcare department is a two-storey building. The lower floor is called the Inpatient unit, otherwise known as the hospital wing. It has a long corridor with locked cells on either side. Most of the cells in the main prison are approximately eight feet by ten feet, but the cells in the Inpatient unit are slightly larger. Sick patients are treated in the Inpatient unit until they are well enough to be transferred back to the main prison. On the upper floor is the Outpatient unit, which is where I am based and where the appointments with prisoners are held.

Our clinic rooms are directly above the Inpatient cells. As the Outpatient and Inpatient units coexist in such close proximity, it is the sounds and smells of the prison that have made a lasting impression on me. Every sound seems to be amplified. I can hear prisoners switching TV channels or singing along to their radios. If they throw furniture around or kick the toilet, or the sink off the wall – and this happens often enough for the sound of shattering porcelain to have become identifiable – it feels like a jolt up my spine. It is almost as if I am sharing a cell with one of the prisoners. Sometimes, like a disgruntled neighbour, I have to go downstairs and ask them to turn down the music because I can't hear my patients during the consultation. Other times I hear a track that I like and pop downstairs to enquire what it is. It's how I first discovered grime music.

Many of the prisoners in the Inpatient unit have been sectioned under the Mental Health Act and are very unwell. They're awaiting beds in community mental-health units, but the number of mental-health beds in England has been cut by 73 per cent, from 67,000 in 1987–8 to 18,400 in 2018–19, despite a surge in requirements. It means some patients have to travel hundreds of miles from 'home' for treatment.

I would be completely without empathy if the sound of another human crying, shouting or screaming didn't affect me. They are tortured sounds, which never become normalized as background noise. On one occasion a man situated directly under my clinic room was having a manic episode. He sang the Pharrell Williams song, 'Happy', at the top of his voice, all day, seemingly without a break. He had a good voice, to give him his due. But after eight or so hours of listening to this I felt uncomfortably close to mania myself. The nurses kindly transferred him to another cell and suggested other songs for him to sing. I could then still hear him, but now he crooned soothing ballads, full of emotion.

The door to my clinic room in the Outpatient unit has a small whiteboard where I write my name every day. My first name is spelled phonetically and is just two syllables Shah-hed. It comes from the Arabic for 'witness'. In my working life I have heard every variation from Sham-med, Shashermed, Shaded, Shade, Shaheeeeed and Shah-red. It is like being called Joan when your name is John. My favourite misnomer is Salad. How a trained nurse, able to pronounce hypertrophic cardiomyopathy, could see my name badge which clearly stated Shahed and read it as Salad is beyond my comprehension. Some of my friends still affectionately call me Salad. My surname, Yousaf, which also has just two syllables, You-saf, is a minefield too. I do not want to be known as Dr Useless, so early on in my career I asked to be called Dr Y. This is how I am still known by my colleagues and patients. If I write my name quickly it reads DRY – much like my sense of humour.

My clinic room looks like a standard room in any
GP practice. There is a desk with a computer and an
examination couch. But the walls are a shade of acid
yellow that seems to pulsate with intensity. When my
eyes are strained from staring at a computer screen all
day I curse whoever decided against inoffensive
magnolia.

In the homeless practice the panic alarm is hidden
under the desk. In the prison's clinic room the bright
green alarms are fixed to the wall at eye level. If at any
point during a consultation I feel threatened and press
the alarm in front of a prisoner, it is likely to antagonize
them further. It is less inflammatory to leave the room
quickly and push one of the silent panic alarms in the
healthcare corridor. An amber light in the ceiling will
flash to inform those in need of help – often great
need – that the officers are aware and on their way.

On the wall above my desk is a light box that doesn't
work. It is covered by a poster of an improbably happy
doctor with a brilliant white smile. It reads in capi-
tals WE ARE HEALTHCARE, TREAT US WITH
RESPECT. Someone has drawn a moustache and glasses
on the doctor's face and blacked out his teeth.

The most notable difference between this space and
a standard GP clinic is the thick bars on all the windows. We are all caged in together, doctor and patients.
The ventilation in prisons is terrible because, despite
the bars on the windows, they can only be extended a
few inches. I'm lucky that my windows have not been
nailed shut, as in some cells, and replaced with ventilation panels. These perforated sheets of metal have
been painted over so many times that the holes are

redundant and there is no airflow. A caged animal would not be held in these conditions. And yet here we are.

The majority of the men I see in offender healthcare are just like any patient in the community. Upper respiratory tract infections like colds and sore throats, chest infections, high blood pressure and diabetes, high cholesterol, back pain, rashes, lumps and bumps, and sometimes cancer and serious illnesses. These individuals are generally more interesting than my patients in the community because their lives are so different from my own and at times they seem to be speaking a different language. When one man came to my clinic complaining of rectal bleeding, I immediately went into panic mode and wondered if he had been the victim of a sexual assault. He waved my concerns away. I excluded red-flag symptoms for bowel cancer and suggested he might have chronic constipation due to the poor prison diet, which mostly resembles slop. The lack of adequate nutrition is highlighted by routine blood tests which show many of our patients have folic acid and vitamin D deficiencies. I asked if I could get a chaperone so I could perform a per rectum or anal examination – I explained it would mean inserting a finger into his rectum.

'I can't, I'm packing,' he whispered.

'Are you going somewhere?' I asked, confused.

'No, I'm *packing*,' he repeated, slowly, as if to a child.

I shook my head, none the wiser. He looked at me pityingly – it was a look I would get a lot when I first started working in prisons. He very kindly explained he had a phone in his rectum. I must have looked very concerned because I assumed it would be a standard-sized phone. He patiently told me it was smaller than his thumb. He needed to wrap it in layers of cling film and often needed to remove and reinsert it quickly.

'I don't even need to use lubrication – I can dry pack – been doing it for years,' he said with some pride.

'That would explain why you're bleeding,' I concluded, and prescribed him laxatives and lubrication. Illicit telephones are common amongst the prisoners – some are designed to evade metal detectors. Inmates want to stay in contact with their families or continue running their drug empires behind bars. The officers are aware of the problem but there's not much they can do. They have bigger issues to deal with.

The computers are very slow, there being an inevitable lack of investment in the technology, and at the start of my working day, while my computer configures my settings, I like to take in the view. A grubby white wall, approximately seventeen to twenty feet in height, encircles the prison. The wall is topped with razor wire which is snagged with plastic bags that flutter like bunting. Sniffer dogs and their handlers guard the perimeter and look for any contraband that might have been thrown over. Sometimes drones fly overhead carrying drugs and telephones. I watch as officers give chase in this game of drones and phones, hoping to get to these parcels before the prisoners can intercept them.

The notice board in my clinic room has patient information leaflets, posters and yellowing 'thank you' cards pinned to it. The most important document is the weekly rota. This shows where all the doctors are expected to be at any time. My mornings begin with a clinic. There are approximately twelve to fifteen appointment slots, each of which is seven and a half minutes in duration. The list can be extended with more patients added to it. This is a remand prison and we often see people within their first twenty-four hours of arrival. The number of patients I am able to see in a clinic depends on how busy the previous twenty-four hours have been in terms of new admissions to the prison. I also see pre-booked patients from our waiting lists.

Each appointment is supposed to be 'one patient with one problem', but the men who come to the Outpatient clinic bring lists of issues so it usually takes more than seven and a half minutes to resolve their concerns. There could also be numerous add-ons, with the nurses asking me to review the patients in their clinics. I can see up to twenty patients in a clinic. Nonetheless, the morning Outpatient clinics have to be finished by 12 p.m. at the latest. Officers will then take the men to collect their lunch and lock them in their cells, and they will have the first of many daily head counts to ensure no one is unaccounted for.

After my Outpatient clinic I used to do a ward round of the Segregation unit, which held up to twenty men. The Seg unit is where the most disruptive prisoners are sent for a period of separation from the general population – and it is in frequent use. Then I would do a ward round of the Inpatient unit, which had twenty beds. I could see up to sixty patients in a morning, which was a very heavy morning by any GP's standards, and would write up my notes during my lunch break. I was also booked in for an afternoon Outpatient clinic with twelve to fifteen slots, which started at 2 p.m. It was only much later that I discovered I should never have been seeing so many patients. Dr A and Dr S had counted the Outpatient clinic as a morning's work and had spent the afternoon dividing up the ward rounds in the Inpatient unit and Segregation unit between them rather than doing an additional afternoon Outpatient clinic. I'm still unsure who thought it was wise for a newly qualified GP to see so many patients in a day. I hadn't signed up to do the work of two doctors. This overworking of newly qualified, and therefore ill-informed, GPs is not uncommon in either prisons or the community. I now insist on doing a clinic in the morning and either a clinic or a ward round of the Segregation or the Inpatient unit in the afternoons, which is a safer and more manageable workload.

The rota also shows who is designated as duty doctor on each day. This is the doctor who, in addition to their other work, will also respond to the many tasks of the duty doctor that are sent electronically throughout the day and will also deal with any emergencies. And there are lots of emergencies. As more doctors began to leave the prison over the first few months after my arrival and either work in the community or move abroad, I became the designated duty doctor on my three working days in the prison. For a young GP, new to offender healthcare, it was a very steep learning curve.

My prison work fascinates my friends, many of whom are doctors themselves. At first they would ask why I would want to work with 'murderers, thieves and rapists', until I explained that I make a point of not wanting to know what any of my patients have done. To me they are people first and we have a duty to care for them. Their criminal records are held on a separate prison computer system called Prison National Offender Management Information System, or P-NOMIS for short, which I've chosen not to have a username or password for. I only have access to my patients' prison healthcare details. The patient sitting in front of me may indeed be a murderer, thief or rapist, but they could also be in prison simply for an unpaid fine or driving while disqualified. I do not need to know.

It is important to me to refer to the men as patients as soon as they enter healthcare. I don't refer to them as prisoners or inmates when I see them in my clinic. I pretend the bars on the windows are absent. I will undoubtedly be aware of who they are and what they've done if they are part of a high-profile case, but I try not to let that cloud my judgement. Often the prisoners are surprised when healthcare staff say we have no idea why they're in prison and don't want to know. One of the dental nurses told me that she had once welcomed a patient into the dental surgery and, by way of greeting, asked him how he was.

'I'm fine,' he told her. 'I am not aroused by children any more.'

'Oh . . . that's good,' she replied hesitantly.

My daily challenges leave my friends and family wide-eyed. I spend a lot of my day running between

emergencies, resuscitating people, stitching injuries and
tending to wounds. One of my friends is my former
office manager Lin from the training GP practice. The
role of the office manager or practice manager who
coordinates healthcare and its staff does not exist in our
prison – we have a head of healthcare and various other
managers. Lin and my family and friends worry for my
personal safety. The best I can tell them is that I always
ensure the patient is seated by the window and I sit
closer to the door in case I need to make a run for it.

We run clinics in the Outpatient unit but also in healthcare clinics in the prison buildings where the men are
housed. These are interchangeably called the wings or
the house blocks and there are half a dozen of them. In
some prisons the house blocks are numbered or named
and in others, like ours, they are given letters. When I
started I was informed by the nurses that the house
blocks of note were D Block, where people with
substance-misuse issues were located, and the VP unit,
where the vulnerable prisoners, who have committed
crimes of a sensitive or sexual nature, are housed.

D Block patients have a history of misusing drugs
including heroin, crack cocaine, alcohol and any manner of prescription pills. Heroin and alcohol use can't
be stopped abruptly because that can lead to seizures
and death. The turkey in 'cold turkey' is cold because it
is dead. If someone is misusing alcohol or heroin they
need to be brought down off it gradually with specialist
help, and that process still has to happen even if they are
in prison. Substance misuse and addiction is an entire
field of medicine and we use medications such as

methadone, Subutex and diazepam, amongst others, to stabilize patients.

A common complaint from the men on D Block is that their methadone dose isn't high enough and they're still suffering from debilitating withdrawal symptoms or 'clucking'. Any doctor who walks on to D Block will immediately be surrounded by a group of men demanding that their doses are increased. These men are often gaunt and pale and sometimes have poorly healing ulcers, sores and blood clots from injecting drugs. The other prisoners sometimes unkindly refer to these men as the walking dead, druggie zombies or drug seekers.

The VP unit is secured off from the rest of the prison by high walls and extra security. The prisoners located here are termed vulnerable because they are vilified by mainstream prisoners who will attack them at any opportunity. The two streams travel through the prison at different times and using different routes to prevent any contact. Not all prisons have a VP unit and some prisons are solely for VPs, but ours is a mixed population where approximately 20 per cent are VPs. They have their own GP clinic room on the VP unit, but if they need to be seen in the Outpatient department they will be secured in a separate waiting room away from the mainstream prisoners. We do everything we can to keep them safe, which is not an easy job when so many people want to do them harm.

The VPs are generally convicted of historical crimes and are decades older than the rest of the prison population. On entering the VP unit doctors may be stopped by men, often in wheelchairs, who want to discuss the particular side effects of their multiple medications.

Whereas the D Block prisoners can be rough in their manner, the VPs are most often effusively and unnecessarily complimentary and polite.

In the centre of the notice board in my clinic room is a poster of a young man on a life-support machine and below it the warning DON'T DICE WITH SPICE! Spice or novel psychoactive substances is a synthetic cannabinoid and very popular in prisons because it can't be detected with a standard cannabis drug-testing kit. The poster I refer patients to the most in my room is in the less than authoritative Comic Sans font and looks a little like this:

FOR THE INFORMATION OF ALL PATIENTS.

Doctors cannot prescribe, or request, the following:

Own trainers / footwear.

Extra / own clothing.

Extra mattresses.

Single cell allocation.

Soft chairs.

This decision has been made following guidance / instruction from the Security Team and the Number One Governor.

The healthcare managers are based in offices directly opposite my room. They generally have a background in nursing or business management. Some are friendly and helpful and others less so. Some never seem to emerge from their rooms and it's difficult to know what they do all day. Although, to be fair, I wouldn't expect them to have an in-depth knowledge of how I organize my working day. But with doors closed it's difficult even to imagine how they're occupying their time. Perhaps they're looking for new jobs. Many leave offender healthcare after just a couple of years and find less stressful work elsewhere. One manager could barely contain her excitement when she announced that she was off to run a guinea pig farm.

There are inevitably tensions between some of the managers and those of us on the front line. Every day we face threats of violence and extreme challenges and it's easy to feel unsupported and unappreciated, especially when we're stressed and feeling vulnerable. The administration staff in particular are grossly overworked and underpaid. Based in an office next door to mine, Helly, Sharon, Lisa and Anne-Marie brighten up what could otherwise be an oppressively dark atmosphere. I love hearing them laugh raucously through our shared wall as I sit at my desk. I relied on them heavily when I first started because offender healthcare had completely different operating systems to community GP practice. They taught me how to book GP appointments and refer patients to the outside hospital. I still need their advice on a daily basis and look for excuses to go to their office – just for a break and often for a laugh.

Helly clamps her hand over her mouth after she swears, which is often. She is a golden ray of light and provides daily updates about her husband Carl's latest misadventures in DIY. Anne-Marie is wickedly funny with a deadpan delivery. Sharon swivels around in her chair and sings the greatest hits of the eighties. When the managers are away we sometimes turn the music up to maximum volume and be silly, dancing away the tension. It's like a pressure valve being released and is vital for our mental health. Nurse Stevie G is always at hand with dad jokes and friendly banter. Nurse Alan always greets me with a handshake and a hair-raising anecdote. Healthcare assistant Sophie starts every day by saying she will give it her full twenty per cent. She actually gives one hundred and twenty per cent because she does her work and some. They are wonderful people. What keeps them, or any of us, coming back day after day? There is a great sense of camaraderie and we look after each other and our patients. We care.

Further along the healthcare corridor are the rooms used by the visiting physiotherapist, optician, podiatrist and psychiatrist. At the very end is a door that leads into the patients' waiting room. The objective is only to send people to an outside hospital if it is an emergency that we can't manage ourselves. If there's no other option then it has to be authorized by the prison officers or governors first. This can lead to friction between healthcare and the prison. Senior officers will often say they don't have the staff needed to escort a prisoner to the outside hospital. They may try to pressurize us into downgrading an emergency. I learned quickly to stand my ground.

'This man needs to go to the outside hospital now. I have already contacted the emergency services and an ambulance is on its way. If you want to turn it away at the gate that is your decision but not one that I can defend medically,' I say matter-of-factly.

The senior officers often, but not always, relent. I have to act in the best interests of my patients and the officers have a duty to protect the public, which they can't do if they are grossly understaffed. The patient will need to be handcuffed and chained to a couple of prison officers, who will escort the individual to the outside hospital, even if he is in a hospital bed. Some prisoners are considered to be so dangerous they need to be accompanied by a small unit of officers. The safety of the public takes precedence over all other considerations. How the prison provides those officers it can ill afford to spare explains why it's something of a stand-off.

The prison officers keep the public safe from the worst of the worst. But the officers are demoralized, underpaid and feel overlooked – they refer to themselves as the forgotten fourth emergency service. If an officer calls in sick it could lead to their colleagues being overstretched and therefore placed in danger. I have known officers with bloodied lips and black eyes refuse to take sick leave. They are under extraordinary strain but always put the safety of the prison, and the public, before their own. I have a lot of respect for them. Relations between the officers and healthcare staff are often cordial and sometimes far more than cordial. I fully appreciate that my experience of officers might be vastly different if I was a prisoner and going out of my mind with pent-up frustration.

At the other end of the healthcare corridor are the stairs that lead down to the Inpatient unit. In the corner is a jumble of boxes and a heap of broken chairs that hurriedly need to be moved whenever there is a visit from the Care Quality Commission to ensure we are maintaining high clinical standards. Here at the end of the corridor is also the coffee room, where we go to unwind. Rather than scrolling through social media when we have a break, the healthcare staff talk to each other, encouraged at least in part by the fact that no mobile phones or smart technology are allowed in the prison. We lock them in our cars before entering the site. Sometimes, in the coffee room, the microwave beeps and we all panic and reflexively pat ourselves down in case we've left our phones in our pockets. We chat about our days, and sometimes we shout. We are directly above the noisy Inpatient unit and often have to raise our voices to be heard. It's good to talk and share information. But healthcare is also an intense and claustrophobic environment that can breed gossip, half-truths and hearsay. Something said in jest can quickly escalate. For example, two nurses refused to work together and hadn't spoken for years merely because one had complained about the other's fishy lunch.

We all need time away from each other occasionally, and our workplace. I gave up smoking in 2012 and by the time I started working in prisons I sorely missed it as an excuse to walk outside of those crushing walls. The air beyond the peeling white edifice somehow smelt fresher and tasted sweeter. I guess it was a lungful of freedom rather than nicotine that I was craving.

There was no staff cafeteria on the site when I started the job, instead there was a snack vending machine in the visitors' centre. In addition, the League of Friends came in three times a week with sandwiches and tea-cakes. In the absence of a cafeteria, most of us bring in packed lunches or ready meals. I am British of Paki-stani heritage and wear both of my identities with pride. I am wholly one and wholly the other, not half and half. There is a little crossover in the middle where the Venn diagram circles intersect in interesting and contradictory ways. My parents were both keen to replicate the bonds of sharing food and hospitality, a custom they were brought up with in Pakistan. As a consequence I have a snack drawer in my office which is brimming with goodies to share and which needs to be replenished regularly. I like to think that any friendly chat with Dr Y will involve a snack of some description.

We are discouraged from eating at our desks by Infection Control. Infection Control has clearly never visited the coffee room. The magnificently stained carpet is a Rorschach test of filth. There is a toaster which smells of burning plastic. The toaster and kettle can't be plugged in at the same time because they trip the department's entire electrical supply. The cluttered fridge benevolently showers food on whoever accesses it. As with any shared fridge, food routinely goes missing – or off. Ceremoniously stuck to the front of the fridge is a mission statement the managers created around the time I started work, designed to give us a sense of corporate identity as we stand in line waiting to heat up our lunches. A little tired now, it reads like this:

Our Vision
Our vision explains that we desire to be a leading organisation that works in partnership with service users and commissioners to provide integrated healthcare solutions in a responsive environment.

Our Values

Our values demonstrate what we believe in and how
we will behave: **CARERS** –

Caring – caring for carers, kindness and concern
   in the workplace
Approachable – pleasant and approachable,
   communicative and helpful
Receptive – flexible and open-minded
Empathic – responsive to the thoughts and feelings
   of others
Reasonable – rational and fair
Sensitive – thoughtful and receptive

'I wouldn't wipe my arse with that,' one of my new
colleagues said.

'It's laminated,' another helpfully pointed out.

Sometimes my friends ask what prisons smell like.
Prisons – due to their disgracefully poor aeration – have
a muggy stink of men's feet, mouldy showers and discarded food. On a hot day the entire prison hums like
an overflowing dustbin. Many of the men are obsessive
about their personal hygiene and try to shower daily if
they are allowed to by the officers. The cells don't have
showers in them and two men often share a cell and a
toilet. They hang a bed sheet up around it for some
minuscule sense of privacy and, rather understandably, a
fight can break out over a smelly poo.

When the officers unlock the men in the mornings
for what's called free-flow, they line up to wait for a free
cubicle in the communal washing facilities. Some of these
rooms have broken showers and inadequate drainage. The

water pressure and temperature are widely variable. The men always wear flip-flops in the showers because they can end up ankle-deep in swampy water. They are understandably paranoid about catching infections due to the low standards of hygiene – the prison's, not theirs – and every rash is feared to be scabies. When the men need to be examined by a doctor or nurse and they haven't showered that day they often apologize profusely if they smell. They are at pains to differentiate themselves from the dirty environment which houses them. At every opportunity they slather themselves with cocoa butter and deodorant, and sometimes this can be a little overpowering.

In between seeing patients my door will always be ajar and staff will wander in and ask for advice or chat or indeed share a snack. Amongst the staff at least, the prison has an informal environment not customarily seen in GP practices or in hospitals. It is Helly's ritual to pop into my room every morning, ask how I am, and weigh herself using my weighing scales.

'Another day in paradise!' she says, as she balances on one foot to make herself lighter. It is the standard greeting amongst staff along with 'Living the dream'.

It isn't, and we aren't.

She plonks herself down next to me and I offer her biscuits and chocolates from my 'secret' snack drawer. I became a doctor because I like people. I am always curious to learn why any of my colleagues also ended up working in prisons. The staff, like the prisoners, all have different stories to tell. Helly admits she came to her prison interview to be nosy, to scratch an itch about what it's like in prison. She likes crime dramas and wanted to see inside. She hadn't expected to get the job. She certainly hadn't expected to stay so long. Her family jokes that they always knew she would end up in prison. The prisoners respond well to Helly's down-to-earth attitude. She treats them like normal people, rather than monsters. That, I soon realized, was the key.

Prison has a reputation for attracting oddballs amongst the staff, a category in which Helly includes herself and me – in a good way, she assures me. There is no other place quite like it, and before too long it becomes difficult to imagine working anywhere else. Every other job would be boring by comparison. Offender healthcare staff can quickly become somewhat institutionalized. We like being in self-imposed exile. We like being cut off from the chaos of the outside world and the feeling you get when you step through the gates that you're leaving your problems as well as your phone behind. Only I had in fact brought plenty of my problems with me. Not too long before starting the job I had experienced the worst year of my life and I don't think many of my new colleagues would have guessed I was harbouring dark thoughts. My way of dealing with it was to choose to hide away. In a prison of all places.

2

Welcome to Hell

I quickly discovered exactly how someone goes from being a free man to being locked up. It was eye-opening, to say the least. And Mr R was my teacher.

Mr R was driving to collect his son from school when the police arrested him. They sealed off the road and ordered him to exit his personalized Ferrari at gunpoint. He told them there must have been a huge misunderstanding.

'I'm an accountant, married to a doctor!' he shouted, protesting his innocence with his middle-class credentials.

The police confirmed his identity. Mr R was hand-cuffed and taken to the police station for questioning, whereupon his belongings were confiscated, including his phone, tie and shoelaces. He was escorted to a small cell until his solicitor arrived. There he was informed by the police of the code of practice they followed. He sobbed when a nurse reviewed him. There were no issues with his physical health, mental health or substance misuse.

'You can't just arrest people like this. I have rights! I'm an innocent man. I need to speak to my wife. My son needs to be picked up from school. No one knows where I am. You have left my unlocked car by the side of the road! This isn't right. This can't be happening to me,' Mr R kept repeating.

The police officers provided him with sugary cups of tea and checked on him every few minutes. If he had been under the age of eighteen or a vulnerable adult, the police would have contacted his guardian or found an appropriate adult from a list they had to support him. This was all standard procedure and when Mr R's solicitor arrived the police interviewed their suspect under caution and it was recorded as evidence. The proviso was the staple of any police procedural: 'You do not have to say anything. But it may harm your defence if you do not mention when questioned something which you later rely upon in court. Anything you do say may be given in evidence.'

The police had been investigating Mr R for months. They asserted that he had been laundering money for a huge drug-smuggling cartel. He shook his head in disbelief. He said they had the wrong man. Mr R assured them he would be taking legal action against them for this wrongful arrest.

They asked him what he was doing with tens of thousands of pounds in the boot of his car. Mr R's car had not been left neglected by the roadside. It had been impounded and was in the care of the police.

Mr R's solicitor advised him to reply 'no comment' to all further questions.

He was held in police custody for twenty-four hours and questioned again. The police applied to a magistrates' court to hold him for longer. He was suspected of a serious crime and this extension was granted. His solicitor argued that the evidence was circumstantial and requested that Mr R be released on police bail. This was on the understanding that Mr R would return to the police station for further questioning. The request for police bail was denied because Mr R had international contacts and was considered to be a flight risk.

The case was passed to the magistrates' court in the first instance and, because it was a serious criminal matter, it was then transferred to a Crown Court. From there Mr R was handcuffed and informed that he would be taken to a remand prison to await trial.

'I'm going to jail *before* my trial?' he asked in disbelief.

Prison transport is uncomfortable. The prison vans are called sweatboxes for good reason. They are filled with small locked compartments no larger than a public toilet cubicle. The vans travel to prisons and courts throughout the country and it can be a very long journey. It's also a claustrophobic experience for the accused that foreshadows the prison cell awaiting them.

When Mr R arrived at the prison site the van passed the entrance sign which had been vandalized. Through a combination of scratchings-out and some good work with heavy marker pens it now read Welcome to Hell.

The prison vans park outside the gates while a series of lengthy checks need to be performed. There can sometimes be a queue of vans, which leads to a long wait for new prisoners who are already nervous. Finally the prisoners are taken off the van one at a time and into a part of the prison called Reception. The word 'reception' conjures images of a warm welcome, of water dispensers and pot plants. But prison Reception is a rabbit warren of corridors, holding cells and rooms. The new prisoners shout to be heard over the din of doors and gates being slammed – the noise is overwhelming and constant. For anyone who hasn't been in prison before it can be terrifying – and Mr R was terrified.

He sat in a corner of the holding cell and tried not to make eye contact with anyone. One of the other prisoners was huge, even by prison standards, with tear-drops tattooed under both eyes. He kept asking Mr R if he had any smokes. Mr R shook his head almost constantly, but the questions kept coming. A dishevelled-looking man sat in the far corner of the cell, pulled down his trousers, and defecated on the floor because there was no toilet. The small room quickly filled with the stench. Mr R covered his mouth and began to gag. The other men started to kick the door and demanded to be let out for fresh air. The door remained closed.

Finally a prison officer collected Mr R. He was strip-searched behind a curtained cubicle. This is humiliating but it's mandatory, unfortunately, and is done to avoid people smuggling drugs and weapons into the prison. Sometimes the men hide contraband behind their scrotums. Mr R was clean. He was given the standard prison uniform of a grey tracksuit and light blue T-shirt.

There are no pockets in the uniforms, which is to avoid the concealment of contraband – and part of the reason why orifices are so popular. Generally, seasoned prisoners store their valuables in their socks. Another sign of someone at home in a prison is the habit of resting their hands on the inside of their joggers as if cupping their private parts. Maybe they feel vulnerable, like footballers defending a free kick, and are similarly preparing for a strike. Or it's more likely that they have cold hands and are keeping themselves warm. It certainly puts me off shaking hands with them. Mr R had to sit on a metal-detecting chair called a BOSS chair. The chair bleeps if it detects metal in a body. He was cleared to move on to the next stage of the Reception process.

His telephone had already been confiscated, but prisoners are given a few minutes to write down important phone numbers, addresses and dates. The officers sort through piles of clothes and the prisoners' belongings, which are logged and bagged for storage. They are collected on release – if they are not misplaced. Mr R was wearing an exceptionally expensive watch – it was studded with flawless diamonds. This presented a problem. If it were to be mislaid it would be a major incident. The number one governor was contacted and permission sought for it to be stored in a locked safe.

Mr R was then asked a number of questions and signed short-term contracts called compacts in which he agreed to abide by prison rules. He was photographed and given a prison ID card, which he was told he must keep with him at all times. And, if he wasn't already feeling sufficiently dehumanized, Mr R was allocated a unique prison number which was as important, if not more important, than his name. A prison number is typically something like A1234AB. It would become second nature to recite his number along with his name in prison. His personal details, photograph, fingerprints and details of the offence were uploaded on to P-NOMIS. He then had to wait for healthcare staff to assess him.

Mr R was a smoker; he was a connoisseur of the best-quality Cuban cigars, which he kept in a fumigator. He was issued with a smoker's pack, which contained a small amount of tobacco and a lighter. Mr R was given a plastic bowl, cup and a spoon. He was also given a single breakfast pack which consisted of a tiny bag of cereal that would barely sate a toddler. He was provided with a small carton of long-life milk, a tea bag or sachet of coffee and possibly some sugar, if available. He would be expected to have his breakfast in his cell before he was unlocked in the morning. All meals would be eaten alone, or with a cellmate, and not around a communal table as we so often see in prison dramas.

Many of the prisoners are familiar faces for whom prison is a second home. The officers greet them with a mix of joviality and irritation. But for first-timers like Mr R the staff do recognize that this 'welcome' can be a terrifying process. Sometimes first-timers are unkindly referred to as Fraggles, the skittish creatures from the children's television programme *Fraggle Rock*. In prison, there is a nickname for everything. To help soften the blow, trusted prisoners are given an enhanced status and can become Insiders or be trained by the Samaritans charity to become Listeners. They are invaluable in providing reassurance for first-timers. Men join the Listeners and Insiders training programmes for various reasons. There are some men who seek the roles for extra time out of their cells and the opportunity to ingratiate themselves with the officers. However, there are definitely those who, possibly for the first time in their lives, are being trusted and asked for help and provide it wholeheartedly.

Listeners and Insiders sit with first-timers during Reception and talk them through the process and allay their fears – as best they can – and offer advice. That is the idea. But it isn't always the case. VP and mainstream prisoners are separated into different holding cells as soon as they arrive in the prison. One of the Insiders liked to torment the new VPs or sex offenders by going up to the VP holding cell and hissing that tonight was 'Rapey Night'.

Prisoners are allowed a two-minute phone call to inform family and friends of their location. Some of these men, like Mr R, have no intimation that they might be going to prison. The majority have not even been given a court date yet. All they know is that they are in prison on remand and awaiting trial, which could be six months or more from now. They will not be returning home for the foreseeable future. Their life as they have known it – family, work, bills – has come to a sudden halt. What if there is no one to pick up the pieces? What if there is a pet at home that needs caring for? Or an ailing relative? Will they lose their house or their flat if they fall into arrears? Will their belongings be repossessed? How can they possibly make sense of all of this and explain these strange new circumstances to themselves, let alone anyone else.

Mr R used his two minutes to explain to his wife that their lives had just collapsed.

'This is all a terrible mistake,' he kept repeating to her until the line cut out.

'Don't upset yourself. Everything will be alright. Just get your head down and tomorrow you can have a fresh start,' a lovely female officer said to him.

'I won't survive here. This is not me. I'm not cut out for prison,' Mr R whispered.

'You'll be just fine, we'll look after you,' she replied gently.

These small acts of kindness can be a shining moon in someone's ominously dark sky. I quickly realized that most of the staff who work here want to help people. However difficult their jobs are, they try to make life a little more tolerable for others: for the prisoners and for each other. We are, as they say, all in it together. The officers and healthcare staff are generally friendly and obliging, and far outweigh the gruff members of staff, the troubled souls who thrive on misery. Those are best avoided, like the officer who, when I returned from some leave, went out of his way to find me.

'Been away?' he asked, pleasantly enough.

I nodded.

'You weren't missed,' he said, and smiled triumphantly.

'Why would you tell me that?' I asked.

He had no answer and sauntered away merrily, his day brightened.

Some months later this officer collapsed at work and I was asked to help him. He seemed to forget how often he had professed to my colleagues that he disliked me. He held my hand and tearfully thanked me for helping him. I wished him a speedy recovery as the ambulance took him to hospital. People are infinitely complicated. It's a privilege to be able to care for them when they need help the most.

Mr R was assessed by Kitch, the Reception Nurse Team Leader, for what is known as a first-night screening. By his own admission, Kitch is an unlikely nurse. He balances a pen behind his ear, which is a habit picked up from his days as a builder. Along with his nursing credentials he has a City and Guilds qualification in bricklaying. He looks like a cheeky schoolboy. Kitch has a habit of pulling up the neck of his top to cover his mouth when facing authority figures. He is the perfect nurse for Reception, where his 'blokey' friendliness puts the men at ease.

After starting off on the building sites, in his late twenties he'd gone to night school for three years and got a BTEC in social care and GCSEs in maths and English. He was accepted on to a mental-health nurse training programme and qualified three years later. He'd then worked in an acute psychiatric ward for six years. While there, he'd been offered a secondment in prison for a year – and that was fifteen years ago.

The full health and well-being assessment of Mr R included a physical, sexual, mental-health and substance-misuse history. He also underwent a basic set of observations including blood-pressure and temperature

checks. There were concerns about how distressed he
was. Kitch explained he would therefore also need to
be assessed by me, the prison doctor. Kitch booked Mr
R on to the end of my ever-increasing patient ledger. I
was already frazzled from seeing a stream of newly
arrived patients, the majority of whom were withdrawing from drugs and alcohol. Some were being sick or
messing themselves, others had infections around their
drug-injection sites. We always check for blood clots in
their calves called deep vein thrombosis (DVT), which
if untreated can lead to a clot breaking off and lodging
in the lung, causing a potentially fatal pulmonary
embolism, or travelling to the brain and causing a stroke
or even death. Some of the patients informed us they
had serious mental or physical health problems such as
epilepsy or schizophrenia and had been neglecting
their medications for months, which meant they were
clinically unstable.

The healthcare computer system used in UK prisons
is not fully integrated with the NHS or community
GP systems. Which is to say, I do not have immediate
access to the prisoners' GP records from the point of
entry. In that first consultation there is little to rely on
beyond what the men tell me – and they might be
psychotic, confused, withdrawing from drugs and
alcohol, physically unwell, tired, hungry, angry, lying,
or all of the above. The GP records will need to be
requested by our admin team and it can take up to a
week before a brief summary arrives. At first this felt
like working in A&E, if A&E was being run by one
relatively junior and inexperienced doctor, who is

blindfolded and using a toilet as a clinic room. And then I got used to it.

The officers frequently remind me that all of the men need to be reviewed and locked up by 8 p.m. at the latest. This may be an achievable task if there isn't already a steady queue of prison transport waiting outside the prison with the men still trickling in at 7 p.m. Rather than burst a blood vessel with rage I explain, as calmly as possible, that I am working as quickly and safely as I can. Whoever can't be seen tonight will be reviewed first thing in the morning. The day staff finish work at 8 p.m. and the prison needs to be shut down and locked up completely by 10 p.m. This is when the prison enters Patrol State and no prison cell will be unlocked until the morning unless there's an emergency. The night officers will then patrol the site and one or two night nurses have to deal with any medical emergencies overnight.

Kitch put Mr R into one of the many holding cells opposite my clinic room, effectively a pen approximately ten by twelve feet with toughened plastic windows and doors. There are some benches bolted to the floor so they can't be used as weapons. Often prisoners in the holding cells kick the doors and demand to be let out to use a toilet. They beg for food or water or methadone and medications. They call to me as I walk up and down the corridor ferrying patients to my Reception clinic.

'Where's my methadone? I'm sick. Please, I'm sick.'

'Are you a doctor? Doctor ... Doctor, don't leave me here, please, I'm dying.'

It's terrible to see them huddled together in such a small space. There is a sweaty stench of fear and desperation. The Reception process is exhaustive and can take hours and by the time they are due to see a doctor many of the prisoners just want to go to bed. The doctors will prescribe emergency medications including alcohol detoxes and methadone stabilizations to make them comfortable overnight, before assessing them properly in the Outpatient clinic the following morning.

Newly arrived prisoners without any health issues are taken to the Induction wing to try to acclimatize. Those with drug issues go to D Block. VPs to the VP wing. If anyone is very unwell they are moved to the Inpatient unit – if there is a space. Over the first few weeks the prison officers will orientate them. They will be shown how to arrange for money to be sent into their prison account. Strictly no cash is allowed. All prisoners are expected to work or to be in education in the prison. Many lack basic literacy and numeracy skills – others with more advanced education, like Mr R, can enrol on Open University courses. If they are in full-time work or education they are paid a nominal amount per week, usually around ten pounds, a sum which is transferred directly into their prison bank account. Prisoners can start working in the industrial units and small factories within the prison, and each prison has different workshops and courses such as bricklaying, painting and decorating, and double glazing. The men can work as wing cleaners and in waste management and recycling.

They spend their money in two ways. They buy

phone credits to call numbers that have been vetted – there are no phones in the cells. The public phones are situated on the noisy landings, so all private conversations have to be shouted over the clamour and can be overheard by a line of prisoners waiting to use the phone. To add to the lack of privacy, all telephone calls are recorded and monitored by the security team. The prisoners also buy food and toiletries, which can be ordered on a weekly mail-order system called Canteen.

Opposite the Reception holding cells is a door with a battered metal sign that reads 'Do not kick the door'. It has been ignored quite spectacularly. This tiny room is in fact a toilet, but it is being used as the Reception doctor's clinic room. When the light is switched on the floor shimmers over the torn linoleum and silverfish dart into the corners. There is a toilet and sink on one side and a small desk and chair pushed against the opposite wall. The room is bare of even the most basic clinical equipment like a blood-pressure machine or weighing scales. The door has to be wedged closed with a piece of cardboard or it swings open of its own accord.

When I was first orientated around the prison and shown this room I had laughed, thinking it was an elaborate joke. I peered at the dust bunnies that had gathered in the corners and the mouldy cups piled in the sink. Folders of patients' notes had fallen down the back of the desk and were wedged against the wall. I noted a red-top newspaper which was four years out of date. There was no evidence of cleaning and everything was covered in a thick layer of grime. Of the two strip lights overhead only one was working, and it flickered with a nauseating pulse. The panic button was out of reach and there was no telephone. There was no room for a couch. If an emergency occurred and a patient needed to be examined, they would have to be laid down on the filthy floor with their head beside the toilet or facing a door that could swing open at any time. I had stipulated that there was no way I would ever examine a patient on the floor. It was disgusting and I refused to overlook the affront to staff and patient dignity. It was in contravention of good medical practice and the General Medical Council guidelines. But I was told there were no other rooms available in Reception.

Over the next few months there were times when, against my better judgement, I laid a patient on my coat and examined them on the floor. All I could do to voice my frustrations about the conditions was to complete an Incident Report. The IR was sent to the managers to review and take action. No action was taken for years, until finally the toilet was removed and a couch provided. I only wish I was allowed to bring my phone into prisons so I could take photographs of this and other rooms to share the conditions in which the prisoners are being treated. It's shocking.

Outside the Reception clinic room the roar of prisoners rages against my door. I try to spend more time with people who have never been to prison before, like Mr R. He was one of sixteen men I would assess on this particular evening. Many have been to prison before; some were only released a few days ago, and here they are again. They greet me like a friend, even though I may not have seen them before, so familiar are they with the whole set-up. And it is, they think, the way to get what they want.

'How have you been, Doc? You're looking well. Can you sort me out some sleepers?'

From the corridor, Kitch unlocked the door to the holding cell for me. He asked who I was due to see next. I showed him the name I had scribbled on my long list.

'Mr Harrison,' Kitch called into the waiting room.

All eyes on us, and eventually a dishevelled-looking man began to shuffle to the front. Ah. The gentleman who had relieved his bowels in the corner of the room. His long grey hair was straggly and his face was swollen and discoloured from chronic alcoholism but, incongruously, he had brilliant white dentures and a wide smile. The huge prisoner with teardrop tattoos under his eyes pushed in front of Mr Harrison as he slowly made his way to the door.

'I'm Jamie Lovell. I'm going in front of this crusty crackhead,' the man announced. He towered over me and Kitch. I tried not to flinch.

'The doctor has asked for Mr Harrison first,' Kitch said.

'I am from the Lovell family. We get what we want.'

'Not today you don't. Get back in the holding cell,' Kitch responded flatly.

'Or what?'

'Or you will get nothing and plenty of it,' Kitch told him. The line seemed to work. Mr Lovell retreated.

I could smell the unmistakable aroma of cannabis over the reek of faeces which had not been cleaned up. Kitch caught it too.

'Who is smoking?' he demanded.

Mr Harrison dropped a roll-up cigarette he had concealed behind his back and began to sway. He fell to the floor and there was a sickening thud as his head hit the concrete. He began to kick out his legs and jerk both arms. A seizure. His head was twitching and he was frothing at the mouth. The other men in the holding cell moved away from him, backs towards the walls – both alarmed and fascinated. Kitch pushed a panic button and an amber light began to flash above us.

'Code Blue, Code Blue in Reception,' he said into his radio, using the shorthand for a seizure, chest pain, or illicit drug use.

Officers and nurses ran out of the rooms that line the Reception corridor. The nurses were carrying large resuscitation bags and portable oxygen tanks. We all entered the cell to begin cardio-pulmonary resuscitation and the other prisoners squeezed further into the periphery. We pumped down on Mr Harrison's chest and breathed into his mouth through pocket masks. As soon as was possible, we passed an i-gel tube to aid breathing down his windpipe for ventilation and attached the oxygen cylinder. I placed a needle in a vein in the back of Mr Harrison's hand so that we could administer medication. All the while we spoke to him to explain what we were doing, despite him being unconscious. Throughout, Mr Lovell provided a mocking commentary.

'Shut the fuck up, Lovell,' an officer eventually yelled.

'Go on, restrain me, I ain't scared of no screws. I'll give as good as I get!' Mr Lovell screamed. He began pummelling his chest like a silverback.

The officer called for assistance on his radio. Within seconds a large group of officers arrived. They leapt over us to restrain Mr Lovell as we worked on the resuscitation. Mr Lovell was fighting them, as promised, but was soon overpowered and laid out on his front with his arms and legs twisted behind his back. I was swimming in an ocean of flailing limbs, shouting, screaming, drugs and insanity. I had never felt more alive.

'Get your fucking fingers out of my gooch, you pervert. You're all a bunch of nonces,' Mr Lovell screamed.

I didn't know what a 'gooch' was or a 'nonce' at the time and made a mental note to research it later. I was watching the trace of Mr Harrison's heart on the automated external defibrillator (AED) machine. It was a flat line.

'It's a flat line and you need to shock him, I saw it in a film, and my wife's a doctor,' Mr R informed me from the sidelines. By now, he and the other prisoners had climbed up on to the benches that surrounded us to give us more room to work. They were watching events unfold in a hushed silence.

'A flat line is an unshockable rhythm, the film obviously didn't hire a medical expert,' I replied more calmly than I felt.

I guided my colleagues through the resuscitation process: two minutes of cardio-pulmonary resuscitation before reassessing. Pressing hard and fast. Every two minutes we swapped places to prevent fatigue. I checked Mr Harrison's cardiac rhythm on the AED machine. It was a quivering line, which indicated the heart was moving in a disordered fashion, like a bag of worms. The AED machine announced in a robotic voice that we needed to shock the heart to stop it and restart it properly.

'Stand clear, oxygen away, charging, shock!' I shouted, and pushed the button. Mr Harrison's body convulsed and we immediately resumed resuscitation.

Before I worked in prisons I knew nothing about spice. It is by far the most popular drug in prisons because it's difficult to detect on standard drug tests. It can be sprayed on paper and sent into prisons within letters that otherwise appear normal. Paper containing spice can be cut into tiny pieces and ingested on the tongue as a tab or smoked. I would soon spend my days with the nurses rushing to Codes and emergencies with spice being the cause time and again. Spice has many names: legal highs, synthetic cannabis, novel psycho-active substances, NPS, PS, rice or black mamba. And, although people also call it 'fake weed' or 'synthetic marijuana', it is much more potent than regular cannabis because it's sometimes adulterated with fish tranquillizer and cockroach killer, laboratory-made chemicals with mind-altering effects. One brand is called 'Man Down' because it promises to almost coma-tose the user. Regular users are referred to by other prisoners as 'spice-heads'. Spice can make people psy-chotic, paranoid and aggressive. In the prison they jump off the landings, bounce off the walls and swallow their tongues. We resuscitate them and, often, they do it all again an hour later. There are so many spice- and mamba-related emergencies that the prisoners refer to the frequent ambulances at the prison as the Mambulance. Deemed not fit for human consumption and therefore outside of controlled drugs legislation, spice was finally criminalized in 2016.

'Come on, mate, wake up!' I said to Mr Harrison.

Right on cue, like some terrible B-movie, Mr Harrison sat up, gagged, and pulled the tube out of his throat. His dentures fell into his lap and he neatly slipped them back in as he blinked himself awake. Around us, the prisoners clapped and cheered. The nurses collected up their equipment and took Mr Harrison to the Inpatient unit to be monitored overnight. The officers hauled Mr Lovell to his feet and informed him they were taking him to the Segregation unit. It would be a period of isolation, possibly no more than twenty-four hours, where he could reflect on his behaviour. He screamed and shouted insults as they dragged him down the corridor.

I called for my next patient, Mr R. We were both exhausted from our long days. It was probably the worst day of his life, but for me, in my new job, it was just Wednesday. Mr R was now dressed in prison clothes with his ID badge clutched tightly in his sweaty hand. And still he looked out of place. The scent of his expensive aftershave lingered. I told him that my clinic was a safe space and it was OK to vent his feelings. I spoke to him as gently and as soothingly as the pervasive clamour would allow. I said I could only imagine how difficult and frightening this must be for him.

He spoke quietly at first. He was polite and dignified. Then he began to cry with sobs and hiccups of misery. He rested his elbows on the small desk and buried his face in his hands. Rivulets of tears flowed through his fingers and down his arms. There was a box of tissues on my desk. I didn't push them towards him in case he read this as a signal to stop. He could take as much time as he wanted.

'I did it. I was laundering money. I've been such a fool,' he sobbed.

3

The Doctor Will See You Now

For the first few weeks in the prison I wasn't allowed to 'draw keys', which is the given phrase for being allowed to have your own keys and to move around the institution freely. I had to wait at the gate to be collected in the mornings and was then accompanied at all times throughout the day. All the doors in the prison, including healthcare, were locked on the outside when not in use. It was embarrassing to have to ask for permission to go to the toilet. Someone would have to unlock the door and wait outside until I was done. My liberty was removed and it was an immersive and important experience of being behind bars.

I couldn't be entrusted with keys until I had passed a 'Key Walk and Talk' assessment. Keys are the most valuable tool we – the staff – possess. They are held on a chain attached to our waist belts and housed in a buttoned pouch. Keys should always be in the pouch when they are not in use; if they're visible, they're vulnerable. To lose our keys means instant dismissal. One of the prison doctors had not too long ago been 'walked to the gate', which meant removed with immediate effect. He had had a habit of holding his keys in his hand and not attaching them to the key chain. He must have left them on his desk in between seeing patients and some-one reported him – they didn't have to be taken, just the possibility of their theft was enough to justify his dismissal. If a prisoner steals our keys it's a major secur-ity breach. Every lock in the prison will have to be changed at great expense. The next 'Key Walk and Talk' assessment was scheduled for six to eight weeks' time. Until then I would need a constant chaperone.

Luckily for me Nurse Graham offered to be my guide. He was the attentive Virgil to my Dante as I first explored this underworld. Graham is in his late fifties with a neat side parting through thick hair and a square jaw. The other nurses joke that he looks like a seventies porn star sans moustache. He is dual qualified, which means he is a mental-health nurse as well as a general nurse. He can stitch a prisoner's self-harm wounds and take a mental-health history at the same time. Graham also worked as a prison officer in a category A prison for years and I couldn't have asked for a more encyclo-paedic introduction to offender healthcare. He has a cheerful manner and he finds the humour in any situ-ation, as if he is panning for gold in muck. His partner Marie, one of the healthcare assistants, shares his warm temperament. Graham and Marie soon became my work mum and dad.

'Living the dream,' Graham will say every morning.

It is the archetypal greeting from prison staff. I soon adopted it.

I had a question. 'Gray, most of the prisoners I have seen have been huge. It's like they're on steroids,' I said.

'They probably are,' he replied. 'Don't let them intimidate you, Dr Y. Some of them will like getting under your skin. It's entertainment for them. They want to see you lose your cool and get angry. Don't give them the satisfaction. It's important to look confident, especially when you don't feel it. Show no weakness. You're the doctor. What you say goes. Demonstrate your authority or they will chew you up.'

I nodded but I felt very unsure of myself. I was a people-pleaser by nature. I was also an introvert, thin-skinned and, like most doctors, a perfectionist. Nothing in my medical training, including my homeless work, had prepared me for patients like these. This was uncharted territory; a fold in the map in a place without maps.

Graham went to collect the first patient from the waiting room for my morning clinic. I stood by my desk and tried to appear authoritative.

'The doctor will see you now,' Graham announced, and the door swung open. A mountain of a man lumbered towards me.

Mr H announced that he wanted to kill his wife. He said it as easily as someone ordering lunch. He had been prescribed an antidepressant but had stopped taking it abruptly because it had given him erectile dysfunction, a known side effect. Consequently his mood had also dipped. He was on remand and was due to be sentenced next month. Before we could stop him he declared that he had been accused of actual bodily harm, which carries a maximum sentence of five years if it's a first offence. Mr H freely admitted it was not his first offence and he had numerous previous convictions. He was looking at a long sentence. I didn't want to hear all this, and yet I couldn't stop listening.

'Would you like to be referred to the prison In-reach mental-health team? They can help you with your low mood. We have mental-health nurses who are based on site,' Graham told him.

'I don't want any of that "funny farms" nonsense; making me sing happy songs,' Mr H replied gruffly.

'I can ask the chaplaincy team to come and see you. We have Listeners who have been trained by the Samaritans?' Graham said, trying again.

'I don't need God-botherers. I just want to call my wife,' Mr H said.

'Is there a message you would like to pass on to her?' Graham asked.

'Yes. If she gives evidence against me I will slit her throat,' Mr H replied. I thought I had misheard him at first.

'That sounds like more of a prison matter,' Graham said quietly.

When Mr H left the clinic, Graham called the security team. He informed them Mr H had made threats against his wife. The security team would inform the police. Threats like this, even if made in jest, were taken seriously.

The next patient was Mr B. As soon as he entered the room he announced that he was having a nervous breakdown.

'The only good thing, if it is a good thing, is that my son is sharing a cell with me. We are on a joint-enterprise charge which means we both committed the same crime. It was drugs, we are farmers and we got into debt. We got talked into running a cannabis farm. It was a big operation but we were just small fish. It's him I'm worried about. I've messed up his life and he's only in his early twenties. The beds aren't helping. I'm sleeping on a wooden board. An actual wooden board! I wasn't expecting a five-star hotel but this is worse than a kennel. I'm not a bad person, I just did something stupid,' Mr B said. He had his head down and was rubbing his rough hands together with anxiety.

I offered to refer him to the In-reach mental-health team Graham had told me about. Mr B declined. Like Mr H before him, he didn't want to be labelled as mad. It's a recurring theme – no one wants to admit they are struggling mentally. I told Mr B we all need a bit of help at times. This was probably the most stressful time in his life, I pointed out. Again, Graham explained we also had Listeners and Insiders he could speak with. Mr B said he had already been warned by other prisoners not to talk to Listeners and Insiders because they were prison snitches. The prisoners thought they reported everything back to the officers and couldn't be trusted – I didn't know if there was any truth in this.

'If you close yourself off to help no one is going to be able to do anything for you or your son,' I told him.

'There's a group for first-timers, they meet on Tuesday evenings,' Graham said. 'And there is a music group that meets in the chapel on Wednesdays. You don't want to be cooped up in a cell all day.'

'I'll tell my boy. He might find it useful,' Mr B said.

'Ask your son if he would like to come and speak to us,' Graham suggested. But that was all we could do for Mr B.

Next through the door was Mr KZ.

Mr KZ was a twenty-five-year-old Polish man who had been to prison before on three or four occasions in the UK and also in Poland. He was fluent in English and didn't require Language Line, which is our telephone translation service. He said he was street homeless and 'on the out' – a phrase everyone used to describe not being in prison – he drank six litres of discount cider a day. I wasn't sure if he was exaggerating the amount he drank, hoping for a higher dose of diazepam, a tranquillizer we use as part of our alcohol detoxification. It was without doubt a lot.

Graham showed me how to send a referral to the Integrated Drug Treatment System or IDTS. I would quickly become very familiar with IDTS but for now this was all news to me. They were the team who would take over Mr KZ's substance-misuse care in prison. In the meantime, I prescribed an alcohol detoxification consisting of diazepam, and the vitamins thiamine and vitamin B. Often alcoholics gain most of their calories from drinking and do not eat well. This leads them to being lacking in essential vitamins. Without these vitamins they can develop permanent damage to their nerves, numbness, muscle loss, and in the worst cases permanent memory loss and confusion.

When Mr KZ left the room I confided in Graham that I felt lost without his support. The referrals to other services were completely different here to community general practice.

'You'll pick it up in no time,' he said reassuringly. I had to believe him.

Graham went to collect the next patient. He returned with the huge man with the teardrop tattoos who had been aggressive in Reception the previous evening. He had been transferred to the Segregation unit overnight and released this morning – chastened, I hoped. No officers were present with him, despite yesterday's aggression. What were we expected to do if he reacted as he had done just a few hours ago?

'You may recall Mr Lovell,' Graham said as he ushered the man in.

'Hello, I don't think we have been properly introduced. I'm Dr Y,' I said and extended my hand.

'You have to sort my meds out, I'm rattling,' he launched in. 'I need my pregabalin for my anger-management issues and I have nerve damage in my hands from punching people. Pregabalin helps me with both.' Brushing past me, he fell into the chair by the window.

'I can try to help,' I replied.

I pulled the British National Formulary book from my bag. The BNF contains details of all the medications that are prescribed in the UK. If there is ever a medication or dose I am unfamiliar with I always check the BNF first. It's standard practice. My copy is well-thumbed and annotated. Pregabalin was not a medication I was very familiar with at the time, but it would not reflect well on me to let the patient see I was uncertain – particularly not a patient like Mr Lovell. Pregabalin is

used for neuropathic or nerve pain, amongst other
conditions; it is something I would expect a neurologist
or psychiatrist to prescribe. It's not a first- or second-line
medication for nerve damage. I would need confirma-
tion from Mr Lovell's community GP that he was
actually prescribed this medication before I could continue it.

'I'm not registered with a GP in the UK, I'm a Trav-
eller. I self-medicate and buy my own medications
online. I can't read or write and I don't need a big book
like that to tell me what I need,' he said.

I had an unsettling feeling that Mr Lovell already
realized I was not going to be able to prescribe pregabalin for him and he was not going to be happy with
my refusal.

'Other than your request for pregabalin is there anything else the doctor can help you with?' Graham asked.

Mr Lovell grunted and began tapping the table with
his fingers. His hands were huge. I noted bilateral boxer's fractures where his knuckles had caved in from
punching injuries. He clearly was not the sort of person who talked his way out of an argument. He had
BRUM tattooed on the fingers of one hand and 0121,
the area code for Birmingham, on the other. He loved
his home town, if nothing else.

He noticed me looking. I hoped I'd been able to
arrange my face into a neutral expression.

'Do you like my tattoos, Doc? Are you from Birmingham?' he asked.

'I'm not allowed to say,' I replied quietly.

'In case I try to groom you?' he said and guffawed at
his own joke.

I didn't reply because he was correct. One of the first pieces of advice Graham gave me was never to give a prisoner any personal information. It might seem like polite conversation at first, but they could later use even the most innocent details to blackmail me into smuggling in money or phones. Other staff had been compromised, sacked, and even sent to prison themselves. I should always suspect an ulterior motive if a prisoner took an interest in me, I'd been told.

'I don't need to groom anyone; I'm top dog,' Mr Lovell continued.

I didn't know what 'top dog' meant in a prison setting but now was not the time to ask.

'You don't sound like you're from Birmingham, Doc. You talk very posh. Very clever. You know big words like you chew on a dictionary. Very lah-di-dah aren't you – I bet you went to private school!' Mr Lovell said, trying to provoke me into giving away information, just as Graham had warned.

He was making an acute assessment of me. He was wrong about the private school, but I had memorized a pocket thesaurus when I was tiny. I'd had a better vocabulary when I was at primary school than I now did as an adult. But being smart was not a guaranteed way to make friends. I'd learned that being amiable was much less offensive. I prided myself on being able to talk to anyone, being humorous, likeable. That plan wasn't working out too well with Mr Lovell.

'Do you have any drug or alcohol problems?' I asked.

'I take fuckloads of drugs. I like a drink and in prison I drink hooch.'

I didn't know what hooch was and looked at Graham for clarification.

'The prisoners brew their own booze with oranges and fruit juice. It's called hooch. If the officers find it they confiscate and destroy it,' Graham explained.

'You don't even know what hooch is, Doc,' said Mr Lovell, turning on me. 'You're out of your depth. Don't give me problems and I won't give you problems. Understand? Prescribe my pregabalin and Subutex and I can be out of here. We don't need to waste each other's time with these stupid questions.'

There was a clear undertone of threat in his voice.

From reading his notes I learned Jamie Lovell was thirty-eight years old. He was currently on remand and had been to prison over ten times. He had started smoking heroin when he was thirteen years old. He was currently smoking £100 of heroin and £100 of crack cocaine each day. He also chain-smoked cannabis and sniffed cocaine on weekends. He said he had never injected drugs and referred to it as a mug's game. He later revised that statement and told me that he injected a combination of anabolic steroids.

I could see that Jamie Lovell was withdrawing from heroin. His hands were sweaty and shaking. He said he had vomited five or six times over the past twenty-four hours and reported having diarrhoea. In police custody he had been given diazepam and dihydrocodeine, a strong opioid painkiller, to help with his drug withdrawals. He reported drinking up to two hundred units of alcohol a week and said he needed a drink first thing in the morning to get started. He described missing the drink more than the drugs.

I worked through all the questions on the healthcare screening template.

'Other than the drugs and alcohol do you have any physical problems?' I asked.

'I hear voices in my head,' Jamie replied, pointing to his forehead.

'That's not a physical problem; it's mental health,' I said.

'But it's in my head, and my head is part of my body, isn't it?' he countered.

'Yes, your head is part of your body, but thoughts and feelings come under the category of mental health,' I clarified.

'I'm sick of answering stupid questions. I've been to prison loads of times, it should all be in my records. Why are you asking all these questions again?' he said, raising his voice.

He waved his hands about and began talking about pregabalin again. Eventually he said a 'head doctor' had diagnosed paranoid schizophrenia or drug-induced psychosis in the past. He said that he smoked heroin to calm the voices in his head.

'I do have dark thoughts. Doesn't everyone? I strung myself up when I was in prison last time. I've taken overdoses and jumped from the landings, slashed my arms all the way up and down,' Jamie said, gesticulating. He rolled up his sleeves and showed Graham and me his scars. They glistened under his tattoos much like the aggression under his words.

Graham explained to Mr Lovell that he was concerned about his mental health. He had harmed himself, and others, on a number of occasions. We would therefore

need to open an ACCT. The Assessment, Care in Custody and Teamwork plan ensured that the prison and
healthcare could work together to safeguard him from
harming himself. They would arrange joint meetings
with him to monitor his mental well-being and the
level of input and care he required.

'The orange folder? That ACCT crap? No, I don't
want that. I don't need an officer asking me if I am
alright every fifteen minutes. That'll do my nut in,' Mr
Lovell exclaimed.

He began to become more irate and raised his voice
louder still. He started to play agitatedly with the papers
on my desk. If I'd had a panic alarm under my desk I
would have used it. I didn't see this ending well.

'I'm trying to help you,' I said as calmly as I could. I
wanted to add, 'Why are you being so difficult?' The
question, heard in my head, seemed so childish that I
was ashamed of myself. I was glad my mouth was too
dry to vocalize the words.

'No, you are not trying to help me,' he hissed. 'You
prison doctors and nurses and officers are all the same.
You're on a power trip. On the outside you wouldn't
dare look me in the eye and in here you're trying to
make things difficult. You're just a little rat and I could
break you with my bare hands. Don't act like you're the
boss. I'm the boss. No one tells me what to do.'

He slammed the desk with the palm of his hand. I
jumped. Mr Lovell laughed. He claimed to be illiterate
but he was reading me like a book. He could tell he was
scaring me and he was enjoying it.

'I need you to provide a urine sample to be tested
for toxicology. I can prescribe you treatment based on

the results,' I said, trying not to let my voice falter. Under the desk my legs were jumping and I was tapping my feet lightly, repetitively, on the floor. Why wasn't there a panic button under the desk?

'Toxic-cology? Why are you using big words?' He had softened his tone as if talking to a child. 'I told you that I can't read or write. Real men don't hide behind dictionaries. I have difficulty pissing, I have a shy bladder, and I can't give you a urine sample. Just give me Subutex and pregabalin and we can end this. We can shake hands and walk away.'

Mr Lovell was not to be mollified. Despite our best efforts he was becoming increasingly aggressive. He appeared to be interacting with unseen stimuli. He was swatting at invisible enemies and hissing at them to shut up. I was at once concerned and also not convinced that it was genuine. In my mind I was making a list of the services he required: the In-reach mental-health team, the IDTS team, Listeners, Insiders and chaplaincy. Pretty much everything on offer.

'Once we have the toxicology – I mean urine – results, if it shows it is positive for opiates like heroin I can start you on methadone, which is a heroin substitute and it's what we prescribe here for heroin withdrawals,' I said.

'I don't want methadone; it's junky juice and I'm not a filthy junky. Methadone is a bitch to come off, rots your teeth and it gets in your bones. The rattle is worse than heroin. Either you're going to give me Subutex or I'll have to buy it on the wing. You're forcing me to self-medicate,' Mr Lovell said.

'Mr Lovell, the bottom line is that we cannot give

you Subutex or pregabalin. The answer is no,' I confirmed.

Jamie stood up abruptly and with a roar he swiped
his arm across my desk, sweeping everything on to the
floor. Graham grabbed me and we rushed out of
the room. He pushed the panic alarm in the corridor.
The thunderous rage of destruction from inside the
room continued.

Graham asked if I was OK. The violence, even
though it had been brewing, had come as a shock. It
was something I'd get used to over time. We began
moving away from the clinic and down the corridor to
the main waiting room. My legs had turned to jelly and
running was not an option. Graham seemed relatively
unperturbed – it was as if he had seen this a thousand
times before. And, of course, he had.

'Why aren't there any officers stationed in the Outpatient corridor?' I asked.

'Understaffing,' Graham replied calmly.

'The screws aren't going to help you,' Mr Lovell said
as he emerged menacingly from the clinic room. I
cursed myself for not asking Graham to lock him in.

We backed away at a quicker pace, but I was stumbling over my own feet. I finally understood why the
victims in horror films always fall over.

'You should have prescribed my fucking pregabalin,'
Jamie shouted, his face contorted with rage.

'Stay where you are,' someone shouted back.

I turned to see a female officer running down the
corridor towards us followed by several of her colleagues. The officer flew through the air and an image
of Storm in the *X-Men* films popped into my mind. At

that moment, the officers seemed to me like super-heroes. An immense sense of relief washed over me. Mr Lovell was throwing punches and the officers defended themselves with skill. They grabbed his arms and held them behind his back. He was wrestled to the ground within moments and finally the fight had gone out of him.

The female officer was half the size of the hulking Lovell but she had restrained him within minutes while at the same time smiling and cracking jokes.

'I'm Custodial Manager Goz, everyone just calls me Goz or Gozzy,' she said, turning to me.

She was shorter than me but was pure muscle. Her platinum blonde hair was shaved apart from a short Mohican on top. I noted the three silver lines of rank on her shoulder epaulettes. Graham had already explained that three silver lines denoted a CM who was in charge of a section of the prison. Two lines meant a senior officer who controlled each house block and one line meant a wing officer.

'Pissing off the prisoners already, Doc? Did you say the trigger word NO?' Goz asked.

'Yes, I did,' I admitted sheepishly.

'Good. We need people to set boundaries. Too many doctors are scared of the prisoners and prescribe what-ever they want. If you ever feel unsafe press your alarm and we will come running – even if it does mean we have more control and restraint paperwork to fill in,' she said kindly. She pointed to my clothes. 'Nice suit. My father used to be a tailor. I do like it when people make an effort with their clothes. It looks vintage, wide lapels, flared trousers, classic brown colour.'

'I have matching underpants now,' I said and tried to smile.

'I like you. I'll be your personal bodyguard in here,' Goz said.

Helly and the admin staff emerged from their office and asked if we were alright.

'I knew you were trouble as soon as I first saw you,' Helly said to me and offered to bring us cups of sugary coffee.

After Mr Lovell had been transferred to the Segregation unit, for the second time in twenty-four hours, I went into my clinic room to review the damage. He had smashed my coffee mug. How was I going to Keep Calm and Carry On now? Graham and Helly joined me, and she handed me that promised cup of sugary coffee.

'I think that went well,' Graham offered, reflectively.

'It couldn't have been much worse,' I said with surprise.

'Oh, it can always be worse,' Graham and Helly replied in unison.

'We've had doctors pushed, punched, slapped, spat at. One was even hit with his own keyboard,' Graham explained.

I was expecting him to break into a smile and say he was joking, but he didn't because it was all true. He was testing my resolve. Would I pack my bag and ask to be taken to the gate? I still don't know why I didn't come to that conclusion. Possibly because however traumatic this new experience was – and it was – I had lived through worse challenges.

Distracting myself from my own thoughts, I asked Graham why he worked here.

He'd grown up in a working-class area in the West Midlands in the seventies. He had two main career options: either working in the local steelworks or joining the forces. With A-level biology and A-level history he'd had the option to become a physiotherapist – though beyond 'the bloke with the sponge' at football matches he had no idea what it involved. He was asked if he fancied becoming a male nurse. 'Is there such a thing as a male nurse?' he'd wondered.

At his nursing interview they asked him what sort of nurse he wanted to be. He said 'a good one'. So he trained for three years to become a general nurse, at a time when there were very few male nurses. As a charge nurse he then spent time working on a British air base in Saudi Arabia and then for British Aerospace. He met someone in Saudi who told him to train to become a mental-health nurse and Graham was always looking for a new challenge.

'I did my mental-health training for three years,' he told me as we sipped our hot drinks, my hands eventually steadying with every passing minute. 'Then one of my friends who was a prison officer advised me to join the prison service as a hospital officer because it was better paid than nursing.'

Graham had worked in a cat-A prison for five years at a time when it was unheard of for a prisoner to swear and shout abuse at staff. Then, officers were more 'hands-on' with the men and violence was met with violence or 're-schooling', as it was called. Officers and healthcare staff drank and smoked at work. Everyone went to the pub at lunchtime and they were merry when they came back for the afternoon shift. There was none of the sense of urgency and blind panic we had now.

Graham explained how, in those days, the doctor was God. No prisoner dared to question a doctor or they would get a beating from the officers. 'We had a high-profile prisoner in the cat-A prison called Charlie. He tried to take a doctor hostage once. The crisis lasted for about three seconds because an officer came in, clubbed him over the head and knocked him out cold,' Graham told me.

I almost choked on my coffee.

'Now they have to get a special team in,' Graham continued, 'to counsel someone to get off a table because it is called "an incident at height". The stories I could tell you, Dr Y! They were simpler times. I wouldn't say they were the good old days by any means. There were definitely some sadists in uniforms in those days who probably got away with murder, or close to it. When I worked in another prison one of the officers had his car stolen. That night the officers found a random prisoner who was in for a similar crime and kicked the shit out of him. I think they punctured his liver. When they unlocked his cell in the morning he was found in a pool of blood and had almost bled to death. They rushed him to the outside hospital and when the hospital doctors asked what had happened to him the escorting officers said he had fallen down a flight of stairs. In those days a lot of prisoners used to "fall down stairs".'

I was disgusted. How could any of the doctors working in that other prison have turned a blind eye to this?

A man had nearly died. I asked Graham about the doctors who used to work here when the prison had opened. What were they like? Graham told me the first two doctors who worked here were 'real characters'. Dr N1 was a lay preacher. If he had a patient in his room for too long, Graham would knock on the door and check he was alright. It wasn't unusual to find Dr N1 and the prisoner on their knees praying. The nurses told him to be careful. Perhaps closing your eyes around certain prisoners wasn't a good idea. He insisted he only prayed with those he thought would be responsive to the Lord. Dr N1 wouldn't give the prisoners any medications. He believed the Lord would look after them. This is not quite what the prisoners had in mind – they thought by praying with him, and obliging him, they were going to get manna from heaven in the form of meds. When that didn't work they would scream and shout. That didn't work either.

Dr N2 was indolent. Graham walked in on him once and found him listening to a prisoner's chest but he didn't have the ends of the stethoscope in his ears. Dr N2 thought this was funny and was grinning. He aimed to do the bare minimum of work and did not always reach this low threshold. He was sometimes found sleeping on the doctor's couch during clinics when he should have been seeing patients. After Dr N1 and Dr N2 left, there had been a series of doctors. Some were very good and some were decidedly not, Graham told me.

Graham's stories were colourful and I couldn't believe they had taken place within living memory. The landscape is unrecognizable now. The balance of power between doctor and patient has not just equalized, it has swung in the opposite direction. There is the constant threat of litigation. There seem to be few or no consequences for patients being abusive towards us. In particular, what could we do about Mr Jamie Lovell?

Graham explained we could complete some Incentives and Earned Privileges documentation which would lead to a negative entry in Mr Lovell's P–NOMIS. This wouldn't achieve a great deal because Mr Lovell was already on a basic regime with no TV and supposedly locked behind his door all day. What more did he have to lose? Standard and enhanced prisoners had more merits and positive entries in their records, which meant enhanced prisoners could wear their own clothes and spend more money on Canteen. At this rate, Jamie Lovell was never going to find himself being given privileges. How could he be rehabilitated and prepared for re-entry into society? What could we all do to stop him from coming back to prison time and again? Form-filling didn't seem to be the answer, but I didn't know how to help Mr Lovell turn his life around.

4

The Lifer

Mr A was a 'lifer'. He introduced himself to me by saying he had been in prison for over thirty-three years and had never met a doctor he liked. He had no expectations of my being any different. I tried not to take it personally. He made no eye contact with me and shuffled around in his seat as if he was about to leave at any moment. He told me he didn't have time to waste talking to me. He was cold and wanted to get back to his cell and wrap up in his blankets. His hands and feet were numb and icy blue, he complained. I sympathized. I was doing the consultation wearing my coat, a hat and a scarf.

British Summer Time officially began on the last Sunday of March and in response the prison heating had been switched off by the governor despite the fact it was snowing heavily. I couldn't feel my fingers as I typed. I told the managers that these were unworkable conditions – I noticed some of them had electric fan heaters under their desks. I was informed they had relayed their own concerns to the governor and had been told the heating would not be switched on again until winter started on the last Sunday of October. The governor proclaimed that the minimum workplace temperature was 16 degrees Celsius and we were currently at 18 degrees. I was unsure if I believed that information – it was snowing outside and the thick walls and concrete floors meant it felt far colder.

'I work in the laundry on my block. All the guys have been begging me for extra blankets. Everyone is wrapped up in all the layers of their clothes and staying under the covers,' Mr A said in his broad Yorkshire accent.

Mr A was painfully thin and weighed himself as often as he could. Access to weighing scales is limited in prison because, as with any heavy object, they can be used as a weapon. There are no weighing scales on any of the wings, so Mr A begrudgingly attended GP appointments to monitor his weight. If patients are underweight we prescribe them calorific build-up drinks twice a day and weigh them in clinic every fourteen days. We also monitor their blood tests every few months to ensure there is no organ damage. Mr A had been booked into my clinic to discuss his kidney and liver function results, which were abnormal.

'There's nothing you can tell me that I don't already know,' he said as I ran through his latest blood results and tried to explain what every value meant. He looked bored and disinterested and stared out of the window.

He had no teeth and wasn't wearing dentures; his lips were pursed in a tight knot.

'Can I ask you a question?' I asked Mr A.

'Knock yourself out,' he said and I thought I could see his breath against the window pane.

'What is a lifer?' I asked with genuine curiosity.

He finally made eye contact. He could see I was trying to learn about his situation. He swivelled slowly in his chair to face me and off he went.

'I got what is known as a mandatory life sentence with a twelve-year tariff. That meant I had to do twelve years in prison and after that I had to go to the parole board every two years, where I could be considered for release. The parole board was an interview with three suited types who went through your prison records looking at everything you had done over the past two years. They would say I had to do this or that course to prove I was rehabilitated. They read out every negative entry in my notes and made me feel like shit. On this date you told an officer to fuck themselves and nonsense like that. I didn't deny that I had said that but what was the context of the altercation – that's the bit they never mentioned. Maybe the officer was being a twat and needed to be told to go fuck himself?

'The parole board would tell me what anger-management courses and good behaviour I had to show before the next parole board would meet two years later. But I was moved around prisons and they didn't even do the courses there. I was being moved around but not moving forwards – it was hopeless. Before I knew it I had wasted nine years of my life on top of the first twelve. Going to these parole boards and getting knocked back and having another two years added on ... Then all this psychology nonsense started in ninety-six or ninety-eight. The psychologists wanted to look at your life and see where you'd gone wrong. They wanted to know if I had a traumatic birth – I said you best ask my ma and she's dead. It was just a series of tick-box exercises. I gave up. I refused to do any courses. I realized I was in for the long haul. I've not been a model prisoner; I have spent a lot of time in the block, the Segregation unit. I don't get along with people. I have an antisocial personality. I think most people are shits,' he said.

'Jeez,' I said.

'No one seems to know what they're doing. Like switching the fucking heating off when there's a blizzard outside. It's people's lives they're messing up and no one could care less because to them we're all trash. Lifers like me just coast through our sentences, go to the parole board every couple of years and get knocked back. I don't think I'll ever get out. I don't even know if I want to,' he concluded.

He waved his bony hands in front of me. This man had minimal body fat and was at risk of hypothermic shock, where his vital organs would shut down and he would die. We needed to warm him up.

'You've been in prison for almost as long as I've been alive,' I said as I set to work.

'Aye, I was thirty-two when I came in and I'm sixty-five now. All I done was cut a cunt's face. It was just a fucked-up Friday night out. We had an argument and to get away from him I had to start stabbing him or he would have hurt me. The way they go on it's like I'm a mass murderer. It was an accident; I must have slipped and nipped his heart and I killed him. I didn't intend to do that. I'd been on the streets since I was eight years old. My ma died when I was six and I had to look after my baby sister. We were going round our relatives for a couple of years, but they had their own mouths to feed and they couldn't keep us for long. I always had a knife on me. I was just a fucked-up kid, then I was a fucked-up man, ya know?' Mr A said.

'How can I help you?' I asked with sadness. And perhaps he heard it in my voice. He looked at me again.

'I could do with some new dentures, I left mine at the previous prison. I was told I was leaving with no notice and left half of my stuff there. I can't eat properly. I don't have much of an appetite – they say it's anorexia. That's just bollocks. I don't want to be a fat bastard, my weight is the only thing I can control in my life. Other than that there's nothing you can do for me,' he said.

'I'll put you on our dentist's waiting list as a high priority,' I said.

'Right, well, I'll be off then. I'll get no thanks if I go back and find they've robbed the laundry of all the blankets,' he said and left the room abruptly before I could complete the consultation. I hadn't even examined him properly. I called after him, but he was gone.

The prison seemed to occupy a black hole where time and space were skewed. After just a few weeks of working here I felt as if it had been years and I understood why the prisoners said at times it felt like seconds turned into hours and hours into weeks. There was a lot I still didn't know. But I knew that I would no longer have a chaperone once I was allowed to have keys. My probationary period would be over and I'd be alone with my patients. Often my chaperone was Graham, but today it was healthcare assistant Christine. She was always cheerful and the men respected her. Everyone called her 'Little Chris' because of her diminutive stature. She was intelligent, witty and kind. As Mr A departed, I turned to Chris with a shocked expression and held up my numb hands.

'He has been in prison for thirty-three years!' I said.

'Mobile phones, the internet . . . he has been completely cut off from the world. No wonder he's not sure whether he'd ever like to be released,' she said and shivered in her coat. I noticed her vape rattle in her top coat pocket.

'Smoking will stunt your growth,' I said, trying to lighten the mood.

'Now you tell me!' she replied with mock surprise and smiled back.

All of the patients I had seen in the morning had complained about the cold. We have high Did Not Attend rates in our clinics; sometimes only 50 per cent of our booked patients arrive. Some don't come to clinic because an officer would need to unlock them and then escort them to the Outpatient department. If there aren't enough officers there will be no free-flow and all prisoners are locked behind their doors. The patients may not have received their medical appointment slips – these are delivered by trusted prisoners but still things go astray. Sometimes patients refuse to attend because they want to use their limited time out of the cell to call loved ones, have a shower, or socialize with friends. Sometimes, like today, it is too cold and leaving the warmth of their beds feels impossible, or they over-sleep after a sleepless night caused by an uncomfortable bed or a distressed man screaming and shouting on the wing. A single prisoner can disrupt an entire wing so that all of the men will be irritable and tired the following day. It is no wonder that one of the commonest requests made to doctors is for sleeping tablets.

I decided that if my patients couldn't come to see me then I would go and see them on the wings. Chris knew that I was more nervous about going on to the wings than she was. She had struggled with her confidence before working in the prison. Interacting with the prisoners and working with hard-boiled staff who had been here for years had taught her to be more assertive. It wasn't possible to survive otherwise. I hoped it would rub off on me too.

One of Chris's roles is to lead the recruitment of prisoners who will complete an accredited health-promotion course and become 'health champions'. They are trained to do simple well-being checks on other prisoners. Every month there is a new health-promotion topic, such as testicular checks or prostate cancer awareness, and they will hand out patient information leaflets. If prisoners have any concerns they can speak to a health champion, who will then provide feedback to Chris. This is a very successful system. Prisoners are surprisingly willing to engage with the health champions and also with Chris. Each health champion will be in position for six months before someone else is recruited and trained. There are always a lot of men on the waiting list to take on the role. They enjoy the responsibility and extra time out of the cells.

Chris and I walked on to one of the house blocks and my heart sank. I spotted a group of prisoners huddled together for warmth and noticed Jamie Lovell was standing with them. I looked around to see if there were any officers on the landing in case he tried to attack us. He'd certainly spotted me. Striding towards us, he brushed past me and stood directly in front of Chris.

'Miss, are you Thai?' Jamie asked, all innocence.

'You mean "Thai-nee", tiny? No, mate, I'm just short,' she replied quickly.

'Miss, you're so cold and blue you look like a cute little Smurf,' Jamie said, refusing to let it go.

'Thank you for the compliment, Jamie, being only five feet tall does have its advantages. I let compliments and insults go over my head.' She paused for effect. Even Jamie Lovell had to smile.

'I've come to ask you if you would like to become a health champion,' Chris continued.

This was news to me, and I thought she was joking. Perhaps it showed on my face, but Jamie thought it was a joke too. Chris explained what the role entailed. Jamie seemed interested, especially when he heard that he could have extra gym sessions. But he looked disappointed when he learned there was a written examination.

'I can't read or write,' he said quietly. Gone was the bravado about his illiteracy which he'd displayed in my clinic room.

'We can sort that out. I'll contact the Shannon Trust

prison literacy charity. They're a brilliant group of volunteers who teach prisoners to read,' Chris said.

'I'm too old to learn anything new,' he replied.

'You're only thirty-eight! Give the Shannon Trust a go. I'll ask them to come and see you. I think you would be really good in the role of health promotion,' Chris said encouragingly. I was starting to believe it myself.

As we walked away I noticed Mr R, the money-laundering accountant – as he would now forever be known – standing outside his cell door. He was shivering in his prison T-shirt and I noticed he had a black eye. I asked him what had happened and he retreated into his cell, allowing us in behind him. As soon as we had followed him in he broke down, explaining that he was being bullied. A gang of men had realized he was wealthy and were forcing him to pay them protection in the form of goods ordered on Canteen. His wife was transferring money into his prison account, which he would then use to buy the bullies whatever they wanted.

The prison black market and protection racket worked on a system known as Double Bubble. If a man owed a pound on day one, the debt would be two pounds on the second day, four on the third day, and sixty-four pounds by the seventh day. If the debt was not cleared it could rise to thousands of pounds. Mr R was in an impossible position.

Most cells I had been into with Chris were piled high with tins of tuna and instant noodles, which seemed to be what the men lived on. Mr R's room was not only freezing, it had been stripped; his mattress, blankets, kettle and television were all absent. The only personal item he now possessed was a single photograph of his wife and child beside his bare bed. Chris and I told him that he should inform the senior officers of his mistreatment, which he refused to do. He made us promise not to tell anyone. I wondered how I was going to be able to help him.

'Snitches get stitches,' he said quietly, a shiver running through him. Fear or cold? It wasn't possible to tell.

It's a common unwritten rule in prisons never to talk about bullying. Being a snitch can have serious consequences, including a terrifying escalation in bullying. Moving to another block will not help because the label of being a snitch quickly follows. Snitches will be further isolated and targeted. Mr R had also been threatened that the bullies had contacts on the outside who could harm his family. While I struggled to think what I could do for him, Chris had had a thought.

'Looks like we've found our newest health champion!' she said. 'It will get you off the wing. Have you seen the size of the other health champions? You'll be part of their team and they will look after you.'

As we walked away Chris explained why she also wanted to recruit Jamie Lovell. She had known him for years. He was part of what she called the 'boomerang gang' of prisoners who were always in and out of prison. She wanted to break the cycle of bad behaviour by giving Jamie a position of trust. He needed space to grow or he would stagnate. Jamie, like so many people in prison, was his own worst enemy.

'In the meantime, we can lift Mr R out of his

terrible situation. Prison is no place for a posh bloke,' Chris observed.

I knew it was wrong to judge Jamie Lovell based on a few, albeit fractious, encounters. I hadn't looked past his tattooed fists. I thought of him as a drug-seeking brute who was violent when he didn't get his own way, and I hadn't wondered what lay beneath. I understood that the guys felt animosity towards healthcare, because they only saw a doctor or nurse when there was a problem and they already had loads of pent-up frustration. The answer was so often 'No'. The main problem was that they felt forgotten about. Of course, there were some men who were always making complaints and you could never satisfy them. Chris was honest and upfront with them and encouraged them to take responsibility. They needed some agency in their lives and she tried to empower them. They were not going to be in prison for ever and they needed to be able to look after themselves. In prison, it was easy to get used to having other people sort out your problems. The men became institutionalized. Helpless. Some guys snapped at Chris and told her to do everything for them. They would say it was her job. She would say it was theirs.

'I've probably bitten back once or twice. All the guys get frustrated being here. We all do at times, but at least we can go home, order a takeaway, watch TV, unwind – they can't do any of that. Working here has been a positive experience and completely changed my outlook on life. It's made me a better person. I think I'll be here for ever,' Chris told me.

I wondered if I would feel the same if I worked here for as many years as Chris had. Would I too become a lifer? Would it have a positive effect on me? Would Mr Lovell and I continue to dance around each other? My family were worried for my safety. However, they had noticed I had grown in confidence. Being cooped up with men deprived of their liberty had made me value my own freedom like never before. If I was cold I was at liberty to turn the heating on at home, if I was too warm I could open a window. I had gained a little perspective.

On the day I saw Mr A I sent an email to the number one governor and included Health and Safety Executive guidelines on minimum workplace temperatures, and also Codes of Practice on housing temperatures. I explained I had seen a gentleman who was suffering from hypothermia and there were many other patients like him on the wings. These men could develop long-term injuries including frostbite, which would leave the prison vulnerable to litigation. My email was not responded to formally but later that day the radiators gurgled into life. It felt like a victory for sanity and humanity; I had achieved something. It's important to take the wins when you get them.

It was only when I was leaving work at the end of the day that I noticed my scarf was missing. I must have taken it off, either in my room or on the wings and now it was gone. I told Chris it was a birthday present and she promised to ask the health champions to hunt for my scarf. She said I would have it on my desk by the next morning. My scarf was never located. Rather than apologize for this failure in her investigative powers Chris chided me.

'Who would have thought there would be thieves in a prison!' she said.

Offender healthcare occupies the grey zone between primary care, hospital care, mental health and substance misuse. It is a place of great unpredictability. Even if I help someone, like Mr A, when I later say hello to him on the house blocks he might well snap at me or ignore me completely. Someone can appear grateful and still try to pick my pocket or take the scarf from around my neck – or, in the worst-case scenario, try to tighten the knot. We have had staff garrotted with their own scarves and necklaces. In this environment complaints and the threat of legal action are common, and it is so rare to receive praise that a 'thank you' card from years ago will still be pinned to a notice board like a lucky four-leaf clover.

Even if I do my utmost to help someone, they may demand my name and say they will see me in court. When I first started working in the prison I was perturbed by the frequent threats of litigation. I spoke with the other doctors about it. They said it was just part of the job. Often the threats were just empty words, but sometimes they came from men with too much time on their hands and access to 'no win, no fee' medical negligence lawyers. I called my medical indemnity provider on a daily basis during my first few weeks of working in the prison. I felt that I had to do everything possible to protect myself as I was still finding my feet.

Other doctors in the prison were doing what they could to improve things, too. One sent an email to the managers and copied us all in on it. The other doctors took this as an opportunity to call for better working conditions. They asked why we didn't have any GP meetings where we could air our concerns. These meetings were the staple of GP practices in the community and would ordinarily be organized by the practice manager – a role we didn't have in prisons, so that in part explained their absence. The doctors also asked why we didn't have significant event meetings in which we could formally discuss the kinds of threatening situations that were happening regularly. Having recently attended a prison healthcare conference they'd learned that some prisons had a significant event meeting on the day an incident occurred and then within three days they had a follow-up. This approach had led to a reduction in the numbers of deaths and near misses; quite simply, people learned from things going wrong. The doctors noted that in our prison staff morale was low. Front-line workers didn't feel listened to. All these were good points.

In addition, the doctors flagged a list of missing equipment and that the clinics needed to be restocked. One of the clinics didn't have a printer or telephone. One needed a couch. One had a broken chair. We were using a toilet as a Reception clinic. The VP clinic didn't have perhaps the most essential piece of equipment, a panic alarm. The list went on and on, and yet there was no forum in which to convey our concerns and know for sure that we were being heard.

The managers were sympathetic and the email was met with a reasonable response saying plans were in place to improve the healthcare infrastructure. But the doctor who sent the initial email wasn't reassured and she left a few weeks later. Another doctor left two weeks after that. Clearly, losing staff at that rate wasn't ideal. Including Dr A and Dr S, over the course of twelve months six doctors left the prison. I'd only just started and I thought of leaving too. It wasn't the patients who frightened me, it was the chaos of the healthcare provision.

Two doctors were required to be on site at all times to manage the workload. But when the permanent doctors started departing and we couldn't find locum or emergency doctor cover to plug the gaps, it wasn't unusual for me to be the only doctor present. It was difficult to find locums willing to work in the prison because despite the additional threats it did not pay more than being a locum in the community. Some of the locums who came to our aid were excellent, but many were clearly perturbed by the difficult environment and would not return. Some doctors, whether they were permanent or locums, didn't have any sense of urgency. It meant others would have to work twice as hard to deal with the relentless churn of patients and tasks. The stress and anxiety were incredible and there was very little downtime because there was always a list of issues to attend to. I would come into work and find old ECGs, or heart traces, left on my desk, ECGs that showed marked abnormalities. Had the patient been reviewed? Was he still alive? At times I felt as though I was running around like a headless chicken. If I left, who would look after my patients?

As a team, the doctors asked for the duty doctor task system to be reviewed. The majority of tasks were generated by nurses after a medication had already run out. There were often over a hundred duty doctor tasks arising each day while we rushed from emergency to emergency. Each one could mean a missed dose of medication as the time increased between a prisoner running out of medication and being prescribed more. This was a clinical concern because the medications could be critical, like epilepsy medication. If there were outstanding tasks on a Friday evening there might not be a prescriber in until Monday morning. This would mean a significant break in treatment and it could lead to patients – and those around them – coming to harm.

Completing the duty doctor tasks could take an entire day – as soon as one task was completed another arrived. In addition to the duty doctor tasks there were blood results and ECGs and letters to go through. Whenever I'd climbed a mountain of tasks and thought I was making progress, I would look up and see another summit. I worked through my breaks and began to stay late for a couple of hours every day. One of the other doctors stepped in and advised me against this. 'We are permanently understaffed and that is a management issue. If you step in and do extra unpaid work out of goodwill you are masking the problem!' he said.

With or without the additional hours, we were busy seeing patients all day. Every few minutes a new duty doctor pop-up would appear on my screen. These were a distraction I didn't know how to switch off. It broke my concentration when I was seeing my patients.

Question? A new task of type 'Miscellaneous' has arrived. Do you want to go to the task list screen? This man has dry skin, please prescribe cream. Task marked as a red flag emergency request.

An emergency request for skin cream, I wondered?

'Do you know how to switch off the pop-ups?' I asked Chris. 'There seems to be a new one every few minutes. Some of them aren't even urgent.'

'The nurses send the tasks as urgent because otherwise they don't get looked at. If you ignore them you might end up with a price on your head,' she said.

'You mean someone would pay to have me harmed?' I asked with alarm.

'Yes – I'm starting a collection,' she said and laughed.

I laughed too, nervously.

It was not unusual to have prisoners shout threats and abuse when they felt their needs were not met. I didn't think it was far-fetched for a prisoner to attack a doctor because he had been refused moisturizer which he could buy on Canteen. What a strange world this was.

I was sprinting from one short-term crisis to another. I continually sought to make long-term improvements to healthcare and service provision. I helped to set up a weekly GP Multi-Disciplinary Team Meeting where the most complicated primary-care patients were discussed with senior nurses and an ongoing plan for their care was formulated. I also sought to improve communication between the different teams and developed a good working relationship with the psychiatrists and mental-health team. I was eking out some semblance of order from the chaos but I was still learning myself. I had to ask for advice from the administration department, senior nurses and pharmacy staff. 'What do I do when . . .?' 'How do I . . .?' 'Can you tell me what . . .?'

I had lots of questions. Barty and Nadeem were senior pharmacy technicians and, in the absence of a pharmacist on site, were invaluable. Barty had worked in the prison for a decade, but Nadeem had joined just before I had.

Nadeem had worked part-time in a community pharmacy since he was a teenager, as a weekend job. It helped fund a law degree, but he had found it hard to progress in the legal field without contacts who could secure a training post with a law firm. He completed his qualifications in becoming a pharmacy technician and began working in the prison out of curiosity and to support his young family. Between them Barty and Nadeem taught me so much about writing out prison prescriptions. To start with, there seemed to be something wrong with almost every prescription I wrote. Barty waved the offending items in my face and took great pleasure in crossing them through with a large green X.

'What are you doing, Dr Y? You need to be more careful,' Barty warned me kindly. 'Offender healthcare is like a game of snakes and ladders. If you make a mistake and someone dies, then you will be off to the coroner's court, faster than a slippery slide. That's a fate worse than death – the barristers will tear you apart!'

Nadeem had a gentler approach and would ask if I had intended to prescribe a double dose of a medication – he had intercepted the prescription before a patient came to harm. There was so much to learn. It was like being at medical school again. Back then, for months before my final exams I'd locked myself in my room to study as hard as I could. On a bad day I'd studied for only

eight hours. On a good day I'd worked for twelve, fourteen or sixteen hours. My wall planner had been
meticulously marked with every break I took. I never
spent more than ten minutes in the bathroom and I ate
meals at my desk.

Now that I was working in the prison service, I liked
learning and found offender healthcare fascinating, so
that wasn't the problem. The problem was that I needed
to learn faster. I booked myself on to substance misuse
and forensic medicine courses and read up on crimin-
ology. I learned about documentation of injuries
including blunt trauma and sharp trauma and was
always trying to improve my practice and the general
standards in healthcare. I learned the dos and don'ts of
prescribing from Barty and Nadeem, and I made a list
that I kept in my diary for quick reference.

1. Do not prescribe any powders in prison, they can
   be blown into staff's eyes and used as a weapon.
   Some powders can be used to make explosives.
2. No medication that comes in glass bottles – can be
   used as a weapon.
3. No aerosols or sprays – they can be used as
   explosives and flame throwers.
4. No muscle rub creams that contain menthol – it
   masks the smell of drugs and confuses the sniffer
   dogs.
5. No mouthwash – mouthwash can inactivate the
   effects of toothpaste and the dentist prescribes this
   for short courses only.
6. No Coal Tar shampoo – the prisoners dry it on
   paper and smoke it.

7. Do not prescribe long courses of sleeping tablets, prisoners can have three nights only or they might become dependent on it.

8. Check all meds twice before prescribing them. Check what else the prisoner is on or there might be drug interactions. If these men can sue healthcare, they will.

9. Do not prescribe nutritional supplements unless the prisoner's Body Mass Index is less than eighteen. Most of these lads are huge and they want the extra protein to put on more muscle.

10. Do not prescribe any medications 'In Possession' unless the prisoner has had an IP risk assessment which confirms they are not going to overdose if allowed to have the medication in their cell.

11. Do not prescribe build-up supplements IP so that they can take them back to their cells. The bigger lads will bully the smaller ones for them. The underweight prisoner must come to the medication hatch twice a day and be supervised as they consume their supplements.

12. IP medications must be stopped as soon as a patient is put on an ACCT and changed to Non In Possession (NIP). If you prescribe IP meds to someone on an ACCT and they die from an overdose you are going to coroner's court. If in doubt – ask.

13. Avoid coroner's court if you want a long career in Offender Healthcare.

5

Teamwork

A medical consultation is just a conversation between two people. Theoretically it can be the easiest thing in the world. However, some consultations are more difficult than others. The doctor's role is to utilize their years of training and expertise to advise the patient about their treatment options. Advise, not tell. The days of the doctor telling the patient what to do are long gone. Our clinic rooms have been reorganized to reflect the dissolution of the old power dynamic. We no longer peer down at our patients from the other side of a desk. This is seen as a barrier to establishing a therapeutic relationship. The desk has been pushed against a wall and my patients and I sit on the same side of it.

In the prison there are some precautions for our personal safety such as never entering a room before a prisoner, never turning our back to them, and always ensuring we are seated closest to the exit – in case we need to make a dash for it. This is to prevent us being punched in the back of the head, strangled from behind, or taken hostage – all of which have happened to staff. I'd chosen not to know what anyone is in prison for – they could be a mass murderer or be here for driving while disqualified. I try to avoid staring at the computer screen, which displays their notes, when I speak to them in my clinic room. Eye contact is really important. I want my patients to feel they are being heard and seen. Four or five years at medical school, two years of hospital foundation training, and three years of GP training teach doctors the importance of body language. I am particularly conscious of demonstrating receptiveness by not crossing my arms and legs.

The start of every consultation is given over to allowing the patient to explore their ideas, concerns and expectations. We try to use layman's language and every medical term is explained. Complex conditions are distilled down to their first principles where we explain how the body works and why sometimes it does not. The term 'patient' itself, with its Latin origins meaning to suffer, is also sometimes replaced by service user, attendee or client. However, some patients prefer to retain the term and think client and service user sound suspiciously mercantile. At the heart of it all, the doctor–patient relationship remains sacrosanct. I can't break patient confidentiality unless I'm told that a crime is going to be committed and I have to make a safeguarding referral.

A quick lesson in prison nomenclature, which has also shifted. Prisoners are sometimes referred to as inmates or residents. They are never to be called criminals, convicts, cons, jailbirds, felons, thugs, scumbags or lags. According to protocols, prisoners should be addressed as Mr or Miss and then their surname. But some prisoners will only respond if called by their soubriquet, such as Mad Dog – which takes a bit of getting used to. Staff do not use their first names in front of prisoners in case it leads to inappropriate informality. I am always referred to as Dr Y by staff and prisoners. The term prison officer is preferred over jailer, guard and warden. Prisoners often call male officers Boss, Sir or Guv, and all women are addressed as Miss or Ma'am, followed by their surname. The slang terms turnkey or screw are only used as an insult by disgruntled prisoners – which means the term screw is still often used.

Communication skills are vital to doctors to aid diagnosis. We attempt to look beyond what is said and to pick up on non-verbal cues. What is left unsaid or the manner in which information is conveyed is sometimes more informative than the words themselves. It's imperative to allow people to feel listened to and to demonstrate that their concerns are important. The simple fact is this: many prisoners lack basic schooling. The disparity in our communication skills can become a stumbling block, if we let it. I've had to learn a lot of slang terms and accept that some prisoners swear every couple of words, for want of a better adjective. There is nothing to be gained by being uptight and prissy. They deserve to have my full attention by the mere fact that they have prioritized seeing me during their precious time outside their cell, known as 'association time'.

Prisoners' frustration with trying to express themselves can manifest itself as a raised voice or expansive body language whereby they wave their arms about. It's unfair to call this behaviour aggressive; no real physical threat is intended. The key is to use de-escalation techniques such as active listening and allowing them to vent their emotions. A consultation should never become combative or retaliatory and we aim for peaceable concordance – where we agree on a course of treatment. This sense of resolution is not always possible, and it is common for an inmate to express dissatisfaction about prison healthcare in general, and prison doctors in particular.

In prisons, inevitably, we sometimes have to deal with individuals who are purposefully intimidating. Difficult patients have often led difficult lives. They have learned to combat challenges with aggression. It means an entire consultation can consist of someone storming into my clinic room, banging on the desk, and shouting at me or threatening violence. No amount of nodding and sympathetic noises, the 'hmms' and 'aahs' of active listening, can pacify someone who keeps referring to me as a dickhead.

Despite all the challenges, I have developed a reputation for being able to pacify even the most irate patient. I think it's because I listen more than I speak. I want to see the situation from the patient's perspective and imagine how I'd feel if I was in their shoes. Also it's because, unlike many of my doctor colleagues, I'm from a working-class background and many of my patients are people I can imagine living on the street where I grew up. Some of our neighbours in Birmingham's Sparkhill area sold drugs from their homes and were in and out of prison. It was no secret. Once, my sister

Shahzadi accidentally locked her car keys inside her car and asked one of our neighbours for help. He very kindly broke into her car in minutes without scratching any of her paintwork. To me, these were just ordinary people with their own desires, challenges and sometimes unique skill sets.

Careful consultation and empathy in my clinic are essential, but it's nonetheless difficult to keep prisoners happy as offender healthcare is often stricter when it comes to prescribing certain medications than in community general practice. Many medications available outside are banned on site, often because they can be weaponized or traded on the prison's black market. Barty and Nadeem are always careful to check the doctors' prescriptions to ensure rogue elements don't slip by. Medications stronger than ibuprofen and paracetamol are prescribed with caution. This puts the prison GP in the unenviable situation of having to explain that a patient's going to detox or slowly reduce and stop a medication. Before this decision is made a Multi-Disciplinary Team, or MDT, meeting is convened to discuss each case. These meetings include specialists from different disciplines. A decision will only be made if a consensus is reached.

It was decided that an inmate named Mr V was a complicated individual who required an MDT. Mr V arrived in the prison first thing in the morning as a last-minute transfer from another site. There were printouts of his urgent referrals on my desk when I arrived at work. Usually when someone is referred to the outside hospital the healthcare department should put that individual on a 'medical hold', which prevents them from being transferred to another prison. It's unusual for someone to be moved to another prison if they have pending appointments, but it does happen, usually as an oversight. I also noted that there had been a Code Blue – Mr V had reportedly had a seizure as he was being transferred this morning. And yet he was still sent to us and that was very suspect. This appeared to be an inappropriate transfer – it seemed like his former prison was trying to get rid of him. Why?

I spoke to our head of healthcare and advised them that Mr V should be returned to his former prison so that he wouldn't miss his appointments. A few hours later I was informed that the sending prison had refused to accept him back. I called the other prison on numerous occasions, but their head of healthcare and doctors were unavailable to speak to me. Their telephones rang out and my emails went unanswered. Some of the nurses said we had been 'stitched up' as a rather poor April Fool's joke. They guessed Mr V was a difficult patient. He would have to remain with us and so we set about creating care plans.

I saw Mr V in his cell with Graham as my chaperone. Mr V spoke in a whisper about his long recovery from a history of substance misuse. He was fifty years old but appeared much older and was frail and tearful. He said he hadn't used heroin for over twelve months and I congratulated him. He was wearing dark glasses and I couldn't see his eyes. The dark glasses, he said, were because he was registered blind, as well as hearing impaired. Then there was his poorly controlled epilepsy due to a traumatic life in which he had suffered many head injuries. He also said he had severe spinal damage from beatings and could barely walk without two walking sticks and, as a result, he had regular falls. But his walking sticks had been confiscated by the prison officers in Reception because his prison transfer notes stated he had used them as weapons. The nurses searched our stores and found him a battered wheelchair instead. He was pleased with that. Mr V engaged well in conversation and I thought he was quite a pleasant individual who'd been through the mill a bit. Mr V told me he was awaiting a parole hearing and was expecting to be released soon. I counted that he had been to prison on twenty separate occasions. I couldn't imagine how the cowed figure sitting in the wheelchair in front of me had such an extensive criminal career.

Mr V said he was prescribed pregabalin for chronic back pain and sciatica. He stated he had already been informed by our nurses that we didn't allow pregabalin for people who were also prescribed opioids, which he was. This was correct – pregabalin and opioids were a dangerous combination that could cause heart and breathing problems and could lead to death. He had also been prescribed Subutex, tramadol, mirtazapine, amitriptyline, epilepsy medications and sleeping tablets. I explained to him that these medications interacted with each other and could increase the frequency and severity of his epileptic seizures. Mr V said he was happy to consider any medication changes as long as he was not left in pain. I said I would refer him to the MDT for discussion.

Our nurses ensured he had a ground-level cell on the house block so that he didn't need to navigate stairs.

Unfortunately, the cell doors were too narrow to allow a wheelchair to access them. He would need to keep his wheelchair outside his cell and stumble around his cell as best he could, blindly holding on to furniture without any walking aids. It seemed inhumane to me. He was an accident waiting to happen. I looked around his cell noting trip hazards everywhere. I explained there were currently no spaces in the Inpatient unit but that he was number one on the waiting list. He reached out clumsily until he found my hands and clasped them between his and thanked me. All in all it was a very reasonable consultation and I derived from it a sense of personal well-being. If only every prisoner could be as amenable to being helped. This seemed like the beginning of a therapeutic relationship where we would both emerge with the satisfaction of a job well done.

The sense of contentment did not last long. The following morning Mr V was caught trying to conceal his medications. He pretended to swallow them all but in fact spat them out into his hand. When challenged by healthcare staff Mr V said he was being victimized for being visually impaired and he became abusive and threatening. An officer intervened and wheeled him back to his cell. Mr V returned to the medication hatch a short time later – with another officer. He informed the nurses that he had indeed concealed the medications earlier but he had since lost them and he wanted more. When they declined his request he became abusive again and the nurses pushed the panic alarm.

Later that day there was a Code Blue and Mr V was found on the floor of another prisoner's cell which was cloudy with smoke that smelt of drugs – possibly spice.

He was having difficulty breathing, his verbal responses were slow, and he seemed to be under the influence of an unknown substance. Oxygen was administered, he was revived, at which he immediately denied using any drugs and said he had suffered an epileptic seizure. He refused any further input from healthcare and asked the nurses to leave him alone. Satisfied that he was out of any immediate danger, they did.

The following morning Mr V attempted to conceal his medications in the roof of his mouth using a dab of toothpaste – it was one of the oldest tricks in the book. When challenged he angrily shot up from his wheelchair and marched away with ease; not even a hint of a limp. Two days later, while a nurse was administering Mr V's medications he was observed to be acting suspiciously. He started to cough dramatically as if he was choking. The prisoner standing behind him in the medication queue whispered to the nurse that he had witnessed Mr V spitting out his medication into his hand.

Mr V was booked in to see the Integrated Drug Treatment System doctor, Dr Emily Winters, who works closely with Toni, a second-generation British-Jamaican IDTS nurse with a Black Country accent that trumps my Brummie accent. A few minutes into the consultation the panic alarm was pushed. I ran to their clinic and flung the door open to find Mr V standing with his face pressed up close to Emily's and his hands raised. He was threatening to strangle her. Toni managed to drag him away by his arm and bundled him past me and out of the door. Mr V then very carefully laid himself down on the floor and began to shake his arms and legs.

'I'm having a fit!' he shouted.

'No, you're not,' I told him plainly.

The officers arrived within moments and asked why the alarm had been pushed. They could see a frail and vulnerable-looking man lying on the floor who looked to be in need of urgent attention while the medical staff around were ignoring him.

'He threatened to strangle the doctor. He was right in her face,' Toni explained.

'No, I did not, you liar!' Mr V shouted from the floor, his limbs still 'convulsing'.

The officers lifted him up from the floor and tried to put him in his wheelchair.

'Fuck off, I can walk,' Mr V shouted and kicked the wheelchair over. He hurried down the corridor and the officers had to run to catch up with him. I had no sense that they considered him threatening a doctor a serious enough offence to warrant him being taken to the Segregation unit. I checked that Emily was OK.

'He's a tricky customer,' she said with typical understatement.

'Your nose is bleeding. Did he hit you?' I asked with concern.

'That's just my blood pressure. I forgot to take my meds this morning,' she told me.

I handed her a tissue, which she pressed to her nose; it was gushing blood. Toni led her to the bathroom to clean up. I cleared the blood off her keyboard with antibacterial wipes.

Emily had a dry sense of humour and was great company. Toni had a booming laugh that could be heard down the corridor before she was seen. The two of them worked well together and we all became good friends. The third member of their team was another senior IDTS nurse called Rich. He had been in a punk band in the early eighties and many of his friends had died from drug overdoses. Watching the devastation around him, he had become interested in substance misuse and trained as a nurse, then began working in the community before transferring to the prison two years ago. Rich, like many of the staff in the prison, kindly took me under his wing. During our Friday lunch breaks we would go to the music room and he would teach me to play the guitar with extraordinary patience. I had owned a guitar for five years and it was gathering dust at home. Rich taught me to make time for my hobbies and for myself. He knew how hard I worked and said I was at risk of burnout. He was keen to impress upon me the importance of downtime. He was a vegan who practised yoga and meditation and lovingly tended an organic allotment – quite the trans-formation for a former punk. His lifestyle outside of work was the perfect antidote for the stresses of prison life. I needed to find a bit more balance myself.

I joined Emily, Toni and Rich for coffee breaks and it was the highlight of our stressful days. For fifteen or twenty minutes we laughed so generously that we for-got we were behind bars. Often I was the butt of the good-natured jokes for my naiveté and simplistic world view. Emily was a great fan of Disney and she thought I inhabited a fairytale world where the whole of humanity could sit in a sunny glade making daisy chains. I liked her version of me but it could not be further from the truth. I didn't tell her about my bouts of depression. I ignored my own problems by staying busy – by putting myself second and worrying about my patients instead. Of course, ignoring my problems did not make them go away. When I was alone it was as if a dark curtain descended all around me and I had to work incredibly hard to engage with my surroundings. Maybe that's why I had gravitated towards the thunderous noise and stench of prison work? It drowned out everything else, and I was grateful for that.

'I'm really surprised by the way Mr V is acting,' I said when Emily and Toni returned from the bathroom.

'His notes show this is a clear pattern of behaviour,' Emily said, still pressing her nose to stem the flow of blood.

'His notes go back twenty years, I only skim-read them,' I had to admit.

'Let me bring you up to speed. He appears to be selling his medications for drugs. He has admitted to buying heroin and spice in prison. This prison is full of drugs. Mr V has a history of attacks on healthcare staff. He is a team-splitter and tries to divide the primary-care, drug and mental-health teams. He presents to each of them with different symptoms and demands medications. He inevitably gets detoxed off pregabalin in prison. As soon as he's released he goes back to his community GP and intimidates them until they are prescribed again. He is a major risk of an accidental overdose,' Emily told me in a flawless summary.

'He is a death in custody waiting to happen. He loves spice and heroin but reacts badly to them. He will die and we will all get hauled over the coals in coroner's court,' Toni added.

Emily, Toni and Rich had an extensive cupboard of sweets and snacks in their room. Toni began to make us all cups of hot chocolate. Sugar was always part of the response to a challenging situation and the IDTS team faced many of them.

'We have to take him off some of his medications for his own protection. I think we should start with reducing the Subutex because he continues to conceal it. If he gives it to someone, they could have an overdose and die,' Emily said.

'If he's not taking it properly then he doesn't need it,' Toni chipped in.

'We need an MDT. We will need an officer to be present because it's going to be a difficult conversation,' Emily said.

'If he dares to try any funny business again I'll knock him into next week. Some swift Jamaican justice,' Toni said with a slap that swished through the air.

The Multi-Disciplinary Team meeting was arranged for the following week. I attended along with Mr V, Emily, Toni, the head of healthcare, and Mr V's drug worker. Also present was one of the In-reach mental-health nurses, Dean.

The first time I had met Dean I was incredibly busy in clinic and he very politely asked me to review a mental-health patient on the wings. There was no psychiatrist on site that day and he thought it was a psychiatric emergency. I reminded him I was a GP and not a psychiatrist, but I would go with him once I'd finished stitching someone's facial wound. I noticed Dean averted his green eyes as if, like many mental-health nurses, he didn't like the sight of blood. When Dean and I walked on to the wings prisoners called to him with smiles. He was clearly popular with patients and officers alike. It seemed there were few people who could resist Dean's Irish charm, wide smile, and penchant for quoting Kylie Minogue as if she was the greatest sage of the modern era. He went to all of her concerts and posed for photographs with her where she, admittedly, looked a little intimidated by his wild enthusiasm. I was interested to see the patient whose psychiatric state he was concerned about. The man was sitting in his cell with his eyes fixed on the ceiling.

'Can you look at me, please? I need to examine your eyes,' I said.

'I can't move my eyes,' the man replied through gritted teeth. He was clearly in great distress.

'He's been prescribed a new antipsychotic and I think the dose might be too high,' Dean explained with concern.

Dean was correct, the individual was suffering from an oculogyric crisis, a side effect of his medications that prevented his control over his eye movements. It was indeed a psychiatric emergency. I contacted the on-call psychiatrist and the patient was rushed to the outside hospital. The episode taught me to trust Dean's patient assessments. He was a very conscientious nurse who wrote essays rather than sentences in his patient notes – just as I did. He had been to coroner's court before and said his take-home message had been 'if it's not written down it didn't happen'. If something hadn't been documented in the healthcare records it was difficult to prove care had been given.

Mr V said he would attend the MDT on the condition that he could bring someone for emotional support; he chose a health champion, Mr R. I was glad to see Mr R again and I had heard from Chris that he was growing in his role and seemed to enjoy it. The men respected him and sought him out for advice. Goz, the small but powerful custodial manager, was also present in case Mr V became violent.

'I'm your bodyguard, Dr Y,' she reminded me. 'If he even looks at you weirdly I will snap him in two.'

'He's blind, Goz,' I reminded her.

'Well then he won't see it coming,' Goz replied.

We all sat in a semi-circle, with no sense of hierarchy, a configuration aimed at putting Mr V at ease. The walls were covered in posters of sunrises and mountain tops overlaid with motivational quotes:

'The Only Way Out Is Through!'

'I Am Not What Happens To Me – I Am What I Choose To Become!'

There was also a poster of the Stages of Change by Prochaska and DiClemente. It demonstrated how to move forward from a relapse and maintain new, healthier patterns of behaviour. The upward spiral showed how the first step was to recognize there was a problem even if there was no commitment to change it. This MDT was for Mr V to contemplate his problems and how we could take action to prevent future relapses.

Goz politely informed Mr V that if he became aggressive the meeting would be terminated and he would be asked to leave. He sat in his wheelchair with his head bowed at first. His next move was to try flirting with Goz. She was unimpressed by his small talk.

'Stop barking; it's the wrong tree,' Goz told him flatly. From behind the dark glasses he appeared to notice her rainbow lanyard and looked crestfallen.

Then he moved into aggressive mode.

'I just want you to know that I am going to sue this poxy prison,' Mr V announced to the room.

'Let me try to help you,' I said. It had quickly become my go-to line. I wanted the patient to feel heard and cared for. I also thought: who says 'poxy' any more?

He replied with a volley of expletives.

'Wind your neck in,' Goz interjected.

'Shut up,' Mr V snapped at her.

'Say that again and I'll tie your limbs in a bow!' Goz said with a stern tone that made it clear she would not tolerate any further bad behaviour.

Mr V began to present his case and he grew increasingly agitated. He was irritable, rude, and swearing profusely – but it was all verbal. There were no physical threats yet. He denied concealing his medications and smoking spice. His notes now made perfect sense. There had been numerous concerns at his previous prison. He also had a long history of being rude and threatening towards staff and, after a sunny start, we had now experienced this at close quarters.

Toni explained to Mr V that when he had arrived in our prison he had signed a number of compacts. One of them stated that if there was any suspicion that he concealed his meds or didn't take them in the pre-scribed manner then they would be stopped. This was for his protection and the protection of others. Mr V asked if the compact had been in Braille. It had not. Therefore, he said, he hadn't known what he was sign-ing. The form should have been read out to him because he was visually impaired. Mr V had an answer for everything.

'My medications were prescribed by hospital doc-tors: neurologists and psychiatrists. You lot are only GPs and you can't touch them. I know my rights. If you even think about detoxing me I will stop all of my meds and die from an epileptic fit. My death will be on your hands. I will make sure I write letters to the news-papers, my MP, and my family. I will let them know that you have murdered me,' Mr V said with vitriol.

He pointed at each of us in turn. His aim was sur-prisingly good for a man with visual impairment – I wondered if anything he had told me was actually true. He sat back in his wheelchair with his arms crossed defiantly. He certainly wasn't going to make this easy for any of us.

'Medication is just a small part of drug recovery. You still have access to your drug worker and the psy-chosocial team for ongoing support and talking therapies,' Emily said.

'This is all shit and you know you can't do anything to me. I dare you to touch my medications and see what happens! The psychosocial stuff is fucking rub-bish. I'm not interested!' Mr V shouted.

Mr R was clearly flustered but was doing his best to calm Mr V and explain that the team were trying to help him become drug-free. Mr V snapped at him to shut up. Goz told him to watch his language. He didn't tell her to shut up again. No one told Goz what to do.

'We don't want to stop your medications but we have no choice. We have a duty to keep you and others safe,' Emily said with confidence.

After hearing Mr V's complaints and weighing up the evidence all staff present agreed that he needed to be detoxed off some of his medications. Emily and I explained we would detox one medication at a time. It was safer and more tolerable than stopping them all in one go. The psychosocial workers would continue to offer support. We would also open an ACCT document to support him in case he tried to harm himself. Dean said he was happy to continue to offer support. It was a textbook solution to anyone who was detoxed off medications in case they reacted badly.

'Fuck off! Fuck each and every single one of you. I hope you all catch AIDs and die!' Mr V screamed at us all. Again taking the time to point a jabbing finger in all our faces with impeccable accuracy.

He terminated the consultation by stepping from his wheelchair and striding out of the room, slamming the door behind him. Goz followed after him. Mr R apologized to us for the bad language, which was very unexpected and much appreciated, before leaving too. I doubted if Mr V really was blind. He had managed to step through a small gap in the semi-circle to exit the room and had reached for the door handle without any hesitation. He was also able to get up and down from his wheelchair with ease. He didn't appear to need walking sticks, let alone a wheelchair. His diagnoses of visual impairment and mobility issues would need to be assessed – but that was work for another day.

I reached over and passed Emily a tissue because her nose was bleeding again. When everyone else had left the meeting other than Toni and Emily, I asked Emily if she was feeling stressed.

'I don't know, to be honest. My blood pressure is alright when I remember my tablets. I think I've gone beyond being worried about my health. There are times I just feel tired and I think I've had enough and I want to go to bed. It could be stress that's causing my blood pressure. Maybe I'm just not bright enough to work out that I'm stressed . . .' she trailed off, pondering that possibility.

'I was teaching medical students the other day. We were talking about burnout amongst healthcare work-ers. I ticked every single box other than feeling stressed. I've got all the other physical symptoms. My BP was 200/100 when I was expecting it to be close to 120/80. I get nosebleeds every time I'm pissed off with some-one. I've started getting really frustrated with myself because you can't have a very good poker face if every time you're annoyed you spring a leak,' Emily told me.

'Have you seen your GP?' I asked.

Emily looked sheepish. 'Ever since the Dr Shipman debacle,' she reminded me, 'GPs aren't allowed to pro-vide medical care for ourselves or our immediate families. We're not even allowed to prescribe antibiotics for ourselves. I went and registered at my friend's prac-tice because I knew he was a good doctor. The medications made me feel worse for the first two weeks.

Every time I crossed the road or did minimal activity, like climbing a flight of stairs, I'd have a pounding headache and palpitations. Then over a few weeks my BP slowly came down and I'm back to 120/80 now, when I remember to take my meds.'

I rolled my eyes at her.

'I think doctors ignore their own ill health until you just have to do something about it,' Emily said with a small laugh. I laughed too and hoped it didn't sound hollow, as I did exactly the same thing.

Emily continued, 'Toni is as bad as me. We have competitions to see who has the highest BP. The winner lies down and the loser has to make the hot chocolate!'

'Why did you end up in prison?' I asked. It was a question so many of my friends kept asking me, and finding my own response had made me think long and hard about how this eclectic group of colleagues had come together. Emily was the mother of three young daughters and was probably one of the smartest people I had ever met. Like me she was passionate about history, but whereas I bought vintage suits she made her own costumes for battle re-enactments. She was the definition of a leader and I found her inspiring. What was she doing here?

'I thought it would be interesting,' Emily mused. 'My first day in prison reminded me of being back at school. I thought, wow, the bullies at school didn't go away. They're all here, in some way or another. Then I did a couple of days in a maximum-security category A prison. There was one guy that I was in a room with. I was there to reduce his benzodiazepines. I was warned that he had killed several people and I knew the last time someone had tried to reduce his benzos he'd attacked them. I was sitting alone in a room with him and there were six officers outside the room, ready to move fast but maybe not fast enough. After that day, whenever I have a difficult situation, I think, "I faced that guy and I can face this." I do have some sleepless nights. I think we all need some mental-health testing for choosing to work here. You included, Dr Y.'

I let a silence settle between us and then laughed it off – as I always did. I could have taken the opportunity to unburden myself but I didn't. Time and again I could have spoken to my kind colleagues about my bereavement and low mood, but I didn't feel ready – it was still too raw. I averted my eyes and caught sight of a poster with a motivational quote from Maya Angelou – *'There is no greater agony than bearing an untold story inside you.'*

Emily particularly loved working with Toni, Rich and Dean. They really cared about the patients. All of our achievements were, we all knew, because someone had helped us along the way. It was now our turn to be the helpers.

'That was brought home to me when I worked with young offenders,' Emily said. 'There was a girl I saw there, a teenager, who had tried to hang herself. I saw her a few days after the attempt and her entire face was one big blue-grey petechial rash, caused by bleeding under the skin. She had a horrible rope burn around her neck and the blood vessels in her eyes had burst so the whites of her eyes were red. She came to see me because she couldn't work out what was wrong with her skin. She had survived a suicide attempt but was now more concerned about her complexion and how long it would take to clear up! She asked me for make-up tips. That was hard. I thought, I'm trying to make you better just so you can go home to the family you're trying to kill yourself to get away from.'

I had worked in the young offender institution with Emily and I knew the girl she was referring to. She had idolized Emily and asked her where she got her brightly coloured shoes from. They were the sort of shoes a Disney princess would wear – glittery and covered in shiny buckles, fabric posies and ribbons. Emily had themed footwear for every occasion. Some shoes were covered in plastic cookies and appliqué hearts. No surface was left unembellished. Emily said the shoes were hand-made by a man in his nineties on the Isle of Wight, the British version of a blind Tibetan monk. I thought it was a joke at first but it wasn't. Her shoes are as extraordinary as she is.

It was being surrounded by such incredible people that made doing the job possible.

The MDT team agreed to see Mr V every week. He refused to attend the clinics we booked to check on his well-being. So Emily, Toni, Rich, Dean and I made it a weekly ritual to traipse to his cell door. The officer unlocked it for us and Mr V would tell us to fuck off and turn the volume up on his TV. Regular as clockwork. He refused to answer any of our questions and would shout at the officer to lock the door. At first the visits lasted for seconds. Eventually Mr V began using more elaborate swears but at least he was talking to us for a couple of minutes – it was progress of sorts. He could be forgiven for his irritability because his Sub-utex was being lowered and would then stop. Dean believed he needed a period without any medication before his underlying mental-health issues could be assessed. Mr V's substance-misuse and mental-health problems were almost inextricably intertwined, but we needed to unpick it all in order to be able to help him properly.

We referred him to the outside neurologist for an opinion on his supposed epilepsy, but Mr V refused to attend the hospital appointment. We arranged for the neurologist to be sent all of his notes and he called me at the prison; there had never been a diagnosis of epilepsy or any problems with his mobility. He advised us to start taking him off the epilepsy medications and arranged a six-month follow-up with Mr V. The prison optician was similarly perplexed by Mr V's assertion that he was partially sighted – he was assessed and found to have perfect vision.

After a few months' stay with us Mr V was off all of his prescribed medication. Dean said he met him in passing one day and prepared himself for a volley of expletives but instead Mr V was polite and said he had never felt better. None of us is prone to back-slapping and self-congratulations, but this had all the hallmarks of a job well done. At least in this prison, at least for now. We wished Mr V well on his long road to recovery.

6

Trauma

The alert crackled over the radios.

'Code Blue on House Block D, A spur. Oscar 1 attend. Hotel 3 attend. Control has called for an ambulance!'

And so it begins.

We use the NATO phonetic alphabet to communicate. Hotel is for healthcare and Oscar 1 is for operational or prison leadership. Hotel 3 is the nurse or paramedic who will attend all emergencies. Hotel 3 is often Nurse Steph.

Nurse Steph is excellent in a crisis: unflappable, and eminently reassuring. She is nicknamed the Naloxone Queen and is skilled in reviving men with the medication who would otherwise have died from opioid overdoses. Steph is a brittle asthmatic who needs hospital treatment every few months herself. The irony of her tending to men who are smoking noxious substances is not lost on any of us. And yet she lifts the heavy 12kg response bag on to her back and starts running. It contains the oxygen tank, and all the equipment and medications she might need as she heads into the unknown.

On another day, Steph might be responding to a Code Red. Code Reds are emergencies where blood is involved. They can be assaults, stabbings or self-harm, all of which are a regular occurrence. Steph runs to the Codes along with a healthcare assistant, either Chris, Victoria or Sophie. They have minutes to get to the location, which could be anywhere in the prison. We all seem to spend our days rushing from one emergency to the next without any time to write up our notes in between. And, it's worth repeating, notes are what will stop the barristers from tearing you apart in coroner's court.

One of the main issues in prison is spice. Some prisoners are addicted to spice and are so desperate for it they'll even allow themselves to be beaten or degraded in order to obtain it. One man infamously would take 'a hit for a hit' and let people punch him in the face with full force for a single puff of spice. He had his jaw dislocated many times and walked around with a lopsided grin. Officers informed me these assaults were sometimes filmed and uploaded to the internet and would need to be taken down by the security team before it damaged the reputation of the prison. We were already renowned as one of the most violent prisons in the UK.

I asked Steph how the men accessed spice and other drugs in prison. The prisoners were searched when they came in, after all.

'They get it on visits from their family, bent screws,

or they bring it in their *prison pocket*,' she replied nonchalantly.

I was stumped. 'What?' I asked stupidly.

'They "plug" it.'

I shook my head . . .

'They stick it up their bum,' Steph explained bluntly.

'I thought that was called "packing"?' I recalled.

'There're lots of different words for the same gross thing. Sometimes if a guy is suspected of bringing in drugs but he denies it, the other prisoners will spoon him,' Steph said, enjoying my lack of knowledge of prison terminology. When she said spooning, I imagined a couple sleeping curled into each other protectively and lovingly.

'It's not what you're thinking,' she said, as if reading my mind. 'Spooning in prisons means they literally stick a spoon up someone's arse and fiddle about looking for packages. It can cause a lot of internal damage and the first we hear about it is when someone presents with a Code Red and they have extensive bleeding from their back passage. We have to rule out rape and call the forensics team in, but nine times out of ten it is the result of spooning, which is still classified as a sexual crime.'

I covered my mouth with my hand in shock, a cartoon image of disbelief.

The most vicious assault, worse than the shankings (or stabbings with prison-made blades) and being beaten with tins of tuna in a sock, is to be sugar-watered. A large bag of sugar is added to a kettle of water and heated. This molten syrup, when thrown at another human being, burns down through all the layers of skin and tissue. It is more severe than an average water burn and leads to permanent disfigurement. If it is thrown in the face it can lead to blindness and even death. The screams from men who have been sugar-watered fill my nightmares.

Victims of sugar-water attacks are always so badly injured they can't be cared for on the wings. These poor men, blinded, screaming and shivering with shock, have to be escorted to the Outpatient department. Gloopy and cold burns dressings are gently applied to their inflamed wounds. We apologize as we tend to them with the utmost care because we know they are excruciatingly painful. We handle the men with extreme delicacy and offer words of reassurance and comfort that are barely audible over their agonized screams.

As well as Code Blues and Code Reds, healthcare staff are also called to every cell fire. In 2011 alone there were almost a thousand cell fires in UK prisons – the system is a positive inferno. A cell fire is likely to be the most traumatic event you can witness behind bars and you never forget your first time. Mine came one morning.

A radio call came in for the doctor to come to the house block urgently. This is never a good omen. I ran to the location as quickly as I could. I followed the smell of burning and the wailing smoke alarms on the wing until I saw a group of officers, big burly men who gloried in how much physical pain they could endure in the gym, huddled supportively in a corner of the landing. They were weeping quietly – clearly in a state of shock. I hurried to the cell in question and saw that the entire room was swallowed up by black smoke. Peering through it, I could see that the mattress had a large hole burned through it and the floor was wet — but the patient was missing.

I was confused. Then an officer stepped in to guide me. It transpired that each cell door is fitted with an inundation unit, which is a round hole that can be detached. A hosepipe can be fed through it without the need to open the door, which would risk a backdraught and further spread. A prison is a tinderbox and a fire could spread from cell to cell with ferocity. Officers had put out the flames through the hole in the door, but the room was still engulfed in noxious fumes. The officers had carefully carried the man to a vacant neighbouring cell to be treated. During the transfer his burned skin had sloughed off in papery sheets in the officers' hands, revealing his charred and blackened flesh. The officers were understandably traumatized by what they had witnessed.

I ran to the new location to help my colleagues who were already hard at work and struggling to find any unburned areas on the man's body to insert a needle for pain relief because his veins were so damaged. In a glance, I estimated that he had at least 60 per cent burns and was at risk of severe dehydration, shock, infection and death. Finally we located a small patch of skin over his foot that had not been burned and I fixed a precious needle to give him morphine and fluids. The nurses told me that the man had been able to give them a little bit of history amongst his agonized cries. He had been using spice and had fallen unconscious. He had dropped the ignited roll-up on himself. He regained consciousness when his synthetic clothes were ablaze and he was immersed in flames.

The Air Ambulance arrived within minutes and they flew him to the local burns unit, which very fortunately was only a few miles away. We spent the next few days wondering how he was getting on, but there was no news. Finally, after a week, all those who had been involved in his care as we'd battled to sustain life – officers and healthcare – were called to the chapel where we were informed that the patient had succumbed to his injuries. The governor and a representative from healthcare had to break the news to his family in person. They were heartbroken – he had left a young family behind.

In addition to the dangers of spice, the risk of fire is always high because the men will sometimes attack each other with kettles of boiling water, which can lead to an electrical fire. Smoking and lighters became prohibited in prisons in 2015. But the men are ingenious and can strip their kettles down to their wires and spark a fire with ease.

Tobacco is smuggled in and sold at a premium. When the prisoners run out of it they smoke plain paper sprayed with spice, coal tar shampoo, or any other chemical they can find. At one point bananas were banned because the prisoners used to steal the skins, which they dried and smoked in the false belief that smoking banana skins gives a natural high. Prisoners will sometimes even inhale burning plastic for a head rush. They seek oblivion wherever and however they can find it.

No one wants to die in prison. We do everything we can to save lives so that prisoners can go home after

serving their sentences. If anyone looks depressed or
withdrawn we question their mental state and ask if
they have any ideas or plans to self-harm. The In-reach
mental-health team receive dozens of such referrals a
day. Dean is particularly skilled at getting men to lay
their cards on the table when it comes to their emotions. He seems to be constantly running around the
prison from one psychiatric crisis to another and making a real difference. Some men cope with their anxiety
by cutting and scratching themselves, which is known
as 'cutting up'. Their bodies are overlaid with scars at
various stages of healing – but they are adamant it is
just a coping mechanism and they don't actually want
to die. At one point there were approximately seventy
men on ACCTs out of a population of just over a thousand. It is a frightening statistic.

Steph received the governor's commendation for
responding to thirty Codes in one day. It was during
a time when the prison was infiltrated with the dangerous opioid fentanyl. It is extremely potent, and
prisoners were smoking it along with spice. Many
went into immediate respiratory arrest or had prolonged seizures. Some remained unresponsive despite
being given repeated doses of the opioid antidote
naloxone. They had to be transferred to the outside
hospital where they required life support. Steph saved
287 lives in one twelve-month period and was given
a fifty-pound voucher and a 'thank you' card by the
governor. An OBE would have been more appropriate. She is a true hero who is too humble to accept the
congratulations.

'Just doing my job,' Steph says.

If Steph is already dealing with a Code and another emergency comes through the radio system, then Hotel 4 or the next available nurse on the rota will attend. If another emergency comes through, and another, then all Hotel call signs will be asked to attend. If it is a very serious Code and the Hotels need support they will call for a doctor – which indicates things are heading south very quickly. I will then terminate any consultation, apologize to my patient, ask them to leave the room, lock the door behind me and run.

We treat each Code like a battle and fight to bring our patients back from the brink of death. Sometimes there will be four or five members of healthcare staff in a tiny cell. Some cells operate as unofficial wing shops where every spare surface is piled high with goods. Others are relatively bare, with just graffiti and semi-naked pin-ups on the walls. In this confined space we have to climb over each other and work on a man to bring him back to life. Each cell is an entire world and photographs of family stare down at us. Blu-Tack and chewing gum are forbidden in prison because they can be used to block keyholes. If a prisoner got hold of a set of keys they could use gum to make a mould, duplicate the keys and escape. It sounds absurd, the stuff of films, but it's possible. So hand-made Father's Day cards, tenuously fixed to the walls with toothpaste instead, will flap in the disturbed air. Beaming toddlers, parents and partners watch over us as we work. I try not to look at the photographs of family, whose faces seem to be imploring me to bring their loved one back. We are all aware, those inside this tiny room, that life is a very fragile thing. It can be snuffed out as easily as blowing out a candle or lighting a cigarette. Sometimes all it takes is a pill that's just a few millimetres in diameter.

It is exhausting work, bringing a man back to life, and we need to take turns in pressing down on the chest wall deep enough to restart this man's heart. Oxygen is administered and we inflate his collapsed lungs. We rub cold hands between our own and watch as his circulation begins shutting down. The inky blue of death gathers first at the fingertips and works its way up the arms. The automated external defibrillator indicates if a shock is necessary. We draw back as best we can in the cramped space and the seemingly lifeless body convulses on the hard floor. Our hands on his clammy chest do the work of his heart and lungs. All the while we call out to the man lying before us. We beg him to come back to us. We tell him that he is loved. Even after thirty minutes we can get lucky and the deathly blue cloak that is hidden under the skin is pulled slowly away. The ruddy warmth of circulation spreads down from his face to the fingertips until, finally, he gasps and opens his eyes.

'Welcome back to the land of the living,' Steph says wheezily, wiping her wet brow with the back of her gloved hand.

'You nearly gave me a heart attack!' Chris tells the man, clutching at her own chest.

'I'm sorry,' the man murmurs as we put him in the recovery position.

Waves of relief wash over us that death has been overcome – on this occasion. Later we smile and laugh and congratulate each other. Another precious life has been saved. A family which has already been strained by the separation of prison has been saved from being broken. We don't expect thanks; it is our job to protect our patients and it's why we come to work. The physical and emotional toll these emergencies take on us is not something we talk about. As Steph says, we're just doing our job.

Sometimes we work for an hour until the patient is revived. We never want to give up unless it's quite clear they are dead. If they have been using spice they can become paranoid and aggressive as soon as they recover and they will hit out at us. They slap and kick us because they're still under the influence of a noxious substance. We shield our faces from the blows. We gather our equipment before retreating to a safe distance and check on the patient a few minutes later. We might need to rest on the floor outside the cell, propped up against a cold wall. Steph will use her asthma inhaler. Another Code will come through while we are still panting with exhaustion and soaked through with sweat. We pick ourselves up and run to the next emergency.

One of the abiding disappointments about Codes is being called back repeatedly to revive the same individuals. And one of the repeat offenders is Mr Harrison, whose latest stint in prison had begun with a spice collapse in Reception and whose behaviour had continued in the same vein. His habit had not abated. His hair had been worn long since the Swinging Sixties and it had greyed so that he appeared to be a relic from another era. He boasted there was not a single drug he hadn't tried. He told me he was good-looking in his youth, a lady's man who had travelled the world fathering children and trading in narcotics for huge sums of money. He described a glamorous life of every kind of excess and counted ageing rock stars amongst his acquaintances. He said he had explored the jungles of South America where a shaman had given him ayahuasca, a hallucinogenic drug with a notoriously high death rate.

'I nearly died, twice,' Mr Harrison told me with pride, as if he was indestructible. I smiled politely but didn't believe a word of it.

Mr Harrison still carried himself as if he was irresistible to women and he took his false teeth out to blow sloppy kisses to the nurses. The nurses kindly pretended to be flattered and called him a 'character'. He was always in and out of prison with heroin-related offences. He was also reputed to be a prison guinea pig. Prison drug dealers tested the strength of new batches of drugs on him, with or without his consent. If there was a Code on D Block we assumed it was likely to be Mr Harrison and were often correct. Each time we brought him back from the brink we told him how lucky he was to be alive.

'This isn't a life,' he said once as we were leaving. The bravado of being a proud connoisseur of narcotics had left him with sore ribs and a throat which was ragged after a tube had been thrust down it. Steph and I were both uncharacteristically lost for words.

Usually she cracks a joke and I will give a prisoner the advice I prescribe for myself. 'Find three things that you enjoyed in your day – it could be as easy as eating something tasty, hearing something amusing, seeing someone you like. Those three things mean it was a day worth living.'

But I didn't say that on this occasion. Instead I was overcome with sadness. It felt as if all we were doing was mopping up the mess of everyone's disastrous lives only for the deluge to break the banks once again, or applying bandages to deep wounds and then being surprised when they did not heal.

Steph said she needed a cigarette and I gratefully accompanied her out of the prison so that I could breathe fresh air. I had forgotten the number of times I'd advised her to give up smoking. I said it again. She nodded knowingly and took two puffs of her inhaler before heading to her car to collect her cigarettes and lighter. As we walked towards the smoking shed at the edge of the car park she could tell I was in a contemplative mood. I realized she was watching my face closely through a haze of smoke.

'It was Father's Day last weekend, did you get your dad something nice?' she asked.

'He's dead,' I said quietly.

'Oh my God, Dr Y, I didn't know. I'm so sorry,' she spluttered.

'It's fine, he was a lovely man and I have fond memories.'

'Do you want to talk about it?' she asked kindly.

'I don't know,' I replied honestly.

She nodded and we let a silence fall between us.

'He died the night before finals,' I said after some hesitation.

'Bloody hell!' she gasped.

'Yeah, it was.'

'When I was at medical school I lived in a student

house,' I recalled. 'My wall planner had thick black lines around two dates, which were my final examinations: the eighth and ninth of May. Those two days loomed ahead of me like huge fists in boxing gloves. The title of doctor I'd been working towards my entire life was finally coming close. The pressure was intense and on top of all of that I had a fear of overworking and still not feeling good enough. It has been a constant anxiety in my life.'

'Go on,' Steph pressed gently.

'Despite all of my efforts I had a horrible premon- ition that something bad was going to happen. Finally the day came: Monday the eighth of May 2006. It's a date I will never forget. The exam went well. I called home and spoke to my parents. My father wished me well and told me he was praying for my success. He was my best friend and he made me feel safe. During that phone call we laughed and joked as we always did. He told me he was proud of me and that I shouldn't worry about anything. I had a good stable background, unlike a lot of the men in there,' I said, pointing behind us to the great white wall.

Steph nodded. 'Your parents sound like really nice people,' she said.

'Yes, good people,' I went on. 'I don't find it easy to share my feelings.'

'Like a typical man,' Steph said and exhaled a plume of smoke.

'It's only working here and confronting death day in and day out that makes me want to open up about myself,' I continued. 'You look at these men's lives and you can't help but think about your own.'

I paused before continuing.

'After speaking to my parents on the Monday night I was about to get into bed when my sister Shahzadi called me. She told me hesitantly that our father was unwell; he was in hospital and I should come. I could hear the false reassurance in her voice. I knew my father was dead. I don't know how I knew but I did. I left the student house quietly because I didn't want to disturb my housemates. I drove home towards Birmingham, but I was crying and completely disorientated. I took wrong turns and drove into petrol stations for no reason other than to park my car and stop my hands from shaking.'

'Oh, Dr Y!' Steph exclaimed.

'The world had suddenly become a strange and terrifying place. It was like the road was pushing me up into the sky and the tree branches were trying to grab me. I was driving around this strange new world and observing everything as if for the first time. I stopped at a red light and lowered my window. "Do you know the way to the hospital?" I asked the man in the next car. His cap was drawn down over his eyes, but even in the state I was in I could see that they were red and his car smelt of cannabis. He struggled to hear me over his loud music. The man gave me directions very slowly. We were still talking when the cars behind us began honking their horns. "My dad's dead," I managed to say amongst sobs. He said he was sorry. I drove away howling into the night like a wounded animal. He was the first person I told. I wouldn't recognize him now. He was just a stranger. But I want to say thank you to him. Thank you for taking the time to talk to me. He talked to me with kindness and I've never forgotten it.'

'I'm going to need another fag. What happened next?' Steph asked as she lit up with shaking hands.

'Shahzadi called and gave me fresh instructions. In her confusion she had told me to go to the wrong hospital on the other side of Birmingham. She was crying now and I could hear the voices of my uncles and aunties in the background; they were all crying. It had taken me three hours to make a forty-minute journey. I ran through the hospital and was led to a side room by a kind junior doctor. He had been informed I was a medical student doing my final exams. He said he could only imagine how difficult this must be for me. He said he was sorry before pushing the door open for me. I don't know his name. His kindness pierced the darkness like a flaming arrow. It meant so much to me then and it still does now.'

'Kindness,' Steph repeated and I could see tears forming in the corners of her eyes.

'The first person I saw was my mother, Bilqeas. She was sitting on a chair directly in front of me. She wanted to be the person to break the bad news to me. "He's gone," she said quietly. My father was lying on a bed to the side of the room. He was still warm and soft. My uncles and aunties were all there. They left me alone with him for a while and I told him what a wonderful father he had been. I said goodbye. I rarely tell anyone what happened to me, to us as a family. I am telling you this because you need to know that you save so many lives and it's not just those lives that you save, it's their families' too. You are a real hero.'

Steph reached forward and hugged me tightly.

'Thank you,' she whispered into my ear.

'No, you're a good person, you help people every day, you make a difference,' I said, my throat tightening.

'You help people too,' Steph countered, pulling away from me and wiping the tears from her face.

'No I don't, not really,' I said. 'The prisoners hate the doctors here, we are all Dr No and Dr Death and Dr Paracetamol to them. They don't think we care – that's the hardest part. I wouldn't be standing here today if people hadn't helped me and I want to do the same for others.'

'They are chatting shit when they insult the doctors,' Steph said. 'When there's a Code and the doctor arrives everyone, myself included, takes a sigh of relief.'

'I don't understand how our patients play with their lives so easily,' I said.

'Because they have nothing to live for, they have already given up. What actually happened to your dad, if you don't mind me asking?' Steph asked gently.

'My mother told me my father had been in bed when he had spoken to me on the phone,' I replied. 'Later he said he had indigestion and asked for milk. My mother had finished praying and was reciting the Quran as she did every night. She went downstairs and warmed up some milk and honey for him. She brought it to him and he drank it and then lay down and continued to pray. He was praying for my success. My mother said his voice became quieter. She called to him but he didn't respond. She acted quickly and called the emergency services and my sister too. They were with her in minutes. The paramedics said he was already gone. "He must have been in a hurry," they said. They took him to the hospital and that's when my sister called me. Within an hour of my speaking to him he was dead. We knew he had heart problems. My sister and I always took it in turns to escort him to his hospital appointments. We thought he had many years left ahead of him. I was devastated. My GP said it was grief and it would get better with time – but there isn't a pill for every ill. Sometimes you just suffer. I buried the hurt deep down inside me,' I admitted.

'Like the prisoners do,' Steph reflected.

'Which is why it's kind of inevitable that I do the sort of work I do,' I said. 'We went home from the hospital and sat up for the entire night leaning against each other and weeping. Our friends were with us, Shanaz and Mumtaz, still wearing their dressing gowns. If you have friends who will rush to your side in the middle of the night in their dressing gowns they're not just friends, they are family. When the morning came I decided that my father would have wanted me to go to my final examination. My mum and sister tried to stop me, but I felt as if I would be letting him down. I called the medical school and they arranged for me to sit in a separate office with an invigilator. Before the exam I locked myself in the disabled toilet and sobbed uncontrollably. My mouth was full of bile and I was sick with real violence. I lay down on the toilet floor in the foetal position. It was all I could do. Someone knocked on the door and asked if I was alright. I said no and shouted at them to go away.'

'Oh my God, Dr Y!' Steph exclaimed and squeezed my shoulder gently. She knew I wasn't a shouter.

'When I was in the office for my exam I was shaking so intensely that I had to hold on to the desk to steady myself,' I went on. 'I could barely see because my eyes were dancing and my head was pounding. The exam paper was soaked with my snot and tears and the ink from my pen bled into it, making a mess on the page. The invigilator sat opposite me, his face flushed red with embarrassment. He tried to hide behind his book. Even if he had wanted to intervene there was nothing he could have done other than offer his commiserations. I wasn't given any extra time for extenuating circumstances. It was all a miserable blur.

'Afterwards, when I switched on my phone there were a lot of missed calls and messages. My friends found me sitting on the steps of the medical school. They took me back to our student house and helped me pack my belongings. I ripped down the wall planner and tore it into pieces – I had lost faith in any kind of future. Then they insisted on driving me home. We collected my father's body from the hospital and took him to the mosque.'

Steph coughed on her cigarette smoke.

'I was the man of the house now,' I continued, 'but still so young, and I was expected to lead with all of the religious ceremonies. I couldn't have done it without the love and support of our family and friends who ushered me around and showed me what to do. I helped to wash my father, anoint him with perfumed oils and wrap him in his death shroud. It was all very hands-on. We dug the grave ourselves, lowered the coffin in gently and poured in handfuls of earth. I was in a deep state of shock and think autopilot must have kicked in. It is Muslim custom to sit on the floor or on low furniture for three days following a death. My friends helped to clear the furniture in our lounge to the side of the room. They sat on the floor with their arms draped around our shoulders. I would like to thank my family and friends for picking up the pieces when our world collapsed. My friends Mumtaz and Shanaz and their families were by our side every step of the way. They still are.

'Our family ran a newsagent's shop. It was closed when my father died and our only source of income vanished. Ten days later I was in the cemetery when I received a phone call from the Dean of the medical school congratulating me for passing my medical finals. My father had died ten days before hearing the news he had waited decades for – I was standing beside his grave. He would have been so happy. But I really struggled to be pleased. I didn't want to go to my graduation ceremony, but my mother and sister insisted we needed to celebrate. My friends hollered and cheered when I was called to the stage to collect my certificate. The Vice-Dean and Dean offered kind words and squeezed my hand tightly. But I was just going through the motions and wanted it to be over. The thing is, I think I have been going through the motions ever since. Afterwards my mother, sister and I went for a celebratory meal in a nice restaurant, and we ate and posed for photographs and stared into space,' I admitted.

'You deserved to celebrate after all of that hard work. Well done!' Steph said.

'A few weeks after that I started working as a junior doctor, but I didn't tell anyone what had happened,' I conceded.

'Help would have been available,' Steph murmured gently.

'It takes time to open up,' I said. 'None of us are text-book examples, are we? – not the prisoners or us. We are all just humans trying to get through life with what we know.'

Steph nodded. I'd have got the same recognition from any of my wonderful colleagues.

Later as I was driving home I called my friend Adil. He has been my friend for ever and is the closest person I have to a brother. He had been a tower of strength during that dark time. He'd always been close to my father and had cried more than I had.

'Is there anything you need?' he asked.

'I don't smoke weed, Adil,' I reminded him. 'Anyway, I told someone at work about Dad today and I feel better, lighter.'

After a long chat punctuated by laughter I parked outside our shop and said goodbye to Adil. One of our neighbours had spray-painted a sign on their wall – 'No fucking parking please' – and it always made me smile. I hesitated before opening the front door of our shop. I closed my eyes and pretended I was back in time. The shop bell would ring over my head and my father would turn to greet me with a broad smile and a bear hug. I opened my eyes and saw that the lights were switched off. I unlocked the door and walked past shelves covered with blankets and sheets. The perishables had long since been given away. There was a hushed silence that should have felt welcoming after the roar of the prison but it wasn't. I didn't put the lights on as I passed through the closed shop. I remember at first I had thought there was something wrong with all the lights in our home because it seemed so dull – I went around and changed all the lightbulbs to 100 watts. It made no difference. I realized it was dark because my father Mohammed wasn't there to lighten the mood with his smiles and jokes.

The first room beyond the shop was the kitchen. My parents had a happy marriage between someone who loved to cook and someone who loved to eat. They bickered over the kitchen stove about spices and recipes and my mother kept the best treats aside for my father. I could smell the spices: cardamom, turmeric, saffron, chilli. These were the spices I knew before working in the prison and discovering the deadly spice. My mother and sister are excellent cooks and renowned for their generosity. They send food to friends and neighbours on a regular basis and I am given the role of delivery driver. Many of our family memories are inextricably linked to food. We discussed recording our recipes in a cookbook. I approached literary agents and publishers to see if they would be interested in a Pakistani cookbook but they declined it. Pakistan is the fifth most populous nation on earth with a huge diaspora and a culinary history that is both ancient and diverse. And yet when I browse the shelves of bookshops I will find many books on preserves and pickling but possibly none on Pakistani cooking. It seems, to me, to be more than an oversight. Beyond the kitchen is a large lounge and I could see the television flickering through the glass in the window. I opened the door and was greeted by my mother and sister who were watching Turkish serials dubbed into Urdu.

'How was your day?' my mother asked in Urdu.

'It was fine,' I replied in English. It was how we communicated, she in Urdu and me in English. It was a typical understatement that did not do justice to the day I had actually witnessed.

We settled down to a delicious dinner of biriyani. Four plates laid out instead of three. We forced ourselves to laugh to cheer each other up. We kept our personal unhappiness private so as not to burden each other, preferring to relive happy memories from the past.

'When Shahzadi was born she was very beautiful, with bright green eyes, pale skin and red hair,' my mother said. 'When I took her out in a pram, people would stop me in the street and say, "Is she half-caste?"'

'Mum, do you mean mixed race? We don't say half-caste now,' I corrected her.

'It was the nineteen-seventies and people used to say half-caste then,' my mother clarified.

We carried on chatting and poking gentle fun at each other. Humour had saved us. In the immediate aftermath of my father's death an oppressive silence had descended upon our home. My mother struggled to sleep in the bed she had shared with Mohammed. We all moved our bedding to the lounge and slept on the floor for months. If someone needed to talk we all listened and the same funny anecdotes were recounted, but we all knew Dad would have told them better. We fell in and out of sleep with the sound of muffled crying wrapped tightly around us. When I drove us home from the cemetery I sometimes glanced at my mother in the rear-view mirror, her hand clasped tightly over her mouth as she stifled her weeping. Once I heard her calling out in the night.

She was talking in her sleep. 'Now is when I needed you the most,' she murmured. She had gone back to sleep to rejoin the memory of him.

'Life is funny, isn't it?' I said as I washed the dishes, taking extra care with my sister's favourite mug with Benedict Cumberbatch's face on it.

'Life is stubborn,' my mother said. 'Even when something happens that you think will kill you, just keep on living, and it's good. We need to keep moving forwards and carrying others forwards with us.' She gently patted my shoulder.

'Working in the prison has been good for you,' my sister said thoughtfully.

'I wouldn't say good,' I countered.

'The spark is back in your eyes,' she replied and smiled reassuringly.

7

Medical History

My father, Mohammed Yousaf, had volunteered in prisons as a translator. I'd loved hearing his colourful stories about this hidden world and had wondered what life might be like within those high walls. He talked about the scary tattooed men and rats as big as cats. He also talked about the men from deprived back-grounds with little literacy who needed help filling in basic paperwork. If they required his help he would provide it wholeheartedly. My father never passed a homeless person asking for money without reaching into his pocket. As a young man, I'd remonstrated that they would probably spend it on drugs. He would warn me against becoming cynical. To be able to help other people was a gift, he would tell me.

My father's example was one of the reasons I became a GP for the homeless and then moved into offender healthcare. I had taken his words to heart. I had no right to sneer at people. But I soon learned that prison was no place for anyone with a saviour complex. Doctors were not popular. Many of the men saw us as being part of the institution that had imprisoned them rather than as caring people who wanted to help.

A couple of months in, I had passed my 'Key Walk and Talk'. I could draw keys and was expected to do clinics and navigate around the prison without a chaperone. I missed having Chris or Graham to turn to for advice. I was on my own.

When I crossed the quads I would watch as seagulls squawked and feasted on discarded bread and instant noodles thrown down from the windows by the prisoners. Rats, pigeons and gulls fought over the food. The rats were fearless. Prisoners called them 'crack rats'. The urban legend was that they had mutated by feeding on illicit substances in the prison sewers. And perhaps it was true. Many prisoners had drugs in their bodies – opioids, cannabinoids, anabolic steroids or psychiatric medications. They were excreted in their waste and entered the sewage system. Sometimes prisoners flushed drug packages down the toilet if they were at risk of being discovered by officers.

I have a fear of rats and mice. I had stopped flinching when a prisoner twice my size, someone like Jamie Lovell, threatened to rip my head off, but when I saw a rat scurrying under a bush I jumped out of my skin. I once saw two huge rats standing on their hind legs and fighting by the Waste Management Unit. Using their tails for balance, they looked like boxing kangaroos. I was sickened but also fascinated and couldn't look away.

The prison rats scrambled up drainpipes and walls. One unfortunate prisoner was awoken by a rustling sound and found a large rat eating the contents of his cereal pack. He was in a second-floor cell and his window had not been nailed shut. He had left it open a few centimetres for ventilation. He had to improvise a series of ramps dotted with food leading back to the window to encourage the rodent to depart.

'It was just staring me out, Doc,' he told me. 'Like it wasn't even scared or anything. It was off its nut, a proper crack rat, just sitting there staring at me and eating my food. If it had jumped at me I would have shat myself. I had to lay down crumbs like the Pied Piper to get it out of my cell. I'll never open my window again. I don't care how hot it gets. I threw away all of my food and wiped everything down with bleach.'

I shared his horror. We sat for a while in shocked silence, punctuated by the occasional shudder.

Pest control workers were regular visitors. They poured industrial quantities of poison into the drains and cleared out the rats' nests. They left the carcasses to rot down as a deterrent to other rats. The stench of death wafted up from the gutters, toilets and sinks. It was an odour that clung to our clothes and put us off our food, but the rats always returned. They were a permanent feature along with the sound of seagulls and the huge white wall.

We were in our own strange world; a fragile bubble surrounded by razor wire. If my father were alive I would have told him about my experiences behind bars – my mother and sister had little appetite for the gruesome details. I also didn't want them to be scared for me. I couldn't tell them how closely danger brushed up to me.

There weren't enough radios for all the healthcare staff because radios were booked on a first-come, first-served basis and the nurses started work at least an hour before the doctors. I rarely, if ever, had access to a radio with its reassuring panic button. The managers assured me that more had been ordered. There were times when I was walking in the house blocks and prisoners would block my path and interrogate me about their medications. Without a panic button of any sort I had to rely on my communication skills to get out of trouble. My heart sank if Jamie Lovell happened to block my path.

'I'm asking for help and you won't help me,' Jamie thundered. 'I need pregabalin and tramadol. Is that too much to ask? You think all prisoners are blagging and trying to get high. I'm genuine. You can't see my pain, so how do you know that I'm lying?'

'I am trying to help you but I have to follow national guidelines,' I replied meekly. 'I can't prescribe you medications without a clear indication. I have to be careful not to cause you any harm.'

'You're all the same!' Jamie shouted and poked me hard in the chest. I had to pretend it didn't hurt to save face, but the physical contact shocked me.

Jamie walked away to join a group of his friends. They muttered insults under their breath and I pretended not to hear. It was best to keep my head down and just keep walking. There was no point in starting an altercation that could quickly escalate. I was on their turf. I was always outnumbered. Why make enemies and end up with a price on my head? A colleague had had his home address and car registration number circulated amongst the prisoners. He feared for his personal safety and that of his family, so he stopped working at the prison and they had to move out of the area.

I genuinely felt I was making a difference. I saw patients who had shockingly little knowledge about their own bodies. Many had dropped out of school early. I took it as an opportunity for medical education.

'Doc, how many kidneys do we have, is it one kidney and two livers?'

'Normally two kidneys and one liver,' I reply.

'Doc, I found these bumps on the back of my tongue and I cut them off with a razor. What were they?'

'They were your taste buds.'

'There's this hard lump in my chest, I hope it's not cancer.'

'That's your xiphisternum at the bottom of your ribcage. We all have one.'

'I found these lumps on my testicles, can you have a look?'

'That's your epididymis and it's normal.'

'Doc, I don't like the taste of water. I do drink fifteen cups of tea a day but I'm pissing all the time.'

'Tea is a diuretic, it makes you pass water. Try to limit tea and coffee to no more than four cups a day.'

'I have these wart things on my knob. I called my girl and told her she gave me warts. She must have been sleeping around!'

'They're called pearly penile papules and are not a

sexually transmitted infection – you need to apologize to your partner, or ex-partner.'

I would draw an anatomical sketch of the body because many men had no idea what a scrotum was or the difference between their 'balls' and 'ball bags'. It was important to me not to talk down to them. No question was too stupid and sometimes I needed to ask them questions for my own knowledge. I learned from a prisoner, for example, that the perineum was referred to as the 'gooch'. Mr Jamie Lovell's outburst in the Reception holding cell finally made sense.

Nurses are not always appreciated in prisons. The nurses and pharmacy technicians who dispense the medications have a very narrow window of time in which to work. Often there is no officer present to monitor the behaviour of the men. Many of the men want time out of their cell and will go to the medication hatch and ask the nurses for paracetamol. Paracetamol is available to buy on Canteen. The queue for paracetamol is often as long as the one for vital medications – we can get through hundreds of boxes a week. The men say they want paracetamol as a ruse to get out of their cells. If prisoners are refused paracetamol, a torrent of abuse might be unleashed, and the men sometimes spit and throw cups of water at the staff.

Some nurses are more popular than others. If I ever want to bask in reflected glory I take to the wings with Nurse Brian. He is a small fatherly man with a deep Yorkshire accent and a shock of wispy white hair. Some of the prisoners affectionately call him Yoda. He has lived a full life, and still at the age of seventy-three he has more stamina than men half his age. He runs around the wings fuelled by a diet of cigarettes and greasy fry-ups. At least one meal a day needs to consist of egg and chips.

Brian and I share an interest in teaching medicine and medical history, and I love chatting to him. Many of his stories from years back are horrific and I'm glad that those practices have become outdated. In one or two hundred years' time, I suspect, people will look back on what we are doing now with a similar sense of unease. We're sending people to prison in the expect-ation that they will complete certain courses – knowing full well they aren't available because of a lack of fund-ing. So how are they expected to show they have been rehabilitated? Lifers, like Mr A, had given up on a system that seems to have given up on them. It's inhumane.

Brian reminds me of my father because, like him, he emanates a warmth that draws people to him. Brian had left school at the age of fifteen to start working in West Yorkshire Foundries as an office boy in Leeds. His father had been a miner and had been injured down the pit in the early fifties.

'He got his femur broken in two places,' Brian told me. 'There was a disaster and people died. They got my father out alive, but he couldn't go down the pit again. He got a job in the boiler house in a hospital. There was a big 2,500-bed lunatic asylum. Remem-ber, those were less enlightened times and people used to refer to them as "loony bins". They used to be called "bins" because that's where society would put all its unwanted rubbish. On the other side there was an 800-bed general hospital. Dad came home one day and asked if I would like to work in the asylum. So my father getting injured was how I ended up becoming a nurse.'

Brian became a cadet nurse at the age of sixteen. Medical and nursing students were taught together and followed the consultants around the hospital in a respectful and nervous silence. Brian was a brilliant man who could memorize textbooks and he sometimes put the medical students to shame with his knowledge.

'We used to have a consultant surgeon and he used to wear a wig,' he continued. 'But it wasn't like a modern-day wig. It was like a lump of carpet stuck to his head. He was doing rounds on the ward one day. Do you remember those drip stands with the curly edges? Well, he walked past one of those and he got his wig caught on that, and he left it behind. God knows how he didn't notice, but no one bloody dared tell him. We waited for him to be gone and put it in an envelope and took it down to his office. We quietly slipped it on to his desk when he wasn't there.

'The doctors were a strange breed in those days; nasty buggers. They'd teach by humiliation. Break you down to nothing. I remembered that when I went on to teach. I never wanted to be like those ignorant sods.'

When Brian was eighteen he began his three years of mental-health training. He followed this with general nursing and gained both qualifications. As we walked the wings, I asked him if he'd ever considered medicine as a career. He told me that he had attended an ordinary secondary-modern school where they only taught basic sciences. In order to apply to medical school he needed to have three A-levels and an O-level in Latin. He tried to do A-levels when he was in his twenties but struggled with full-time work and bringing up a young family.

'There were very few doctors from working-class backgrounds until the grammar schools evened the playing field,' Brian said with no bitterness for missed opportunities.

I thought about my own experiences at medical school. Many of the students around me had come from comfortable backgrounds. It was not unusual for one or both of their parents to be doctors. Many had been educated in private schools that had pumped them full of confidence. They expected people to listen when they talked. They had a swagger when they walked. Their wealth insulated them from insecurity. Any minor disappointment or setback was met with disbelief – as if life owed them something. They had no idea how hard life could be.

'If we fail,' my friend Amdad from medical school used to say, 'we'll go back to sweeping floors. It's a long fall with no one to catch us. If I get kicked out of medical school or don't pass my medical finals I'll have to go back to live with my family in Cardiff. I'll be working as a waiter in my dad's Indian restaurant by the end of the week.'

I believed him. If I failed medical finals the logical step would be to take over running our newsagent's shop – working fourteen hours a day, seven days a week, for forty years with minimal gain – just as my parents had.

When Brian and I went to the wings to see patients

he picked up on my sense of unease. The healthcare staff and officers were friendly towards me but it was a different story with the prisoners. My reluctance to prescribe sedating medications like pregabalin and zopiclone, which was a sleeping tablet, had led to resentment amongst some of the prisoners. Wherever we went Brian was met with broad smiles and pats on the back and I was met with a stony silence. Sometimes the men laughed and joked with Brian, but when I tried to take part they stared at me with hard eyes. Brian tried to make me feel better about my lack of progress in building a rapport with them.

'Did I tell you about the first patient I ever met?' he asked me.

I shook my head.

'I got my nose broke on my first bloody day by a patient called Raymond,' Brian said.

'Why did he do that?' I asked.

'Raymond was in the lunatic asylum and he was mentally subnormal, as it was known then, learning disabilities they call it now. They sent me up to the refractory ward with a message. Raymond was stood there. He blocked the door and he said, "Lazenby." I said, "What?" He said, "Lazenby!" So I said, "Move out the way." He twatted me right on the bloody nose. I found out later that Lazenby was a golf course somewhere and that was his trigger. You had to say, "Oh that's a nice place" and then you were OK, but I didn't know that and no one had told me,' Brian said.

I shook my head in disbelief.

'There was another patient called John and he would stand outside all day with his arms outstretched. A nurse told me to go and get the lad in. So I called him and said, "John, come in." He twatted me as well. Apparently they called him Jesus because he thought he was the second coming of Jesus Christ. After that I would just say, "Jesus, in for your dinner!" He was alright with me after that. You just have to give it time and become a familiar face before people start trusting you,' Brian advised.

In case that day never came, I had started to introduce myself as Brian's friend. This worked to melt some of the glacial chill I encountered from the men. I was indeed Brian's friend and I sought him out as often as possible so I could hear the stories from his long career in healthcare. Some of his anecdotes were painful to listen to, but they would help me to put my own working practice into some kind of perspective, and they'd always remind me of why I was there in the first place.

We were treating a man who had bite marks on his arms from a prison fight and injuries to his jaw. Bite marks were common in the prison. We washed his wounds and gave him a tetanus injection and a course of antibiotics.

'Do you know what they used to do to biters when I was young?' Brian asked him.

'You're ancient; were you ever young, Brian?' the man joked.

'When I was about your age I worked in a lunatic asylum. If there was a biter they would take their teeth out. Just the front incisors, so they couldn't bite, but they still had their molars so they could chew. If any of them were punchers or kickers and violent towards staff or refused to take their meds they would be given pre-frontal lobotomies. There were dozens of them walking around like zombies with their frontal lobes severed. In the United States they used to go in through the eye socket. In England it would tend to be through the temporal lobe. Just put a hole in the temple and put in a scalpel and smash it in and out a few times. That was it, zombified,' Brian said.

The man's smile faded and he looked at me to see if it was a joke. I shrugged my shoulders. I didn't know if this was true or not. Perhaps it was just a story that Brian told to make prisoners more mindful of their own behaviour, or at least grateful for small mercies, that they were here and not there.

His own experiences had made Brian deeply mistrustful of doctors and medicine.

He wasn't even registered with a GP. He purchased his medications online. When he filled in the questionnaire which asked if he had seen a doctor recently, he always said yes because he worked with doctors and saw one every day. He wasn't lying.

'I was in Southern California in 1974 when the doctors went on strike. And, do you know, the death rate fell by 25 per cent. I read somewhere that in Israel the doctors were on strike for an entire year and they had a 70 per cent drop in the death rate. What does that tell you?' Brian chuckled.

Further into his career he was offered a position as a Director of Nursing at a Saudi drug-abuse hospital. In reality it was a prison, he told me. The prisoners were given three chances to detox, but if they were brought in for a fourth time it was game over. It wasn't like here where we were seeing the same faces again and again.

'They would detox them and put them in the back of a pickup truck and take them to the market, the souk as they called it, after Friday prayers,' Brian went on. 'I had to sit there in my bloody white coat, shirt and tie in the fifty-degree heat next to the Prince. They would chop their heads off. That's how they kept crime down; drugs, theft, violence, any of that business, their criminal population would automatically get dispatched. Our driver, Riaz, was a morgue technician and he used to collect the bodies and the heads. We'd go back up to the hospital and he would sew the heads back on, and then the families would take the bodies and bury them.'

My eyes widened.

'I would give the prisoners diazepam before they got in the truck. I'd give them a good dose to get it into their system faster. They wouldn't feel a thing. Give them a nice send-off,' he said.

Brian's life is his work and his family. We are his work family. He tucks into bacon butties prepared for him by the officers in Segregation. The women in admin bake cakes for him. Whenever I see him I check that he's taking his medications. It is our way of showing him we love him. Like my own father, the man has a charmed aura that dispenses light on all those around him and I take a lot of comfort from his presence.

Brian's stories were interrupted by a Code Blue on the radio and we ran to the wing to find Jamie Lovell. He had clearly been in a fight. He had bloody teeth marks on both hands, presumably where he had punched someone hard in the mouth.

'I fell against a wall,' he said casually.

'A wall with teeth? Don't lie to me, Jamie. I've already seen another lad with bite marks on his arms and injuries to his jaw. I assume you two had a disagreement and decided to knock seven bells out of each other? You'll need antibiotics and a tetanus shot,' Brian said as he washed Jamie's wounds.

Like me and all the other prisoners, Jamie succumbed to Brian's fatherly attention and seemed calmed by him. Then he became aware of me on the other side of the room and his body language shifted.

'I don't want him anywhere near me,' Jamie said, nodding towards me. 'He's a shit doctor. Everyone calls him Dr No.'

'Dr Y is one of the best doctors going,' Brian said, a willing cheerleader. 'What he doesn't know isn't worth knowing. He has written books!'

I almost blushed. To have Brian's support meant the world to me. I had written a book on medical mnemonics as a final-year medical student and a follow-up book a few years later.

Brian called me to his side and I examined Jamie's hands. He had broken the metacarpal bones in both hands. His knuckles had receded, which was otherwise known as boxer's fractures. He had old boxer's fractures too and it was difficult to see which of his injuries were new. I strapped his fingers together to stabilize them and help them to heal straight. As he aged it would be increasingly difficult for them to mend well.

'Would you like a patient information leaflet about boxer's fractures?' I asked mindlessly, keen to advise him on his health condition.

'You know I can't read,' Jamie said, fixing me with his gaze.

'Well, do something about it, you daft bugger,' Brian told him. 'We have classes in the prison that will help you to learn. What's this on your elbow?'

'My elbow was hurting so I bandaged a couple of paracetamol tablets to it. I feel much better now,' Jamie said.

Brian undid the bandage and retrieved the tablets.

'No one expects you to be the next Shakespeare,' he said. 'But if you learn to read and write a little bit you'll avoid embarrassment. Every medication comes with instructions. If you can't read them you'll be brushing your teeth with haemorrhoid cream. Oral paraceta-mol is for swallowing, not strapping to your skin, you numpty.'

'I'm too old to read and write. I made sure my kids went to school. My grandkids can all read. They write me letters with little pictures. Cute as you like,' Jamie said with pride.

'Wouldn't you like to write back to them? You could then pass the written exam and become a health cham-pion and work with Chris,' I chipped in.

Jamie was quiet for a few moments. I took the opportunity to say I would gladly contact the Shannon Trust prison literacy charity for him.

'I taught myself to write short stories. I just pick up a pen and start writing things down, when I'm in the mood, not as much now as I used to do. You could start with writing poems and I could read them if you like, give you some pointers,' I said, sensing that he might be receptive.

'So you can laugh at me?' Jamie asked.

'Why would I laugh at you? I'm not cruel,' I replied with surprise.

Jamie smiled at me for the first time. He nodded when Brian asked if he would join the literacy programme.

'Will he get away with the fighting?' I asked Brian as we walked back to the healthcare department.

'No, they'll drag him off to the Segregation unit for another twenty-four hours. You wait until he learns to read and write. There will be a new complaint from him on a daily basis,' Brian joked.

'Brian, did you see the state of his hands? Forget writing complaints, he won't be able to hold a pen,' I said.

'He's not as daft as he looks. I won't tell you what he's in for, but I will say it takes brains – I don't know how he managed it without being able to read and write. He's sharp enough – when he wants to be. He just needs to be ready to want to learn.'

'Brian, you have all these stories, and everything that goes on in prisons is so fascinating.'

'Well Dr Y, all the medical records from the mental hospitals will have been destroyed by now, they only keep them for three years after death or twenty years from the last contact with healthcare. It's for data protection. The Raymonds and Johns and all those poor lobotomized souls are long gone and forgotten about apart from in here,' he said pointing to his head.

'What a tragic loss, all those lives, all of that history just shredded,' I said quietly.

I kicked myself for not recording my father's stories. There was no video footage of him. How was I going to keep his memory alive? I made a promise to myself to start writing again – just little vignettes – fully anonymized. Stories about this incredible time in offender healthcare – recorded for posterity.

Brian could see I had withdrawn into myself as we strolled through the walkways and landings of the prison. He knew I liked complicated cases and often when we were walking around he would present a clinical scenario with signs and symptoms. If it sounded important we would head towards the individual and review him.

'I've got one for you,' Brian said as we were walking back from seeing Jamie. 'Mr C, he's a thirty-year-old gent, recently transferred here from another prison. Very pleasant and polite. Says he has been having looser stools for three months, passing blood occasionally but it's painless – no history of haemorrhoids. He thinks he has found a lump in the left side of his abdomen above the left hip. I've done his blood tests and it shows he has iron deficiency.'

'Brian, that meets the criteria for an urgent referral to the lower gastrointestinal surgeons, we have to rule out bowel cancer. We have to go and see him now!' I said with alarm.

We both rushed towards Mr C's cell. An officer unlocked the door and we were faced with a muscular young man who appeared breathless and was sweating profusely.

He could see the panic on our faces and raised his hand to placate us.

'Just been doing a cell work-out: 500 burpees, 500 sit-ups, 500 press-ups,' Mr C said between gulps of air.

'This is Dr Y. Run through your symptoms with him and he will sort you out,' Brian said kindly.

Every detail Mr C provided me with fitted the criteria of rectal cancer. The only symptom he didn't have was weight loss, but that could be down to his exercise regime and the mountains of protein he was consuming. His room was piled high with tins of fish and protein shakes. I examined him and there was indeed a worrying lump in the left side of his abdomen, which could be a cancer. But he politely declined a per rectum examination which would allow me to feel for any lumps.

'Nah, no disrespect, Doc, but I'm not about that lifestyle. One-way traffic only, you get me?' he said with a strong London accent. I wondered what he was doing in the Midlands, so far from home.

'Look, I have to tell you that I'm concerned,' I said. 'Your symptoms and your blood results are unusual – your iron levels are low, which could be due to you bleeding from your back passage. We need to do other blood tests and I think it's best if I refer you to the outside hospital to rule out a tumour of the rectum. As you know, this is a prison, we're not allowed to tell you the date and time of any hospital appointment, because prisoners have in the past tried to arrange escapes. But I will push for you to be seen in hospital in the next two weeks.'

Mr C nodded, slowly absorbing this information.

'If your symptoms worsen, if you pass a large amount of blood through your back passage and feel weak and unsteady, push your cell bell,' I said, pointing to the button on the wall. The cell bell is used by prisoners to get the attention of officers and is supposed to be responded to within minutes.

'The officers don't respond to cell bells,' Mr C said quietly. He sat down on his bed with his head in his hands.

'With your permission we can tell the officers you have something wrong,' Brian said. 'We won't break medical confidentiality and give them details, but we can say that you are a high priority. If you push your cell bell they will call healthcare straight away, OK?'

Mr C nodded, but the fight had gone out of him.

'I told them at my last prison that something was wrong. I told them. They just ignored me. I know my body. I'm a fitness instructor on the outside. I have a life, a girlfriend, a kid on the way. How am I meant to tell them I might have cancer? I don't want to die in prison. What about my kid? I don't even know if it is a boy or a girl. What if I never meet my kid and they don't get to know me, I'm just going to be a photograph to them,' Mr C whispered, suddenly a shadow of his former self.

'I am going to see you in my clinic every week, same time, same place,' I said. 'If you don't come to me because there are no officers to bring you to the Outpatients clinic, you don't need to worry because I will come to you. I know it's easier said than done but let us do the worrying for you. You're in good hands with us.'

'Are you my doctor? I mean, I don't want to be seeing different people every time I go to healthcare and have to tell them the story right from the beginning again.'

'Yes, I am your doctor. If you have any problems just ask for Dr Y,' I said to reassure him.

8

Black-Eye Fridays

Fridays are Canteen day when men take delivery of the items they have ordered the previous week. This is also when debts are settled. The inevitable fighting means that, in between seeing patients booked into my clinic, there is a steady stream of injured men to review, some with head wounds and missing teeth, so the dental team and I work closely together. On this particular sunny Friday in June I was walking into the prison with my friend Helen, a dental nurse. Helen changes her hair colour on a regular basis. Today it was candy-floss pink and lifted my spirits ahead of the hectic day to come. I discussed with her Mr C, the thirty-year-old individual with the suspected rectal tumour. He had requested dental treatment but he was also anaemic and it was probably best to hold off non-essential work that could lead to further blood loss.

'He's only thirty years old. What if it is rectal cancer?' Helen asked.

'Then he'll need investigations, chemotherapy and possibly surgery,' I said, trying to keep the emotion out of it.

'Poor lad, imagine going through all of that in here of all places,' Helen replied.

As well as her role in the prison Helen also works in the community with special-care patients, dental-phobics and children with autism. Helen makes tiny denture palates for babies with cleft lips and palates so they can feed. She tries to care for the prisoners with the same diligence. Helen is one of the kindest and most empathic people I know. She had trained to become a certified counsellor in her fifties and we share a close bond built on a love of food, food and more food.

We also see eye to eye on how the prisoners should be treated and often talk about our shared vision for offender healthcare. Many of the men in prison have low self-esteem. You can tell by their demeanour that they are resigned to being mistreated. They shuffle into our clinic rooms with hunched shoulders and poor eye contact. They may have been waiting a long time to see us because dental and GP waiting lists are invariably long in prisons due to chronic understaffing. When they finally get to see us it is as if they are expecting us to say, 'Who cares if you've been waiting, you don't deserve decency and respect.' And when we don't they are surprised, but it takes time for their defences to thaw. Many have had a horrendous upbringing, often in care homes. They might otherwise present with bravado and a hostile exterior because this is a violent and threatening environment. They don't want to be seen to be weak and vulnerable.

Helen and I try to engage with the men with compassion. I had managed to persuade the governor to switch the heating on during cold weather, to be responsive to what was happening outside, whatever the season. Helen had arranged for Mr A, the 'lifer', to have a new set of dentures fitted. It is the simplest things that can make a huge difference to the men. Some guys say they haven't smiled for years because of their teeth. They bring their top lip down when they speak or rest their hands over their faces. A nicer smile gives them confidence and that means they are more likely to apply for a job when they are released, and a job can mean the start of a new and better life.

As Helen and I entered the prison together on that Friday we both fell silent. We noticed how eerily muted the men were but we were both too superstitious to use the Q-word. It was always the case that if someone said it was quiet, and there was a momentary breather, uttering the words would bring about a circus of chaos. This morning, the ubiquitous shouting and banging were absent. This was usually a sign that the prison was 'bubbling' and something big was being planned, like an assault on an officer or an attempted break-out. The silence was deeply unnerving.

The sounds of this noisy place usually distract from the odour. It is almost as though our senses can't take in everything at once. In the absence of the thundering sound of a thousand frustrated and angry men I noticed the strong smell of effluent. Manure was being sprayed on to the surrounding fields. The distant hum of farming machinery was punctuated by gunshots from the neighbouring firing range. We both took in the great white wall that surrounded the prison. Burnished with golden light, the tops of the trees in the fields beyond could just be seen. The seagulls and pigeons, disturbed by the farming activity, weren't confident enough to swoop down and pick up the scraps thrown by the prisoners. Food lay rotting in the quad. We stood still for a moment and listened. Silence was never a good sign. It contained an element of surprise, and not knowing what would happen next.

'In the first couple of weeks of working in the prison I found it all quite overwhelming,' Helen told me then. 'It was the noise, the people shouting and the heavy atmosphere. I was unnerved by the radios screeching every few seconds and alarms echoing down the corridors. On the first day someone was banging the pipes in the cell below the dental surgery. I couldn't hear myself think. I was on high alert, every noise, every bang would make me jump. It took about six months to find my feet.'

I had been working here for four months. The novelty of the prison environment was beginning to fade, but I could see how it would never become ordinary.

'Don't go on to the wings alone today, Dr Y. Something doesn't feel right. Make sure you're within shouting distance of a colleague at all times,' Helen warned me. Neither of us was carrying a radio.

We crossed the messy quad and climbed the flight of stairs to the external entrance to the Outpatient unit waiting room. The corridor that led to our clinic rooms lay beyond it. We could now hear shouting and the tumult of furniture being overturned. We looked at each other and realized why the prison had been so quiet – a fight was underway. A flustered officer appeared at the door and ushered us in. There was blood all over the floor and more splattered on the walls. Nurses were tending to half a dozen injured men who were sitting or lying on the floor. The fight had clearly been huge, with chairs used as weapons. A large group of officers was busy separating two groups of prisoners, and one of the men caught up in the tumult was Mr Jamie Lovell. Despite what had felt like progress over the past few weeks, it was hardly a surprise to me that if there was trouble Mr Lovell would somehow be involved.

'Doctor Y, Helen, we need you,' Graham called out.

I hadn't even taken my coat off. I knelt beside the patient Graham was tending to. He was an older man who was pale and clammy, with beads of sweat on his forehead, but I couldn't see any injuries on him. Graham gave me an update. The man was sixty years old, he had high blood pressure and diabetes but had not been taking his medications. He had walked into the waiting room, witnessed the carnage and collapsed.

'I don't like the sight of blood,' the man explained.

'Graham, he's had a shock,' I said. 'Monitor his blood pressure and blood sugar. If the blood sugar is low give him some sugary tea and monitor it again after twenty minutes. If there are any problems come back to me.'

'Doc, can you have a look at this man?' one of the officers called. He was beckoning me over to see Mr

Lovell, who was bleeding heavily from his mouth. His T-shirt was soaked through with blood. The other officers were restraining another huge man, who had bloodied fists and was still shouting threats at Mr Lovell.

'I don't want to see Dr Dolittle!' he hissed as I approached.

'The prisoners had a fight and were banging each other's head off the walls before the nurses called a Code Red and we could come and separate them,' the officer informed me breathlessly.

'Show me your mouth, Mr Lovell,' I said.

Mr Lovell spat something out. It landed by my feet. A tooth. Most of his front teeth were missing. Helen bent down and collected the tooth in a clean handkerchief; she found more teeth on the blood-splattered floor, handling them with extreme care, especially the exposed roots. She asked for a glass of milk. When it was brought to her she gently dropped the teeth in. They swirled around, leaving raspberry-coloured ribbons.

I looked over at her, eyebrows raised.

'The milk preserves the tooth for a short while so we can try to put it back in,' Helen explained. 'The milk can keep it going for slightly longer because it contains calcium and keeps it more sterile. But there's no guarantee that it'll work. We'll get the teeth back in his mouth and splint them initially to try and save them.'

Mr Lovell was led into the dental surgery where Helen assisted Katie the dentist in trying to salvage his smile. I helped the other nurses tend to the other men's injuries. Steph, Chris, Graham, Brian and I stitched up the wounds, and I prescribed antibiotics to prevent infections.

The men freely admitted that they had planned on teaching Jamie Lovell a lesson because he always refused to pay his debts. They'd decided to knock his teeth out. They had beaten him with socks filled with tins of tuna. How they had managed to smuggle the weapons into healthcare worried and surprised me. Mr Lovell had fought back with more skill than they had anticipated and had made full use of the waiting-room furniture. It was a brutal cyclone of violence and everyone was injured.

Once the rest of the men were patched up the officers took them to the Segregation unit. Helen called me into the dental surgery. Mr Lovell was sitting in the dentist's chair and Katie was assessing him.

'I think he has broken his jaw, Dr Y. Can you have a look?' Katie asked.

I approached Mr Lovell. His face was smeared with dried blood and he had two black eyes forming and swellings in front of his ears where his upper jaw articulated with the lower jaw. I felt a loose crunching sensation when he opened and closed his mouth. His jaw was dislocated.

'You need surgery in an outside hospital,' I explained.

'Fuck that shit,' Mr Lovell said and spat out a large blood clot.

'You won't be able to eat or talk properly if your jaw isn't fixed; it will only get worse,' I said.

Mr Lovell shrugged his huge shoulders. He said that the men had done him a favour. They had knocked out his teeth which were rotten anyway. He blamed his lifestyle, drugs and upbringing. His parents didn't care about teeth. He had never been to the dentist and, despite being covered in tattoos and injecting anabolic steroids, he said he was scared of needles. He wanted expensive implants made of solid gold like his friends had paid for in Turkey. If not gold, he would settle for porcelain veneers. He said the prison had let him down by not protecting him from being assaulted and he would sue unless we gave him what he wanted. Helen started to speak to him in her soothing voice. She didn't say anything I would not have said, but maybe it was the softness with which she communicated that reached him.

Whenever I'd seen Mr Lovell I immediately became uptight, expecting a barrage of abuse. I was once walking past him on the landing when he was using the wing telephone to call home. He was speaking to a child, it seemed, because his voice was soft and he asked if the child was being good and doing their homework. He said Gramps would be home soon. The entire time we maintained eye contact as I walked past him. I didn't trust him not to block my path. He was thirty-eight years old – only a few years older than me – and yet he was a grandfather. I felt like a boy in his presence. He could pick up on my ambivalence towards him however much I tried to conceal it.

Helen had always been a great communicator but since becoming a counsellor her listening skills had vastly improved. Mr Lovell could see that she was actively listening to him and engaging with him fully. She made him feel that this was his time, his space, and he began to let down his defences.

It was as if Helen had stepped into his world. Barriers were gently broken down and his gruff facade faded.

When I spoke to him he even smiled at me, an empty gummy smile. He was interacting with us in a way I hadn't known before. I candidly admitted that I thought he always went out of his way to try to intimidate me and my heart sank whenever I saw him. I was surprised when he apologized to me. We all felt listened to. He then told me he had taken my advice on board and was engaging with the Shannon Trust prison literacy charity. He had begun to write simple poems and said he would send some to me. I was so pleased I shook his bruised hand. He winced in pain.

'Call me Jamie, Mr Lovell is my dad,' he said.

It felt like a major breakthrough.

Jamie agreed to go to the outside hospital to get his jaw fixed. I contacted the maxillary facial doctor on call at the local hospital, who said they would see him immediately. I informed Graham, who in turn informed the senior officer managing the prison shift, referred to as Victor One. Due to his level of threat to others, four burly officers were required to escort Jamie to hospital. They fitted him with heavy handcuffs and chains, which two of them then attached to themselves. They were all squashed together in the back of a taxi with my referral letter. We were all surprised by how compliant and polite Jamie was being. Secretly I wondered how long it would last. There was still a good chance he might change his mind, discharge himself from the hospital, and come back demanding a set of gold teeth after all.

Later, after a busy morning of clinics, Helen and I finally sat down to lunch. However hectic our work was, we always ensured that we had lunch together with our friends and colleagues. It was a moment to ground ourselves and feel 'normal' in this abnormal environment. Helen and I took turns to bring in cheese and antipasti and piled each other's plates with delicious morsels. Some of our friends complained about the smell of our Gorgonzola sandwiches and spat out the wasabi peas we offered them, but for Helen and myself this was the highlight of the day. I asked her how she had managed to connect with Jamie.

She explained that some of the men had bad manners and they wouldn't listen or would talk over others. Not the end of the world, perhaps, but few people go to work every day to be verbally abused. If the men were particularly abusive in their language she was able to say, 'Stop that right now. You're not talking to me or to the dentist like that!' The majority of men would apologize immediately, but it had taken a while for Helen to feel comfortable challenging them. We certainly both recognized our advantage of having stable and loving backgrounds. These men were used to speaking to other prisoners with language peppered with expletives. They sometimes needed to be reminded that this was our professional working environment.

Some of the men might be irritable and abrupt with us. We understood that pain and frustration could make anyone aggressive and it was our job to stay calm. A couple of people had reached up and grabbed at Katie the dentist during a treatment, Helen said. They did this to me when I put in stitches too. It was dangerous for everybody, especially if there was a sharp instrument involved. Helen had been working in prisons for almost twenty years and had only come across a handful of men who had made her feel uneasy. Men like this instantly reminded her of where she was. In the same way that I did, she kept an eye on the exit in case she needed it.

'If I feel one ounce of pain I'm going to beat both of you black and blue!' one man had threatened during a dental appointment. Helen was so appalled that she had terminated the treatment. When he refused to leave the room, both Helen and Katie had exited quickly and pushed the panic alarm in the corridor. When the officers arrived to take the man away, he pretended it was all a joke. But as he was being hauled down the corridor he drew his finger across his throat and stared at them with a distinct lack of joviality.

'It's the sort of job where you either run for the hills very quickly, or you stay,' Helen said. 'The challenge and excitement it offers wins out over any fear.' I felt exactly the same way.

We both liked the fact that probably 90 per cent of the time we didn't know what crimes the men had committed. Not knowing what they had done removed a burden of judgement from us and we could treat them all the same. Sometimes the men would volunteer what they had done, especially if it was a lesser crime or if they were maintaining their innocence, and it was interesting to hear their side of the story even if it was clearly delusional.

Helen didn't ask what anyone was in prison for because, she said, it was simply none of her business. But also because her beloved brother had been killed when he was in his early twenties by a drunk driver. If anyone said they were 'only' in prison for driving offences, then immediately her hackles were up. We were human beings too. It meant we were always aware of how we might treat somebody if we really didn't like what they had done, so it was best not to ask.

'There used to be a male dentist working in another prison who would always ask the men what they had done,' Helen told me quietly. 'If it was a violent crime or something of a sexual nature he would use less anaesthetic and cause more pain – it was completely unprofessional. I reported him immediately and he was removed from working on the site.'

I shuddered involuntarily.

'I think we, or rather you, have made a breakthrough with Jamie. I always find him hard work. He calls me Dr No, Dr Dolittle, Dr Death. It's not very endearing,' I said, just about managing to keep the disappointment out of my voice.

She laughed. 'Before you came into the dental clinic today he wasn't being very complimentary about your clothes. He said you dressed like you had mugged a tramp. He asked if you went skip-diving.'

'That cheeky git! These are vintage clothes, Helen, I put a lot of care . . .' I started to protest. But then I had to laugh too. Jamie had sustained a brutal beating and even with a broken jaw he still found my clothes, and by extension me, laughable. I had made some sort of impression. And not taking myself too seriously was surprisingly liberating.

9

Segregation

The Segregation unit has been renamed the Care and Separation Unit, CSU, but everyone still calls it Segregation or Seg. The prisoners here might have broken prison rules by fighting, destroying property, or been found in possession of drugs, alcohol or contraband. Alternatively, they might choose to be in Segregation for their own protection. These are usually short stays, but some men remain here for weeks or months at a time with a governor's review every fourteen days.

Segregation can feel like a de facto mental-health unit. From my perspective, it's only marginally better than tying a troublesome person to a tree at the edge of a village and walking away. There is a crisis in acute mental-health services which means there are always a number of mental-health patients awaiting beds in the community. The number of community mental-health beds has been slashed by 25 per cent since 2010 despite a vastly growing need for them. All of which means the most difficult part of my job is identifying someone who should not be in prison but has nowhere else to go.

The United Nations called for prolonged sentences in solitary confinement to be banned in 2011. The psychological harm of solitary confinement is well documented and particularly damaging to those already suffering from a mental illness. Before anyone can be moved to the Segregation unit a paper form needs to be signed to confirm they are 'fit' for the unit. It lists physical, mental or substance-misuse problems – this would exclude most of the Segregation population. The World Health Organization and UN Office of the High Commissioner for Human Rights deem it unethical for doctors to certify someone as fit for solitary confinement. I resolutely refuse to sign any of the algorithms that 'fit' anyone for Segregation – my primary duty is to promote the health and safety of my patients.

The Segregation unit follows a 'basic' regime without access to a television or kettle and extra privileges such as the gym. The men are locked up in a tiny cell for twenty-three hours a day. They have an hour a day in which they can make a phone call, shower or utilize the exercise yard, a high-walled garden of scrubby grass and cigarette stubs. The prisoners chain-smoke until they run out of tobacco and then they smoke plain paper. The books in the Segregation bookcase have had their pages torn out. Even the Bible has gone up in holy smoke.

Due to intense boredom and mental-health issues, it's no wonder that the prisoners demand regular courses of sleeping tablets. Without them, no one sleeps well because some of the mentally unwell prisoners shout and bang their doors all night. Food is brought to the prisoners and they eat in their cells. Their only company consists of the officers and governors, sometimes an external judge or legal team, the chaplaincy, a daily visit from a nurse, and three times a week a doctor will poke their head into this little corner of living hell and ask if they are OK. It always feels like a pointless question.

I was asked by Dean, the In-reach mental-health nurse, to review a particularly troubled man who had been moved to Segregation. Mr S had recently arrived in the prison and Dean felt Seg was not an appropriate location for him, but, as usual, there were no spaces in the Inpatient unit. He was a VP and had initially been moved to the VP unit but had been so loud and disruptive, day and night, that the other VPs couldn't sleep and had threatened to kill him. He had been locked behind his door in the VP unit for his own protection. The transfer to Seg was not a drastic change in his circumstances.

Mr S, I learned, had a history of going to A&E with 'tummy pain' and requesting rectal examinations. He then accused the staff of assault. He played the little boy lost and said he needed a hug and then fondled staff. Mr S also communicated via his hand puppet, Binky Bear. I was standing beside his cell doorway in the Seg unit, speaking to the officers, when his emaciated arm appeared with the puppet on the end of it, peeking around the corner. I saw my reflection in Binky Bear's glass eye; I was trapped in the dark centre, surrounded by a ring of fiery amber. The other eye had been pulled out and hung from the empty socket by tattered threads. Binky had a chewed plastic nose and a torn smile. His grey fur was mangy and bare in patches. He waved at me with a scruffy paw from the doorway of the prison cell.

'I'm Binky Bear. Will you be my friend?' Binky asked me in a high-pitched voice.

'I've come to see Mr S,' I replied warily. I was already quite disturbed by the situation.

'He's in here with me,' Binky said and beckoned to me with his paw.

'Back against the wall, Mr S,' Officer W commanded.

Officer W was also known as Officer Silverback because, quite simply, like a gorilla, he was huge and hairy. His face was covered by a beard that seemed to start just below his eyes. It was impossible to see if he was smiling. He didn't like heat and it was a blisteringly hot July day. There were inflamed red patches below his eyes. His startling appearance didn't usually stop the officers joking with him. But today, with the heat and the strange case of Mr S, didn't seem like an appropriate day for levity.

Officer W, Custodial Manager Goz and a third officer entered the cell. I followed.

Mr S was a slight man in his mid-sixties. His white stubble crackled when he brought Binky Bear to his face. He was sweating despite only wearing an adult nappy and Binky Bear on his right hand. His wrinkled skin glistened and its old scars gave him a toad-like appearance. His clothes were in two clear bags beside his bed: jumpers with cuddly animals on their fronts, brightly coloured trousers, and what looked like a clown's outfit.

Despite the summer heat he was shivering and my first impulse was to go over and check his temperature. But what I knew of his history kept me from touching him. One of the officers had divulged that he was a violent paedophile. I wish I had been unaware of this fact because immediately a barrier went up in my mind. I couldn't help but filter everything he did through that dark prism and it turned my stomach. He had served long sentences in prison, completed all of his sex-offender courses, and was eventually deemed to have been rehabilitated and released. Within a matter of weeks he breached the terms of his licence by attend-ing a children's party and he was recalled to prison. He had a lifetime ban from having any contact with chil-dren and was also prohibited from owning animals. It was going to be difficult to treat him dispassionately and with empathy, but I had to try.

I was unsure why he hadn't dressed himself, unless he was waiting for someone to help him. With or without his juvenile clothes he gave the impression of being an overgrown toddler. I imagined his stunted growth was from poor nutrition in childhood. He had a malformed chest wall with ribs that had been broken – I shuddered to think how – and healed in a tangle of neglect. He was thin with a hollow belly and protruding hip bones. His large eyes reminded me of Binky Bear's glassy stare. Mr S was examining me as closely as I was reviewing him. He did not blink.

'This is the doctor. He's going to take us home,' Binky whispered to Mr S.

Mr S was a poor ventriloquist and he held Binky in front of his mouth when he spoke.

Mr S whispered back into Binky's threadbare ear and I watched Mr S's fingers working the mouth of the puppet.

'He would like to know when we can go home?' Binky asked in a childlike voice.

'You'll be staying with us for a little while. You have breached the terms of your licence, which means you are on remand and will be here until you're seen in court,' I said.

Binky Bear responded but I was having difficulty hearing him. The Segregation unit is the noisiest part of the prison and shrieking and crying surrounds it like a thunderous dark cloud. High-profile prisoners – the extremely violent, people withdrawing from drugs, white supremacists and Islamist extremists – are housed in adjoining cells and this leads to a uniquely charged environment. Everyone was shouting threats at everyone else all the time.

'They are being nasty to us,' Binky said, and Mr S gestured to the men outside his own four walls and pulled the corners of his mouth down.

Dean had requested I complete a learning disability assessment of Mr S to see if he needed extra support, because he appeared unable to take care of even his most basic needs. A social care package would then be discussed with the occupational therapists to see if he needed help with feeding and dressing himself. I hoped to build up trust with him so he would put Binky down and we could communicate directly.

'Why don't you put Binky on the bed so we can talk, Mr S,' I said.

'He likes having my hand up him,' Mr S replied.

'Poor Binky Bear,' Goz sighed.

'He is very sorry for what he has done, he just wants to go home,' Binky said, turning to Mr S.

Mr S's face crumpled. He began to cry and then to howl. Tears streamed down his face and he used Binky to wipe them. He toddled a few steps towards me with his arms outstretched as if to hug me. In any other scenario I may have allowed him to embrace me, but the officers motioned for me not to approach him.

'Don't get too close!' Officer W snapped at him.

'I'm sorry,' Mr S sobbed and, with his free hand, began to slap his own face with force.

All three of the officers were stony-faced, their body language exuding brute force. The more emotional Mr S became, the stiller the officers became, as if primed to pounce. Despite any misgivings, I still had an ethical duty of care to him. I stepped forwards and cleared my throat.

'Mr S,' I began.

'Talk to the bear!' he screamed, spittle trickling down his unshaven chin.

Compliantly, I shifted my gaze.

'Binky, I am here to help Mr S. I need to make sure that we are offering you all the help you need,' I said.

'Everyone is being mean,' Binky said in a small voice.

'I can see that you're upset. Would you like me to come back when you are less distressed?' I asked. I was already moving towards the door. The notes from police custody described Mr S's history of admissions to mental-health units followed by periods of homelessness and long stretches in prison. He needed to acclimatize and I would come back at a later date.

'Aren't you going to stick a finger up my bum?' Mr S shouted at me.

I stopped and turned towards him. This time he wasn't speaking through Binky Bear. The high-pitched squeal had been replaced by a gravelly voice full of vitriol.

'You haven't asked why I am wearing a nappy,' Mr S hissed.

I found my voice. 'Why?' I asked.

'Because doctors like you keep poking your fingers where they don't belong,' he screamed.

'Ignore him, Doc,' Goz said.

'At least I said sorry. No one said sorry to me!' Mr S whimpered. His scrawny arms were flexed with rage and his lips were drawn back over chipped and discoloured teeth.

'Mr S, the decision to locate you in the Segregation unit is for your own protection. We are trying to help you,' I said.

'Piss off!' Mr S shouted. Then his lips twisted into a crooked smile. The artifice of victimhood had been shed as easily as he could shed Binky Bear.

'OK,' I said simply, grateful to be out of there for the time being. 'See you next time.'

'He seemed nice,' Goz remarked lightly as she locked the cell door behind us.

I paused, searching for the right words. 'He's certainly

a complicated gentleman – I think he needs to be assessed by a psychiatrist,' I offered.

'You doctors love understatements,' Officer W said and led me into the Segregation office.

The office is full of magazines featuring bronzed men and women on the covers, with bulging muscles, thick veins, spray-tan faces and bright white smiles. The officers consume huge amounts of protein and are always ready to go to the gym and, in fairness, they need to be fit and strong to do the job. I had neglected myself since becoming a doctor. I was always too tired, or at least that was the excuse I gave myself. However, since working in the prison I had developed a new appreciation of wide-open spaces. I had started running for the freedom it offered and as a consequence I had become much leaner and developed a pencil neck. I joked that I got tired from lifting a pen. Kindly, the officers pointed to my head and said I was using the most important muscle.

Most of the officers have a background in the armed forces. They run the Segregation unit with military precision. Each of the prisoners has to be locked and unlocked separately, whether this is to provide them with meals, a shower, a telephone call or exercise on the yard. They are not allowed to meet and it requires impressive organization to keep them apart. I sat down next to a wall-mounted whiteboard on which the cell location, name and number of every prisoner is written. In Segregation, there are twenty cells over two floors. Some of the cells can't be used because the prisoners have broken the sinks, blocked the toilets and flooded their rooms. They knock holes in the walls and pull the electrics out of the sockets. The Estates department need to repair the cells on a weekly basis.

Sometimes the prisoners will initiate a 'dirty protest', also known as 'bronzing', and smear faeces on themselves or on their walls. It is a way of externalizing their frustrations and trauma. Many of them have already been sectioned under section 47 of the Mental Health Act 1983 and are awaiting a transfer from prison to a community mental-health bed, when one finally becomes available. The officers try their best but they are not medically trained for this – these patients should not be in a prison. Once a prisoner starts a dirty protest it needs to be contained, because it is a biohazard and there is always the fear that other prisoners might follow suit. It isn't unusual to have two or three dirty protests occurring at the same time.

The officers informed me that dirty protests first started to gain notoriety in the Maze Prison in Northern Ireland during the Troubles. Prisoners used dirty protests for many reasons, one of which was to demoralize the officers. The officers in the Maze responded by pulling prisoners on dirty protest out of their own cells and swapping them around. While protestors could just about bear to sit in their own mess, they were disgusted to sit in someone else's shit. This is not a practice I have witnessed.

'Have a nice cuppa, Doc,' Goz said, handing me a mug of tea.

The vast majority of officers are unfailingly protective and friendly towards healthcare staff. The officers will often supply me with custard creams and chocolate Bourbons, but today I politely refused.

'Thank you, but I'm fasting. It's Ramadan,' I said.

'You can't have a drink? Not even water?' Goz asked with incredulity.

'Not even water,' I replied.

Islam is a practical way of life. It is not good enough to say you have empathy – you have to prove it. Every year, for one month, Muslims are expected to experience hunger and thirst from sunrise to sunset. The Islamic months follow a lunar calendar, which means Ramadan can be in winter with shorter fasts or in summer with fasts of almost twenty hours. During those long summer days it is difficult to maintain a fast but it is meant to be, and the time goes by quickly when I am rushing around from one emergency to another.

Nadeem, the pharmacy technician, and I were for a time the only two Muslim members of staff in healthcare. If we were not overworked we attended Friday prayers in the prison – with the governor's permission. We took care to sit together at the very edge of the congregation of prisoners with our keys hidden under our clothes, like the Muslim officers did. I had been so angry immediately after my father's death that I couldn't look up at the sky. For months I had hesitated before attending the mosque for communal prayers. When the imams preached about divine goodness, kindness and justice, I would look down at the patterned prayer rugs to avoid eye contact. The words and sentiments seemed lofty and far away from my personal experience.

Even now, with Nadeem by my side, I habitually trace the designs on the prayer mats with my finger whenever the imams give a sermon. One imam said

people were like ants who crawled over a beautiful carpet without appreciating the intricate design. Maybe
one day I'll gain some perspective and will understand
the bigger picture, the divine pattern, and why bad
things happen to good people. In the aftermath of my
father's death a lot of family and friends distanced
themselves from us – as if we were tainted or unlucky
and it might somehow rub off on them. They were all
people who would consider themselves to be good
religious folk. On the other hand, many of my friends
were atheists and I knew that being religious bore no
relation to being a good or moral person. The VP unit
is further testament to this fact – it houses clergy of all
faiths.

Nadeem is religious and also deeply moral and ethical. Once a nurse had wandered into my room to see
the two of us huddled over my computer screen. At
first she was concerned it might be something not safe
for work but then laughed when she realized we were
salivating over images of burgers and fast food during
Ramadan.

In the Segregation office, Officer W handed me a
clipboard with the list of twenty patients currently
housed in the Segregation unit. I would be seeing all
of them and asking if they needed anything. The officers unlocked each cell in turn, always ensuring I was
at the back so that they could stand protectively in
front of me in case a prisoner rushed out. The healthcare managers warned doctors against prescribing
non-essential medications, but prisoners routinely
directed their pent-up rage towards us if we declined

to prescribe them something as simple as moisturizer. This put me in a quandary – between a rock and a hard place.

'I need shampoo and moisturizer, acne cream. I need deodorant and I want some sleeping tablets,' the first prisoner said. 'I refuse to buy anything in prison, the government put me here and they should pay.'

'I'm here to prescribe medications not toiletries,' I replied, my standard response.

'Well, they are medications; I have eczema, a dry scalp, excessive sweating and insomnia,' he replied triumphantly.

'Put your shopping list away. This isn't Asda!' Goz snapped and closed the door. 'The next cell is empty, Doc,' Officer W informed me. 'Mr Jamie Lovell is a regular visitor but he's currently in hospital having his jaw fixed. Just cross him off your list.'

Next we saw the patients on dirty protest – some had smashed their window panels and broken up the items in their cells to post through the narrow space. One of the men had torn up his mattress into little pieces and thrown it through the observation hatch and out of his cell, where it now sat in a filthy pile sopping with urine. I couldn't understand why he would do that – other than that he was clearly not in a rational state of mind. We had to tread carefully around brown pools and broken glass while being aware further missiles might be lobbed at us. Biohazard screens surrounded the doors of the prisoners on a dirty protest. Sometimes men on dirty protests targeted passers-by with squeezy bottles of their effluent. This is grim for us all. The officers work here for long shifts and maintain a cheerful outlook – I don't know how they do it but I take my hat off to them.

'I'm the doctor,' I called feebly from a distance. 'Anything I can help you with?' What the hell was I going to offer these poor souls?

When doors were unlocked we'd find most of the prisoners were in bed trying to sleep away their sentences. Some of the men did regular exercises or 'pad work-outs' until they had attained muscular 'prison bodies'. They became obsessed with weighing themselves to see how much muscle they had gained. Others turned inwards and read books, passing the time by transporting themselves elsewhere and inhabiting someone else's shoes for a while.

A door was opened to reveal a heavily tattooed young white man sitting on his bed reading a copy of the Quran. It was not unusual to have a former white supremacist now sporting a beard and greeting me with '*Assalamu alaikum*' – 'Peace be upon you' – when they heard my name. Yousaf is the Arabic translation of the prophet Joseph, who was imprisoned in Egypt. At first, I found it jarring to see someone so committed to racism that they would literally mark their belief on their skin having converted, or reverted, to Islam. Especially because as a belief system Islam has its foundation in anti-racism – no human can claim superiority based on skin colour or ethnicity. The man had lips as dry and parched as mine and he too was obviously fasting for Ramadan. He shook his head when I asked if he wanted anything, although he clearly wanted for much.

There are many reasons for becoming a Muslim in

prison. It affords protection in numbers – a sense of belonging to a bigger family who refer to each other as brother and sister. Another possible attraction, not to be downplayed, is the food. The halal options in prison are far more palatable than the bland and overcooked non-halal mush. While there may be 'Prison Muslims' who don't follow their faith on release, I have also met Muslims who continued their faith beyond prison.

Another door was unlocked and another door and another door. Patient after patient. I was running out of space to write my notes. My final consultation was with Mr E. He was a British South Asian man possibly only a few years older than me. Mr E said he had suffered a catastrophic life event a few years previously and since then had been unable to feel any emotions. He said he didn't feel ready to talk about his past. I understood how that felt. I gulped, regained my composure, and slipped into my professional role again. I asked questions about his mood and anxiety and listened to him carefully. I noticed how exhausted he appeared. I asked if he wanted to start taking antidepressants. He politely declined. Mr E didn't think he would ever feel like his old self again. I asked Mr E if he was religious, noting that he had a Muslim name.

'I dunno, I don't pray or fast, I drink and take drugs – but I draw the line at eating pork,' he said and shrugged.

I asked if he might want to speak to the prison imam who was part of the chaplaincy team.

'I avoid "Screacher-Preachers" and "Beardy-Weirdies" – as soon as they start flapping their gums I switch off. All they do is say life is a test and I will be rewarded or punished in the afterlife if I don't repent,' Mr E responded flatly.

'You can't go on like this, you'll burn yourself out,' I said.

Maybe there was something in the way I spoke to him that made him realize I had survived a trauma too. He finally made eye contact. Somehow I seemed to be able to connect with him. He agreed to speak to the imam. Accepting help felt like a breakthrough for both of us. I was using my own personal experiences to reach out to others. My work, I felt, was done – at least for the day.

But throughout the ward round Mr S had kept calling out to us.

'Please help me, help me. I'm sorry, I'm sorry,' Mr S shouted.

The other prisoners shouted abuse back at Mr S. They bellowed 'Nonce' at him until it became an angry chant. Nonce. Nonce. Nonce. Nonce. There were threats of horrific violence. They said they would shank him and pull his guts out. No wonder Mr S was disturbed. He screamed even louder.

'We'll have to see what he wants before this escalates further,' Officer W said with a sigh.

As soon as his cell door was unlocked Mr S sank to his knees and held on to Officer W's legs, Binky Bear nuzzled against his thighs.

'Get that thing off me or I will break its neck and your wrist,' Officer W growled as he disentangled himself from the bear's clutches.

I was feeling a little kinder. 'I'll ask Dean from the

In-reach mental-health team to come and see you. He can give you a distraction pack, which contains puzzles and colouring books and crayons. It'll give you something to do until the psychiatrist can see you in clinic,' I said as gently as I could.

Mr S nodded gratefully and crawled back into his cell, all the while nuzzling Binky Bear, and once again the door closed on him and his misery.

After a few days he was transferred to the Inpatient unit when a space became available. We discussed him in the weekly multi-disciplinary team meetings with the primary-care and In-reach mental-health teams. It was agreed that strict boundaries needed to be adhered to. No member of staff should see Mr S alone due to his history of making false claims of abuse. Dean was assigned as his case worker and began to keep detailed progress notes, an ever-watchful eye on the coroner's court.

Despite the best efforts of the staff, Mr S continued to present with challenging behaviour. He was observed holding his breath until he was blue in the face. Sometimes he shouted that he was having a heart attack and would clutch his chest and ask for mouth-to-mouth resuscitation. He appeared to want female attention and was always disappointed when he opened his eyes to find me kneeling beside him with an oxygen mask. I was disappointed too – I didn't seem to be able to help him. But I was particularly disturbed by Mr S's behaviour because there were so many sick and vulnerable men located in the Inpatient unit and he was taking up valuable time and limited resources. He needed our help too, that much was obvious, but it was difficult to give.

*

Mr C, the thirty-year-old individual with suspected rectal cancer, had been moved to the Inpatient unit too. Events had progressed quickly with him. He was reviewed by the cancer team in the outside hospital within two weeks of my referral and they organized investigations. He was diagnosed with a malignant tumour of the rectum and it appeared to have spread to his liver. Breaking the news to him was particularly difficult. He was in prison and therefore away from his family, with no one to hold his hand. The only contact he had was short family visits with an officer present and limited physical contact. Mr C didn't want to worry his family, especially his partner who was expecting their first child. He was clearly trying to put a brave face on events and was always polite and appeared surprisingly upbeat when I spoke to him.

On the outside all hospital letters would have gone to him directly, but in prison these personal documents were delivered to the healthcare team. I visited him in his Inpatient unit cell on a regular basis to keep him updated on his care, just as I promised I would. He was having chemotherapy in the outside hospital every two weeks and would be exhausted for a couple of days afterwards. He had been moved to the Inpatient unit because he needed plenty of rest and the nurses there could keep a close eye on him.

'I'm going to beat this,' he promised me.

I hoped he would, and although I prayed for him with each of my daily prayers, Mr C didn't get any better. Despite it all, he rarely complained and if he did it was just a mild remark that he had been unable to sleep because Mr S had been screaming and shouting all night. Mr C deserved better. Behind the scenes I had been speaking with the prison about organizing an Executive Release for him. This is compassionate early release without the need for a parole hearing and could be granted by the Secretary of State because Mr C only had a few months left to serve on his sentence. There was no doubt he would be better cared for at home. I was pleased to be able to have a meeting with Mr C's family and his Offender Manager, who provided a positive report and recommended an early release. But it could take months for this to be finalized and Mr C didn't have months. It was the first time I had worked closely with the prison managers and I found them to be much more helpful than prisoners had led me to believe. The prison system was working under huge restrictions, despite all of the many well-intentioned individuals who were trying their hardest. But good intentions only went so far – and Mr C was suffering.

Whereas Mr C minimized his pain and always presented to staff with a cheery 'Good morning', Mr S was often found sobbing and rocking in the corner of his cell. The psychiatrist reviewed him and made a diagnosis of an antisocial personality disorder and schizoaffective disorder. His medication was adjusted, which had a sedating effect initially but there was no overall change in his behaviour. His angry outbursts continued. He threatened to stab members of staff. A plastic knife was retrieved from inside Binky Bear. The puppet was confiscated and Mr S was placed on 'finger food' without access to any cutlery.

The next step was for Mr S to be discussed in a

Multi-Agency Public Protection Arrangements security meeting to assess his risk to the public if he was released. I was called to provide my opinion. His security records showed he was able to navigate the internet and access several social networking sites. The MAPPA coordinator reinforced that he posed a significant risk to the public. Dean and the psychiatrist deemed Mr S was fit to attend court. He was reported to be crying when he was placed in the van on the morning of his trial. He was given a long sentence and transferred to a VP prison.

Binky Bear was found a few weeks after Mr S's departure. It had been stuffed behind a washing machine. Both of its eyes were missing and the stuffing had been pulled out. It was double-bagged as contaminated waste and thrown away. I hoped Mr S would receive better care than Binky had and wondered if he would ever be rehabilitated. Maybe he would die in prison.

That same week Mr C received his Executive Release. He had completed three exhausting cycles of chemotherapy, each two weeks apart, and he appeared to be responding well. His rectal cancer marker, a chemical called carcinoembryonic antigen, had halved, which was a promising sign.

The morning I was informed that Mr C had been granted immediate release from prison was a good one. His family were on their way to collect him. I met him in the Inpatient unit. He was giving away most of his belongings to the other men. He was moving out of the area and the chemotherapy nurses from our local hospital had already arranged a follow-up with a hospital near his home. I said goodbye to him and told him I wished him well in the future.

'Please let us know how you get on. The thing about offender healthcare is that after your patient is released from prison their care automatically gets transferred back to their community team. I won't get any more follow-ups and your records will be closed to me – for patient confidentiality. I won't hear how you are progressing. I won't be your GP any more,' I said sadly.

'You will always be my GP, Dr Y,' Mr C said warmly.

I haven't seen or heard from either Mr C or Mr S again, but I don't think I will forget either of them.

10

The Vulnerable Prisoner Unit

I spoke with my friend Matthew once or twice a week. As students, we'd randomly been allocated the same small study group on the first day of medical school. When I'd first heard his estuary accent, taken in his shaved head and frayed jeans over muddy trainers, I'd thought he was a football hooligan. I had quickly surmised that we had nothing in common and I had sought out friends with a similar background to me. It was only later that I realized my understanding of kinship had been wrong. We'd been thrown together in our housing and that gave us the chance to sit in the kitchen and talk. He would laugh at my jokes and smile easily and often. When I told him that I had initially thought he was a yob, he spat out his tea and almost choked. He said he'd shaved his head because his floppy blond hair made him look like Princess

Diana. He wanted to look 'hard' and it had worked, on me at least.

We left the halls of residence after the first year and found a student house with other friends, Sadat, Gerry and Ade. Matthew would wake us up in the morning by politely knocking on our bedroom doors with a cup of tea. He would ask if we had slept well. He'd cheerfully make our breakfast as we got ready. He loved the traditional Pakistani clothes I wore to bed, the shalwar kameez, and I gave him some pairs. He wore them as soon as he came home each day and enthused about how comfortable they were. Late in the evenings, before we went to bed, Matthew would make us White Russian cocktails, consisting of vodka, coffee liqueur and fresh cream. I didn't drink alcohol so he'd prepare a Virgin White Russian for me, which was a glass of milk. His parents Brian and Gwyneth were as warm and generous as my own.

Calling Matthew was often part of my going-home ritual. It helped put more distance between me and the prison each evening. I told him about the strange world I had discovered behind high walls. He shared experiences from his work as a pathologist. We fell back on humour to make us more human in the dark environments we'd come to inhabit.

'What's a "nonce", Shah?' Matthew asked.

'Nonce is a slang term for a sex offender. More specifically for a paedophile. Why do you want to know?' I asked.

'You never know, it might come up in a pub quiz,' Matthew said.

It was his day off and he told me he was doing some carpentry.

'What are you making? Is it another gimp suspension unit? Mine keeps breaking,' I joked.

'Yes, an extra-strong GSU. Gimps seem to be much heavier than they used to be,' Matthew said, deadpan.

'We all know too much S&M on any GSU can lead to repetitive strain injuries and visits to A&E,' I replied.

In truth, it's no laughing matter. And perhaps one of the most challenging parts of my job comes from my work on the Vulnerable Prisoner unit. While I never ask prisoners what they are in for, if they are housed in the VP unit I effectively know it is for a crime of a sensitive or sexual nature. But what I think about them isn't the issue. I have to separate myself from my feelings in order to do my job. The mainstream prisoners have the opposite mindset. The VP unit is like a red rag to a bull and they look for any opportunity to attack its inhabitants. In the morally ambiguous world of the prison a wife beater can boast about punching a rapist. The VPs and mainstream prisoners have to be kept apart at all times.

Joyce is the lead VP nurse. Known as Joycie to her close friends, she is softly spoken and beautifully dressed in clothes she makes herself. As a mental-health nurse she is exempt from wearing a uniform. She reminds me of the sugar-coated tamarind balls she brings back for me from her trips to visit family in Jamaica. There is sweetness over delicious tartness but with a centre that can break your teeth. She asked me to review one of her patients on the VP unit.

We navigate the prison via the upper walkways used

by the mainstream prisoners. The VPs travel using the lower concrete walkways but never at the same time as the mainstream prisoners. The metal passages rattle around us as the mainstream prisoners stomp and shout. The walkways are encased in mesh tubes to prevent the throwing of missiles and contraband. Sometimes birds become trapped in these labyrinthine cages and they build nests from the fluff shed from the prisoners' uniforms. Joyce and I had to look down to avoid the bird shit and human spit splattered across our path. We heard someone hollering to us from behind.

'Oi, you stopped my meds. I'm going to knock your head off!' a man shouted over the other prisoners.

We pretended not to hear the booming voice but increased our speed.

'I said, I'm going to knock your bloody head off!' The threat came again and it was impossible to ignore.

Joycie and I turned around to face whatever was coming and I saw that she had her finger over the panic button on her radio. I instinctively placed myself between her and Mr Jamie Lovell as he loomed over us. We looked for an officer but couldn't see one. If Joycie pushed her alarm it would be two if not four black eyes before the officers came to rescue us.

'If you're going to knock my block off you had better do a good job because if I get up I'm going to knock your block off!' Joycie said with a low growl. I wasn't sure why I'd thought she needed protecting.

'Only joking!' Jamie exclaimed and began to laugh. He pushed a folded piece of paper into my hand and ran off along the walkway, disappearing into one of the house blocks.

'That dickhead thinks he's hilarious!' I exclaimed, attempting to hide my relief.

I had noticed that his teeth had been transplanted into their gum space and his jaw had been fixed following his visit to the maxillary facial surgeons. The dental nurse Helen and dentist Katie had been able to salvage his smile and it was surprisingly pleasant to be on the receiving end of it.

I unfolded the piece of paper and saw that it was a poem Jamie had written. His handwriting was large and clumsy, as if he had wrestled each letter into submission. The poem itself was simple and good. I smiled as I folded it back up and put it in my pocket. I was glad he was taking steps to improve his literacy. Later I would send him a gentle critique and suggest poets he might like to read in the prison library. If I had any spare time I liked to visit the library myself. Being surrounded by books had a calming effect on me and I could forget I was in prison and put my hectic day to one side. Within a few pages I could be transported anywhere. I thought it was a shame that more prisoners didn't choose this method of escape rather than dangerous drugs like spice. That fairytale world again.

Joycie and I continued our walk to the VP unit. Despite the upper walkways being busy with mainstream prisoners we had decided against using the shadowy lower walkways, even though they were empty of VPs. The chief reason was my fear of rodents and the lower walkways are where the vermin traps were placed. I once saw a rat crawl out of its hiding place in the agony of its death throes. I couldn't look away as it convulsed and I wasn't brave enough to end its suffering. The cherubic Nurse Alice who was accompanying me had dragged a wheelie bin over and crushed its head in what she described as an act of kindness. I hadn't used the lower walkways since.

I asked Joycie if she liked working with the VPs. She had been doing it for ten years, which seemed to answer my question.

'I've always been based with the VPs,' she told me, 'because no one likes working with them. Some of the other staff call them "Creepy VPs". The nurses and some of the doctors feel the unit has a horrible atmosphere. I have to mentally separate myself from the VPs. I don't want to know what they've done because if I did then I couldn't work with them – it's a job, and most of the time I love it.'

The VP unit was a prison within a prison, partitioned from the rest of the site by a huge wall covered in a mural of a forest. The mainstream prisoners had painted the outside of it in their art class and had expressed their disgust at the VPs with broad strokes. The cartoonish painting was splattered with blood-red poppies and every fallen apple had a fleshy maggot protruding from it. Swear words and threats were scratched into the mural constantly until the paint flaked away. *Very Perverted Unit. Kill YoSelf! 1 Bullett = 1 Less Problem.*

I unlocked the door and found the handle was sticky; all the doors and gates in the prison were tacky from accumulated filth. I always carried a small bottle of alcohol gel with me. I liberally doused my hands before nudging the door open with my foot. My path was blocked by a row of old men in wheelchairs.

'I'm sorry, are we in your way?' a well-spoken man in a wheelchair asked.

'We can squeeze by,' I said, carefully side-stepping them. Joycie locked the door behind us.

I had met this man before; he was a former private-school master.

'We're watching the tournament,' the schoolmaster told me.

The VP unit was three storeys and, following his gaze, I looked over the railings to the floor below. Men were playing boules. There was a convivial atmosphere that seemed more like a residential home than a prison. The average age was fifty, with some men in their sixties, seventies and even eighties. Many of them used walking sticks, walking frames and wheelchairs. Despite their health problems they took pride in their environment, and it was one of the only places in the prison that didn't stink. The bins were emptied and the air was heady with rose-scented disinfectant.

'You're a good man,' the schoolmaster said to me. He reached out to pat my hand. Before I knew it he had curled a wrapped sweet into my palm.

'For later,' he said.

'I am not allowed to accept gifts,' I replied. I handed it back.

'Ah, come on,' he said with a wink.

'You don't want to get the doctor into trouble,' Joycie said firmly.

The schoolmaster took back his treat. People tended to do what Joycie said.

The men interrupted their game to call hello and wave at us. There were a few famous faces in the crowd and we were made to feel like celebrities by celebrities. Some of the men slowly made their way up the stairs to meet us. They complimented our clothes. They said we were looking well and asked for 'little favours' like creams and shampoos. We smiled and nodded and I used alcohol gel as an excuse not to shake hands. I didn't want them to force sweets on me and to feel in any way favoured or indebted.

Joycie explained we were here to see a prisoner called Mikey. The men shouted down the landing. An athletic-looking young man emerged from a door and bolted up the stairs towards us.

'Hi Joyce, is this the doctor? Hi Doc, I'm Mikey,' he exclaimed.

He thrust his hand towards me with a wide grin as if we were childhood friends. I was taken aback by his exuberance. I'd never encountered anything like it in prison. I looked at Mikey's hand and then his split lip. Despite the injury, he reminded me of the groomed young men who appeared on TV shows with 'celebrity' or 'love' in their titles. His bleached white teeth shone against his deep tan. Despite being Caucasian his skin tone was darker than mine.

'Nurse Joyce tells me you've been in an altercation. She has asked me to assess you,' I said coolly, to establish boundaries. Mikey put his hand away.

'It's nothing, Doc,' he said. His wide smile caused his lip to crack and start bleeding.

'You're injured. I'll assess you in the clinic,' I said and led the way.

The VP clinic room, like all the clinics situated on

the wings, needed double security. A heavy gate was fitted in front of the door and both needed to be locked. This was to prevent prisoners from breaking in to steal equipment and medication. It was a prison rule that all gates had to be in a fixed position – they either had to be locked shut or secured to the wall with a wall lock. A wall lock was a metal device, which as its name suggested was on the wall and a gate could be attached to it. An unsecured gate was heavy enough to be used as a weapon with which to strike prisoners or staff. Those were the rules in the mainstream prison, but there was no wall lock for the VP clinic gate. I refused to lock myself in a room with a VP in case I needed to make a hasty exit. Many of these men were either on remand or convicted sex offenders and I didn't want to take any chances. Staff in other prisons had been sexually assaulted by convicted rapists.

Joycie and I were on the same page. 'Don't lock the gate, Dr Y,' she said. 'Some of the nurses don't think twice before locking themselves in with the men. No offence to Mikey but I don't trust anyone.'

I hated using this room if Joycie wasn't there. I didn't have a radio or personal alarm. The room lacked a panic button and a telephone despite our frequent requests for them. The officers were stationed at a hub at the end of a long corridor. If I didn't have a chaperone I would be alone in a room with a prisoner who could attack me, despite all my best efforts to protect myself by following procedure.

'Nice atmosphere,' Mikey said, stepping inside and looking around at the peeling posters and overwatered plants.

'I just work here,' I said distractedly.

He was being charming and working hard to engage Joycie in conversation. She smiled and laughed along, but I could tell her guard was up too. Her body language appeared a little stiffer as if her muscles were primed to run. Her movements were usually fluid and relaxed when she was amongst people she trusted. I wondered how difficult it must be for a woman to navigate this underworld, even a woman as tough as Joycie.

There was a small pile of sweets on the desk. Despite the doctors and nurses explaining that gifts were forbidden the VPs always insisted on leaving 'treats' for us at the end of our clinics. The mainstream prisoners never did this; they were hard-pressed even to say thank you. Maybe it was because the VPs were generally older and more used to being deferential towards healthcare staff. But I thought of it as grooming and swept all of the sweets into the bin.

'I was going to have one of those,' Mikey joked with mock disappointment.

'You don't know where they've been,' Joycie said. She laughed revealing only her front teeth.

When Joycie and I were otherwise alone and I was being silly she would laugh freely with her eyes closed and her head thrown back so far I could see her molars. Sometimes she laughed so hard at my inane jokes that there were tears in her eyes and it made me happy.

'Do you know the legend of Persephone?' I asked Mikey as I logged on to the computer.

He raised his manicured eyebrows quizzically.

'She was a Greek goddess who was kidnapped and

taken to the underworld by Hades to be his wife. She was tricked into eating something, a pomegranate seed I believe, and thereby cursed to remain there.' I paused, possibly for dramatic effect, before concluding, 'There are no free gifts in a prison.'

I switched into business mode. 'Anyway, what happened to you?' I asked pointing out Mikey's injuries.

'It's because of the way I look,' he said with a sigh.

I was surprised by his answer and cast a closer eye over him for clues. He was a muscular young man with his hair slicked back into a neat bun and he had a trimmed beard. He was an enhanced prisoner, exempted from wearing prison clothing, and was dressed in a tight T-shirt with a deep V neck that revealed his hairless tattooed chest. He was dressed fashionably with skinny jeans and expensive trainers. I could imagine some women, or men, would find him attractive. I unkindly assumed that he spent a lot of time gazing into his phone's camera.

'It's my teeth,' Mikey said and flashed me a smile.

'Your teeth?' I was none the wiser.

'Most of the guys in prison have bad teeth,' Mikey said. 'I have expensive veneers; I got them done in Turkey and I got a hair transplant there too. Most of these lads are dirty; they don't wash. I am very clean and I shower at least twice a day if the officers unlock my cell. I look and smell good and I have nice things. They think I must be an undercover cop or a reporter.'

There had been an undercover policeman and reporters in prisons sometimes posing as prisoners or officers, but they hadn't stood out as much as Mikey did. I brought up his medical records. It was his first time in prison and there was very little history. Maybe he *was* a policeman or a reporter. I noted with surprise that we shared the same date of birth.

'What do you do on the out?' I asked. It was a phrase I heard the nurses use. Everything was delineated between 'in here' and 'on the out'. Some of the Londoners said 'on road' to mean outside.

'I'm a personal trainer and I have my own gym,' Mikey said proudly. 'I like to help people become the best versions of themselves. I try to stay upbeat and positive, but being here is depressing. I'm losing muscle and gaining fat. They feed us carbs: bread, chips, no protein. Have you seen the "food" they give us?' His manicured hands performed air quotes.

I nodded. I couldn't help but feel some sympathy. The meals smell so bad that I have to hold my breath when I walk past the food trolleys. The sight of the soggy baguettes makes me feel nauseous.

'It's all rotten,' Mikey continued. 'The white bread is grey and it starts curling up in front of you. Loads of times I've had to pick green mould out of the bread. No word of a lie – they are giving us food that you wouldn't feed a dog. I can't eat it. The breakfast packs are a joke, everyone is always hungry; the men will fight over a single roast potato. I never knew prison would be this bad. I wasn't expecting a holiday camp, but this is like a concentration camp. It's affecting my mental health and I'm usually a glass-half-full kind of guy. I heard a rumour that the mainstream prisoners prepare our food and they meddle with it, that they shit in the beans,' he said incredulously.

'Of course they don't shit in the beans!' I said. 'If you

don't trust the food the prison provides you can supplement your diet with things you can buy on Canteen. You need to have credit on your account before you can use the Canteen mail-order catalogue but you can buy clothes and food.'

'I don't want to buy anything in here, Doc,' Mikey said. 'I'm in court on Friday for my trial; you mark my words, I will walk from court because I am innocent.'

'Right,' I said. I avoided eye contact with Joycie. We rarely met a guilty prisoner. There were over a thousand innocent men in this prison – even the ones who had been convicted.

'I can tell you don't believe me. I don't like anyone thinking badly of me. It bugs me. How old are you, Doc? You can't be more than five or ten years older than me?'

'Five or ten years older? *Five or ten years?* I'm the same age as you!' I exclaimed with a sudden outrage that shocked and then embarrassed me.

Mikey found my reaction hilarious. He covered his sore mouth with his hand and began to laugh, his bulky shoulders shaking.

'I'm so sorry, Doc. I didn't mean to piss you off, oh my days!' he exclaimed.

Joycie was trying hard not to laugh. She too had covered her mouth with her hand.

'This,' I said, pointing to my weathered face, 'is stress. Cortisol is the stress hormone and it ages us. Looking older than I am is my badge of honour; it means I care.'

'I needed that. I haven't laughed in weeks. You look so vexed!' Mikey said. He was still grinning, his face was flushed and his eyes were wet.

I saw my reflection in the computer monitor and it was as if I was seeing myself for the first time in years. I did look old and tired. Why hadn't I taken better care of myself?

When I'd begun working as a house officer or junior doctor I was allocated to hospitals in Birmingham. Many of my cohort had graduated from Birmingham Medical School and already knew each other. For me it was a fresh start. But not only had I worked in the same hospital I had rushed to on the fateful night of my father's death, I had also resuscitated patients on the very same bed where his body had lain. I couldn't have done this without shutting down core parts of my own emotions.

One of my new junior doctor friends had pointed to my photo ID and remarked on the baby face. I had inherited large brown eyes from my mother and I had my father's jaw and smiling mouth. My new friend quipped that I shouldn't have used a photograph from five years ago. I didn't tell him it was a recent photograph from just a few months back. I had visibly aged over the course of a harrowing summer. My thick wavy hair fell out in handfuls. My smooth skin was creased and I had dark circles under my eyes. I hardly recognized myself any more.

Not long before my father died, I had written my honours dissertation on a branch of medicine called psychoneuroimmunology, the science of how stress can make us physically sick. This was either coincidence or a foreshadowing. Following his death, our whole family aged as if years had passed over just a few weeks. My mother and sister were known for being beautiful women, and now when they caught a glimpse of their reflections they laughed at the absurdity of their appearance.

'Please don't be offended, Doc,' Mikey continued, 'but you look like you need fresh air and some changes in your lifestyle. I drink at least three litres of water a day and I make sure I get my seven or eight hours of sleep a night. I take vitamin supplements and use a sauna or a steam room to keep my skin fresh. On the out.'

There were certainly no saunas or steam rooms in the prison.

'Any other advice?' I asked. Amusement was replacing my irritation. Mikey glowed with vitality and I was tempted to ask him what moisturizer he used.

'No offence but you could do with going to the gym,' Mikey said. 'If you come to my gym I'll do you a diet and exercise plan. I reckon you would look completely different in six to eight months with the right guidance. Fill out your arms and shoulders a bit. You need it, especially in this environment. You've got good legs, they look strong.' I took the compliment greedily.

'I can't come to your gym or have any contact once you're released. It would be unethical. Once you walk out of those gates I won't see you again unless you come back to prison,' I told him quietly.

'I am never coming back to prison,' proclaimed Mikey. 'I can write you a little exercise plan, if you like? It would give me something to do.'

'OK, that would be nice,' I replied. 'But first I need

to fix your lip. Are you going to tell me who hit you? I'm concerned.'

'There are these two lads on the unit who have been bullying the old guys,' Mikey said. 'Tipping them out of their wheelchairs for entertainment, hitting them, stealing from them. I stood up for the old guys and the two lads didn't like it. They started telling everyone I was an undercover cop sniffing around for more information on their crimes. A group of them ambushed me in the showers. They thought I was a pretty boy who couldn't fight but I gave them a pasting. They won't be bullying anyone for a while.'

I couldn't help but be impressed. It was almost unheard of for anyone to stand up for VPs, even the VPs themselves. However much they protested their innocence they accepted their lowly status in prison society.

'I know the men he means,' Joycie added. 'Both of them are nasty. I've told him to report it to the officers but he won't.'

Mikey gave me permission to examine him. There was a five-millimetre laceration to the lower lip and it was swollen and oozing a little. I handed him a tissue. I looked inside his mouth with my torch. There was a slight swelling to the left cheek but no bruising. He had some tenderness when I pressed on the temporo-mandibular joints which articulated the lower jaw. It appeared to be a soft-tissue injury and there was no obvious bony abnormality or any sign of a jaw dislocation. He was able to open his mouth widely and there was no damage to his tongue. I checked for blood or clear fluid issuing from the nostrils and ears, which might indicate a fractured skull.

'No broken bones, I can glue your lip, no need for stitches,' I told Mikey. 'If you could lie down on the couch I'll get my things together.'

Joycie helped me search the medical cabinets for glue. They were a jumbled mess and badly stocked. We rummaged through containers and made a pile of medications that were out of date and to be disposed of later.

'Can't you hear that?' Mikey asked us.

'Hear what?' Joycie asked as she searched for glue.

'The abuse,' Mikey said. 'I'm not a nonce.'

I stopped what I was doing for a moment and turned towards the window. The clinic was overlooked by an entire house block of mainstream prisoners. A big group of them was staring at us from a short distance and screaming and shouting. There were no curtains or screen to block their view into the VP clinic room. This was despite the doctors and nurses having requested curtains for this room for a long time.

'Pae-do, pae-do, pae-do!' they chanted. It was deafening and yet somehow I had blotted out the noise because I was so accustomed to it.

'I'm not a nonce,' Mikey repeated quietly, almost like a mantra. I could see he had shrunk into himself, the broad shoulders were drawn in.

'We don't want to know what you've done,' Joycie said quickly.

'I'm sure everyone says they're innocent but genuinely I haven't done anything,' he replied.

There was a dull thud against the window. Something that looked like mud splattered on the glass just above our heads. It was toilet paper soiled with faeces.

'That's disgusting,' Mikey said.

'Yes, it is.' Joycie and I shared his repulsion.

I hated using this room because of the chanting and missiles thrown at the windows. It surprised me how I had conditioned myself into not even hearing the abuse until Mikey brought it to my attention. I applied glue to his lip and held it together until it had set. I needed to get this done so we could all leave.

'It should heal nicely,' I said.

'I reckon the scar will make me even more handsome, make me look rugged,' Mikey joked, but his humour was forced – he was still clearly troubled by the chanting outside the window.

He was the picture of wellness. He was right. Even his swollen lip looked like it had been recently pumped full of cosmetic filler rather than swollen from an injury.

'The swelling should go down in a couple of days. Is there anything else I can help you with today?' I asked.

Joycie and I began to tidy up the equipment, but Mikey wasn't finished.

'Doc, you have to understand that I'm a typical lad. I get a lot of female attention,' he said.

'We're not here to judge you,' I interrupted him. I didn't want to hear what crime he was accused of. I had treated him and treated him well. My job was done. I didn't understand why he wanted me to believe in his innocence. Maybe he just wanted to offload on to somebody, anybody, but it was important for me to preserve a professional distance between me and my patients, especially the VPs. I crossed my arms to demonstrate this was not a conversation I was comfortable with.

'But the damage is done. I come from a small town, my reputation has been ruined. People are going to say that where there's smoke there's fire,' Mikey continued quietly.

'If someone has made a false claim you can take legal action and clear your name,' Joycie said.

'It's never that easy, Miss,' Mikey told us. 'This is going to hang over my head for the rest of my life.'

I switched off the computer. As I was turning to leave the room I caught sight of the faeces sliding down the window pane, leaving long smears that would dry and stay there until it next rained. It really was disgusting. I hoped it would rain soon.

I was surprised to discover the gate had been locked. An officer must have walked past and locked it without us noticing. My hand shook as I reached for my keys. For all of his apparent charm Mikey could have attacked us and we wouldn't have been able to escape.

'Doc, you and Joycie need to be careful,' Mikey said with concern, aware too that we'd been locked in and that anything could have happened. I didn't want him to see my shaking hands.

'Fingers crossed you'll be out on Friday and you'll never have to think about this place again. Don't eat any pomegranate seeds,' I advised him.

I made a point of trying to give him a reassuring smile. But with my old man's face I'm not sure I pulled it off.

Outside the room, the schoolmaster and the other men in wheelchairs were still watching the game of boules.

'Who's winning?' I asked.

'No one,' the schoolmaster replied quietly.

I couldn't disagree with him. There were no winners here, only the victims who had brought their violators to justice.

'Thank you, Doc,' Mikey said as we shook hands. He added, 'You've got cold hands. You know what they say about people with cold hands? They have warm hearts.'

'No, just poor circulation,' I quipped.

He patted the left side of his chest lightly, over his heart, two quick taps. We both smiled before he walked away.

Another prisoner, older, with a grey complexion more like mine than Mikey's, was standing at a little distance. He was staring at Joycie and appeared to be sniffing the air.

'You're not wearing that perfume I like,' he said. 'Every day I come here and you're wearing that perfume. I look forward to it and now you're not wearing it.'

'You creepy so-and-so. I don't wear my perfume because you keep sniffing up to me. Go back to your cell and don't bother yourself with my perfume,' Joycie snapped at him.

The man retreated but kept turning back to look at Joycie as he went. It was almost as if he enjoyed being chastised by her. I could understand why female staff were hesitant to come to the VP unit, I found it difficult enough myself.

'Come on, let's go,' I said to Joycie, keen to get both of us out of there. It was a long walk and we chatted as we made our way back to the healthcare department. I had a pressing question for her.

'Do the mainstream prisoners shit in the VPs' beans?'
I asked.

'The mainstream prisoners work in the kitchens,'
Joycie told me. 'The food comes pre-cooked but they
heat it up. It gets moved around the prison in trolleys
and is taken to the different wings. I have heard that
they spit in the food that goes to the VP wing but I
think it's just a rumour. I think once, in another prison,
some mainstream prisoners did shit in the beans that
were going to the VP wing. Now it's an urban legend
that the VPs eat shit. But you saw the state of the windows. The mainstream prisoners hate the VPs. If they
could get away with it they would do it.' It was simply
a fact of life.

'You've been here for ten years. What keeps you
here?' I asked.

She thought about it for a moment. 'It's the prisoners that keep me interested. I like talking to the
prisoners, not about what they have done, but about
ordinary things. Sometimes they're not nice but I don't
really care. There was a prisoner, I can't remember his
name, he said to me, "You fucking black bitch!" I said,
"Thank you very much for being so observant that I'm
black. If you carry on talking to me like that I'll show
you what kind of bitch I am." That was enough to
make him walk off. But the next minute I heard him
shout and the officers were running around, trying to
get to an incident. Some other prisoners who had heard
him call me a black bitch went into his cell, stripped his
clothes off him, and threw him outside naked. Then,
later, when he went to get his food, another prisoner
who'd heard what he said to me held his hand down on

the hotplate. Just kept it there. It burned a big chunk out of his hand,' Joycie said thoughtfully, and not without some pride.

'That's not a heart-warming story, Joycie!' I said with some admonishment. We couldn't condone this behaviour.

'No, but it's a hand-warming story!' she replied.

I checked Mikey's records the following Friday. As he had predicted he was indeed found innocent and immediately released from court. He would now have to live with the stigma of his accusation. Like Persephone he would always be marked by his trip to the underworld.

11

Mr Freddie Mercury

I love Halloween. It's my favourite time of year.

When I was a child I was the only Goth at my mosque. Explaining my leaning towards that very British subculture to the imam was an interesting conversation. He took it reasonably well and earnestly said he would pray for me. I told my parents that I was a vampire and refused to eat garlic. They reminded me we were South Asian and garlic was an integral part of our diet. They also informed me we were Muslims and only ate halal meat which had been drained of all blood. My ever-obliging father provided me with jars of pickled beetroot and said there was no reason I couldn't be a vegetarian vampire. I chewed beetroot and let the juices drip from my mouth menacingly. I pretended that sunlight was harmful to me. I decorated my bedroom with skeletons and skulls that glowed in the dark. I read every conceivable book about witches, monsters and magic. As an adult we still carved pumpkins as a family. My sister Shahzadi and I indulged in horror-movie marathons. It was fun to dabble with fear when you felt safe. But I grew out of my love for horror when I began to feel less secure in the world. Now, as a prison doctor, I was witnessing horror on a daily basis.

On Halloween I was asked to review Mr Freddie Mercury. Mr Freddie Mercury had changed his name by deed poll. He was previously Mr Michael Jackson and before that Sir Elton John. Most prisoners were identified by prison numbers printed on their ID cards, which had to be carried at all times. Mr Mercury was not a number; he chose his own name, he broke rules, fought, took drugs. He had served fifteen years for a three-year prison sentence. He didn't meet any of the criteria to show that he was reformed and rehabilitated. His was an interminable cycle of bad behaviour and punishment. He was deemed a danger to himself and the public. And Mr Freddie Mercury had recently become my patient.

Imprisonment for Public Protection (IPP) sentences, like Mr Mercury's, were introduced in 2005. They were intended for people considered dangerous but whose crimes didn't warrant a life sentence. They had been abolished by the European Court of Human Rights in 2012 as they were deemed to be a human rights violation. But the abolishment was not retrospective, so Mr Mercury, and thousands of others like him, languished in hopelessness. Put simply, he was never going to get out of prison.

I was called to the Inpatient unit to see him. Mr Mercury was on a constant-watch observation, which meant that at all times an officer was monitoring him through the glass panel in the cell door. It was his job to make regular entries in the Assessment, Care in Custody and Teamwork (ACCT) document. As was so often the case, the glass in the observation panel had been smashed and our shoes crunched as we stepped closer to the door. The officer was known as Ginge, for obvious reasons. He was ex-armed forces, always incredibly cheerful.

'What's up, Doc?' he asked as I approached.

'Another day in paradise, mate! What's up with Mr Mercury this time? The hands or the feet?' I asked.

'The spoon,' Ginge told me.

I feared the damage Mr Mercury could do to himself with a spoon.

'Why does he do it, Dr Y?' Ginge asked.

'Can I see your hands?'

Ginge held out his hands with some hesitation, uncertain where I was going with this, and I examined his nails.

'You and Mr Mercury both bite your nails. The difference is that he is an autocannibal and he swallows his fingernails. He eats himself. He cuts off and eats his hair, fingers, his toes and ears. He also eats metal, plastic and poison. It's a psychiatric condition called pica,' I said.

Ginge withdrew his hands with a look of disgust.

'Just eating your hair is called Rapunzel syndrome,' I said. 'It's a rare but dangerous condition. Undigested material forms a lump in the intestines called a bezoar. In medieval times it was used as a cure for multiple ailments.'

'How do you know this stuff?' Ginge asked me incredulously.

'I read,' I said.

I felt a tap on my shoulder and turned to see Nurse Vicky's manicured finger. Vicky was the Inpatient unit manager and was always perfectly groomed – often in various shades of pink. I was constantly startled by her joyful appearance in such a drab setting. And she was quick to remind me that as a mental-health nurse she didn't have to wear a uniform. Today, ahead of our meeting with Mr Freddie Mercury, she pointed out that she was wearing expensive designer clothes and didn't want to get splashed by any blood. Some men who had blood-borne infections, such as HIV or hepatitis C, would threaten to throw their blood at us if they were displeased. We knew that with Mr Freddie Mercury there would be blood.

Through the shattered glass Vicky and I watched Mr Mercury going about his business. He was a man in his mid-thirties and was sitting on his bed, naked apart from his stained underwear. Despite his long history of eating himself, he was morbidly obese. Both of his ears had been sliced off and he had missing fingers and toes. We could see there was a deep gash on his left inner thigh. With a plastic spoon he was scraping the fat from his bloodied muscle and eating it.

Every time I felt as if I was finding my feet in this place I would be confronted by some new scenario that would shock and horrify me. I had been asked to stitch his wounds. The blood trickled down Mr Mercury's leg and congealed on the floor. He didn't appear to be in any discomfort. Quite the opposite; he seemed to be in a trance. It was a sight I wish I had not witnessed.

'That poor man!' Vicky whispered with her hand over her mouth.

'It's tragic,' I had to agree.

'Mr Mercury is a hostage-taker, you can't go in alone,' Ginge said.

I whispered a thank you, and when an additional officer arrived the door was finally unlocked.

'Good luck and happy Halloween,' Ginge said as we ventured in.

I staggered back as a hot wave of stench washed over me. It smelt like a butcher's shop: lard and blood. There was also the unmistakable odour of faeces. It was an unseasonably hot October day and yet the heating was on at maximum capacity. A humane solution would be to allow the men to adjust the temperature in their cell and improve the grossly inadequate ventilation. Assuming it was cold in October and warm when springtime began in March was too simplistic. There are so many layers of complacency and indifference in a prison it's surprising to me that more prisoners don't lose their minds completely.

'Hi, Mr Mercury. I'm Dr Y. Can I come in?' I asked. I stood in the doorway and breathed through my mouth.

'I said no Pakis and no Muslims!' Mr Mercury yelled in my direction.

I was winded for a moment by the racist gut punch. Any difference in a prison could be exploited and weaponized, I knew that. All races became slurs; women were called bitches or, in a throwback to far less enlightened times, lezzas. I thought I had developed a thick skin by working in this environment. One of the reasons I chose offender healthcare was because I wanted to toughen myself up. Prison was teaching me to reassess and value what was truly important to me. But I was still stunned.

The P-word stung. I had been called a black bastard before, but I had managed to sidestep the intended offence because I was unsure if I really was considered black. Did black in the political sense encompass all non-white people? Was the world divided neatly into the binaries of black and white? These were complex issues to be contemplated at another time. For now, I rationalized that in my hierarchy of slurs the N-word trumped all insults. If Mr Mercury had called me or anyone else that, I would have terminated the consultation and asked a colleague to take over from me. But the P-word wasn't too far behind.

Vicky raised her voice to admonish him: 'Mr Mercury, the NHS will not tolerate abuse towards its staff. Is that clear?'

'Shut up, you fake plastic bitch,' Mr Mercury yelled.

'Don't forget this "fake plastic bitch" gives you your medications!' she retorted.

He scoffed. There was blood trickling from his mouth. How could I be offended by someone like him? I had to reach inside myself and find extra depths of compassion.

'I'm the only doctor working today. You can either see me or wait until tomorrow,' I said in a conciliatory tone.

'Whatever,' Mr Mercury said dismissively. He licked his spoon clean.

'OK,' I replied half-heartedly, realizing that this reluctant acceptance would have to do. I was, he'd concluded, better than nothing. I followed the officers into the cell, avoiding the large blood clots on the floor, some dried, some still very fresh.

Prison is almost entirely grey. Grey cement floors, grey-painted brick, grey tracksuits and grey faces. Mr Mercury's whole persona added to the unrelenting gloom. He filled the room, making it appear far smaller. His single bed was secured to the floor in the corner. I observed there was no way someone of his size could fit into a single bed, so he must have trouble sleeping. The cell was stagnant with the reek of his unwashed body and infected ulcers. I wondered how I was going to get close enough to him to do his stitches without gagging. I tried to push open the small window to let some fresh air in, but it was nailed shut. As usual, the perforated air vents on either side of the window were blocked and redundant. The sun was shining outside and yet he kept his room dark by plastering the windows with old newspapers. He was illuminated by the stark overhead light which made his grey skin seem almost translucent. He reminded me of a Francis Bacon painting.

Prisoners were encouraged to personalize their cells to make them homely, even on their limited budget. Amidst the general gloom there was a beacon. A bright collage of images was plastered to the wall beside Mr Mercury's bed, secured using toothpaste. The toothpaste leaked through the images like fresh bruises. The effect was that the happy families and beautiful beach holidays appeared to have shadows eating into their hearts. I looked closer and realized what I had assumed were personal photographs, the product of happier times in Mr Mercury's life, had been cut from magazines. He had superimposed photographs of his huge head on to the men's bodies in a heartbreaking composition of wishful thinking.

I had to turn away. His misery was leaking into me like toothpaste on a photograph. I cleared my throat and tried to find something positive in this hellhole. There was a pile of books beside his bed, mostly novels by Stephen King and Dean Koontz.

'You like horror?' I asked.

'Can't you tell?' He smiled to reveal dark gums and missing teeth. No horror story could compete with his existence. This was all too real.

'I used to like horror,' I said quietly.

'Not any more?' Mr Mercury asked.

I shook my head.

'A rich doctor like you – I bet you live in a palace,' he said with scorn.

'You'd be surprised.'

Mr Mercury had made excellent soap sculptures of teddy bears and skulls, which surrounded him like a substitute family. He was very talented at carving. I congratulated him.

'The officers don't let me have crayons and colouring pencils because I keep eating them and putting them inside my wounds,' Mr Mercury told us. 'I have to carve using a spoon and sometimes they take that away from me too. But, the thing is, nothing feels as good as hurting myself. I feel better as soon as I see the blood leave my body; it takes the pain with it.'

I had read his file. I was aware he had begun to bite himself when he went into care as a child. Self-harm was his oldest coping mechanism.

'Why did you pull out your stitches?' I asked, pointing to the gaping wound in his leg.

'I'm protesting because I'm in pain and no one is helping me,' Mr Mercury said.

I carefully explained that his leg was hurting because he was putting a spoon into a wound. Pain was the body's defence mechanism against injury. A general rule of thumb was not to push past the pain barrier.

He wanted to have his dose of tramadol increased. I explained he was on the maximum dose of 400mg in twenty-four hours. It would be unsafe to go beyond it because he could damage his liver and kidneys. He could develop problems with his breathing and slip into a coma and die.

He extended his spoon towards me. The blood-stained fat wobbled on the spoon.

I shook my head. No.

He shrugged and licked the spoon clean.

'The psychiatrists are coming in tomorrow, Mr Mercury. You can discuss your medications with them. Are you happy for me to put some fresh stitches in now?' I asked.

'I can do my own stitches with a bit of metal and strips of blanket. It's getting more difficult because the scar tissue is tough. When I had MRSA the stitches fell out after two days,' Mr Mercury announced to the room, taking in the officers for the first time. He seemed to enjoy shocking us.

Ginge's colleague suddenly heaved and was sick on the floor. The colour had drained from his face. He looked as if he was going to faint. I escorted him out of the cell for fresh air. Ginge covered the mess with toilet paper until a member of the cleaning team could attend to it.

'I was in Helmand, Afghanistan. Nothing fazes me, Doc,' Ginge said.

But I could see his face had become paler too. I needed to get the stitches into Mr Mercury's wound so we could all leave.

'It is probably best not to perform surgical procedures on yourself,' I told him.

I took the spoon from him tentatively, trying not to exhibit any obvious displeasure. Vicky arrived with a surgical trolley and a suture pack.

'Will you be my glamorous assistant, Vicky?' I asked, in an attempt to lift the mood.

'My pleasure, Doc,' she replied with a tight smile. The colour from her sunbed-tanned face had also paled. I needed to work fast.

I gloved up and assessed the ten-centimetre wound on his leg. It was fetid. I breathed in and out through my mouth. Although Mr Mercury had eaten the fat he hadn't cut away the overlying skin. The wound edges hadn't curled and died. He was covered in scars and prison tattoos. Wispy spiders, birds and fish appeared to flit in and out of his putrid wounds. Most of his tattoos were in blue ink as if he'd doodled on himself with a heavy hand. There was a list of female names on his arm, presumably ex-girlfriends and hopefully not victims. Lines were crossed through them.

I anticipated that soon after I put in the stitches Mr Mercury was likely to undo them again. He would insert pens, spoons, dirt or faeces into the weeping sores. He had been prescribed protracted courses of

antibiotics and was a case study in how to develop drug
resistance. When his wounds became septic he was
transferred to the outside hospital, with an entourage
of officers, for intravenous antibiotics. The hospitals
found him difficult to manage because he scared the
other patients. He was abusive and swore at staff. He
stole and swallowed jewellery, pens, batteries, spoons,
whatever he could find. He had perforated his bowels
on numerous occasions. The hospital doctors wrote letters to the prison expressing their frustrations, which
we understood, but we were his advocates and had to
ensure his care was not compromised by his abrasive
personality. Nonetheless, he was temporarily banned
from many of the local hospitals because he had threatened to harm staff there. He now had to be taken to the
edge of the county for surgery, somewhere his reputation didn't precede him. Sometimes he discharged
himself and was returned to the prison where he and
his wounds festered.

The psychiatrists had diagnosed Mr Freddie Mercury with an emotionally unstable personality disorder.
This was previously known as bipolar personality disorder and isn't to be confused with a bipolar affective
disorder. A personality disorder is not classified as a
mental illness, which meant he was not eligible to be
sectioned under the Mental Health Act or to be transferred to a mental-health unit.

Our thoughts, feelings and behaviour define our
personality. Mr Freddie Mercury's personality caused
long-standing problems for him and the people in his
life. He had difficulty navigating his intense emotions,
which fluctuated faster than he could manage. He acted

impulsively. He reported feeling numb apart from when he was self-harming, and he had been suicidal for years. It was our job to keep him alive despite his daily efforts to kill himself; he had taken multiple overdoses and had tied ligatures around his neck many times. Sometimes it felt as if we were merely prolonging his death rather than giving him a real life. Even as I tended to him I felt troubled by the futility of my actions.

I took swabs of all his dirty wounds to send to micro-biology to see if he was growing any unusual bugs. Then I gently cleaned his sores with saline. As I brought the edges of the leg laceration together I noticed the skin was overlaid with a huge swastika tattoo.

'Well, this is awkward,' I said.

Mr Mercury sighed loudly.

'The swastika is Indian and so was Freddie Mercury,' I murmured.

He pulled away from me, slightly. 'Why don't you go back to your country and look after your own people, Doc?' Mr Mercury asked me.

His tone wasn't hostile. I had been asked this ques-tion before, usually by older middle-class people unaccustomed to so many black and brown faces in healthcare. It seemed obvious to them that because I was brown I couldn't be English and must be from somewhere else. My friend Matthew had an Australian father and Welsh mother but with his blond hair, blue eyes, and accent as English as mine, he was never ques-tioned about his origins, he was never told to go back to where he came from.

My answer for Mr Freddie Mercury was rehearsed but heartfelt.

'You are my people,' I said.

His eyes flickered and there was a breakthrough in our communication. He softened towards me. His body language relaxed and he maintained eye contact when I looked at him.

I injected the edges of the gash with lidocaine to make them comfortably numb. After a few minutes I prodded with the needle to see if the anaesthetic had worked.

'Does it hurt?'

He shook his head.

'OK, I can start putting the stitches in. Are you ready?' I asked.

'I need to put my song on. It relaxes me. It reminds me of the good old days when I used to get high on heroin,' Mr Mercury said.

'Is it The Killers?' Ginge asked.

'No, it's "Pass Out" by Tinie Tempah,' Mr Mercury said, the joke clearly going over his head.

'So you're not a Queen fan?' I asked as he fiddled with his CD player.

'No, why would I be? I hate that queer. I just like the name,' Mr Mercury said.

'Don't be nasty,' I reproached him, but he only shrugged.

His song began to play and I had to hold on to his jumping leg. The song began with a sigh and then the singer's voice announced groggily that he was ready to start. Vicky and Ginge knew the words and began to sing and dance in the confined space. The other officer was nodding his head to the beat from the doorway. I smiled at how ludicrous this entire situation was. I wondered what outsiders would think if they saw this. No one would believe it.

I silently said a prayer before I put in the first stitch. It was an old habit of mine to invoke God's name at the start of any healing process. Every interaction with people like Mr Freddie Mercury taught me to count my blessings. Despite the suffering in the world there was also good and I could be part of that goodness. I inserted the needle. I started in the middle of the wound and used forceps to hold the broken skin tightly as it went in. I pulled the stitch through the tough scar tissue with some difficulty. Forward knots, back knots, forward knots, back knots, and trying not to get them snagged on the forceps or Mr Mercury's hair. When the song finished he played it again, and again. The trance-like tune formed a trippy loop that matched my stitches, forwards, backwards, forwards and backwards. I stared down into the putrid wound with intense concentration and tried not to breathe. As I held my breath the wound appeared to expand and contract before my dancing eyes. The music, heat, lack of ventilation and stench made me want to heave. It would have been easy to pass out. But I had to keep working until the job was done.

'It's not the stitch that bothers me. It's the skin and muscle being pulled back together that hurts. It must be quite satisfying fixing something that's broken?' Mr Mercury asked over the music.

'It is,' I said with relief that it was over. Though I knew that this surface wound was the least of what was broken in Mr Mercury.

I wiped away the blood and cleaned his leg. I covered

the swastika in a dressing. Vicky and I collected up the needles, thread, forceps and swabs. We needed to ensure we didn't leave anything behind that could be used in self-harm or as a weapon, so the procedure was always to count them out and count them back in again. Mr Mercury was already on antibiotics and the sutures could come out in five to seven days; if he didn't take them out sooner. There was always that risk. Vicky said she would assess him later. I implored him not to pull out the stitches I had worked so hard to place.

'You did a good job, Doc,' Mr Mercury said.

It was the closest thing to a thank you. However difficult someone was I always tried to find their humanity. Sometimes I had to search quite hard for it. I noticed his eyes were turquoise with flecks of gold – like a tropical ocean in one of the images beside his bed. I felt a sudden pang of sadness for this troubled man. He handed me a soap sculpture of a skull with heart-shaped eye sockets.

'I can't accept gifts, I'm afraid,' I said.

'It's for Halloween,' Mr Mercury replied, trying to press it on me.

'I can't, I'm afraid,' I repeated. It felt mawkish to wish him a happy Halloween.

As I walked away to wash my hands in the sluice room, I tried to comprehend what had just happened.

'You're a brave man, Doc,' Vicky said quietly, following me over to the sink.

'How can we stop him harming himself?' I asked.

'They've tried everything with him over the years,' Vicky replied. 'Nothing has worked. If you read his history you can see he has "Shit Life Syndrome". He never stood a chance from the moment he was born – he has a mother who is in and out of the picture. With the amount of self-harm he has done it is only a matter of time before he goes too far.'

I surveyed the chaos of the Inpatient unit Mr Freddie Mercury called home. It was always filled to capacity and the vast majority were mental-health patients awaiting community mental-health beds. If an emergency admission came in we would need to vacate a room to accommodate them. A long white corridor, it had ten cells on either side. Walking along it reminded me of the scene from the film *The Silence of the Lambs* where Agent Starling first meets Hannibal Lecter and has to walk past all the other cells to get to his, with all manner of disturbed behaviours on display. Like Mr Mercury's, each of the locked doors had a small observation panel at eye level. And, like Mr Mercury's, many of the panels had been smashed. Arms reached out through the broken glass. The din of screaming and kicking doors was deafening. There was an overpowering smell of stale urine and decay. A few of the inpatients were sexually disinhibited and wanted to make eye contact as they pleasured themselves. It became second nature to duck as we passed by. We kept our eyes on the filthy floor to avoid slipping and falling.

For me one of the strongest senses of being in prison is the vibration felt when a heavy gate is slammed shut. It takes time to acclimatize and no longer jump or shudder when your bones are rattled. Maybe this is what the staff mean when they say prison gets into your bones. The thing is, once you are used to this environment it is difficult to leave. Even just a few months in, the thought of going back to being a community GP with a list of 'normal' patients filled me with dread. I liked not knowing what each day in offender healthcare would bring. I told myself that I thrived in the chaos.

'This is a very strange place,' I said to Vicky.

'Oh yes. A very strange place full of strange people. It's always full of surprises.'

Mr Freddie Mercury was found hanging in his cell a few days later. The officers cut him down and started basic life support until the healthcare team arrived. I was in my morning clinic at the time and not carrying a radio. I was unaware that a Code Blue was in progress but I had a feeling that something was wrong in the prison. My mouth turned sour and the hairs at the back of my neck stood up. It was as if I could smell something vinegary and sharp that prickled my nose. I can't explain my sense of foreboding but I hastily concluded the consultation I was as in. I then spoke to Helly in the admin team, who informed me about the emergency on one of the house blocks. I ran all the way. I prayed to God it was not Mr Freddie Mercury, who had been discharged from the Inpatient unit and relocated to that house block only the day before.

We had discussed him in the MDT yesterday. Doctor Emily and I both felt he was on an unsafe cocktail of medications. Throughout his years in incarceration in various prisons, doctors and nurses had repeatedly documented that they were extremely concerned about Mr Mercury's drug-seeking behaviour. I was also alarmed

by the polypharmacy, which meant he was being prescribed many medications which could have adverse
interactions with each other. The list was long: Con-
certa XL 72mg once daily, pregabalin 300mg twice
a day, zopiclone 15mg at night, diazepam 10mg twice a
day, nefopam 60mg twice a day, tramadol extended-
release 400mg once daily, Oramorph 5mg four times a
day. Two other patients had both died in the past twelve
months while taking similar combinations of medications. It had to stop.

Over the years Mr Mercury had harmed himself so
severely that he must have been in discomfort. The
question had always been how best to manage his pain?
He was referred to hospital for traumas on multiple
occasions. The spinal surgical centre and pain clinic
documented his multiple, sometimes contradictory,
symptoms. He was offered treatment by orthopaedic
surgeons like trigger-point injections and cervical
facet-joint injections, which could help reduce any
inflammation around his joints and thereby reduce his
pain. He declined. He stated he wanted stronger pain-
killers. We couldn't give them to him because they
were unsafe. He was reviewed by the psychiatrists who
variously diagnosed Munchausen's syndrome, prolific
self-harm and personality disorder traits.

He typically self-harmed and took overdoses if his
demands for more opioids were not met. He lay on the
floor for hours and said he was paralysed. Sometimes
he was incontinent of urine and faeces. When he was
unaware of being observed he got up and walked
around. Sometimes he acted as if he had suffered a
stroke and slurred his words and dragged the right side

of his body. A few hours later he would ask to go to the gym or would be seen running around the exercise yard and shadow boxing. He went through a phase of making his nose bleed, swallowing the blood, and then complaining of haematemesis or vomiting blood. If we had any external visitors, such as the Care Quality Commission, he would shock them by lying on the floor and present to them in a state of neglect. When they left he would pick himself up and merrily show us his middle finger.

In the MDT we had also raised concerns that he had spat at the nursing staff and threatened to harm them. He was also known to bully the other patients in the Inpatient unit for their medications. We suggested to him that we start bringing down the doses of his medications and tapering them off. At first he'd sat with us in the meeting with his head downcast but as the meeting progressed he became very hostile. He complained that we were punishing him, that we wanted him to be in pain. He said he would escalate his self-harming behaviour if we touched his medications.

We informed him a patient with spina bifida who used a wheelchair had recently arrived in the prison and he couldn't be managed on the wing due to his complex needs. Mr Mercury would need to relocate to the main house blocks to make room for him. He refused to leave the Inpatient unit. He said it was his home. I explained this wasn't a permanent move but an urgent requirement. We had no other spaces for the man with spina bifida in the Inpatient unit. He began to swear at me. Mr Mercury said he would swallow razor blades and his death would be on my hands. He said he had concealed a razor blade in his mouth and threatened to slit my throat. At that outburst we terminated the MDT. The officers took him away and searched him for razor blades – they were not found. I had updated his ACCT document to record his threats to harm himself and others, and he was forcibly moved out of the Inpatient unit and on to the wing.

I arrived in his new cell just as Steph, the Naloxone Queen, shouted, 'Get a doctor!'

Mr Mercury was lying on the floor. Steph, Nurse Brian and healthcare assistant Chris were working to resuscitate him. His heart had stopped and he wasn't breathing. There was a deep red laceration to his neck where the ligature had cut into his flesh. His skin was blue and his eyes were bulging out of their sockets. We had brought back others who were as far gone as he was and, ever the optimists, it was all hands on deck. We compressed his chest and tried to oxygenate him through an i-gel tube that had been passed down his throat. The nurses were struggling to gain IV access because his skin was such a patchwork of scars and his veins had collapsed. The cell was tiny and he was a large man. We were reaching around and over each other, like a piece of modern dance or a bizarre game of Twister. I found a vein just behind his wrist and inserted a needle so we could administer medications. I was determined to give him another chance.

Mr Mercury had spent much of the past decade on an ACCT due to regular self-harm and suicide attempts. On his discharge from the Inpatient unit yesterday his ACCT had been downgraded from constant-watch supervision to four observations an hour. An officer had to check on him every fifteen minutes, day and night. During the night this involved shining a torch on him to ensure he was breathing. But this was the afternoon and I couldn't understand how he had been left unattended for long enough to hang himself.

The young officer who was supposed to be monitoring him through the observation panel was standing outside the cell, ashen-faced. Clearly traumatized, the poor man kept asking if Mr Mercury was going to be alright. We said we were doing everything that we could. When the officer was out of earshot the nurses told me that Mr Mercury had reportedly asked him for something. The officer was away for longer than expected. When he returned he'd found Mr Mercury hanging from his upturned bed by torn strips of bedding. The bed had been bolted to the ground but he had managed to unscrew it, over some time presumably, without anyone noticing. Now, when the opportunity arose, he'd flipped the bed up and suspended himself within minutes. Maybe it was a cry for help and Mr Mercury thought the officer would return sooner than he did. He might have struggled to undo the ligature that had tightened around his throat. However it happened, his last moments would have been agonized and full of fear.

As I attempted to resuscitate him I was aware it was only a matter of time before he killed himself, we all knew that. And yet here we all were, kneeling around his body trying to bring him back. We didn't question whether or not he wanted to come back. We worked on Mr Mercury for thirty minutes until the paramedics arrived. They confirmed what we didn't want to admit.

He was dead. Defeated, we stopped working on him. We watched the cold darkness spread inwards from his fingers and toes until it lay over his face like a veil. I noted the time of death. We slumped in his room, exhausted, trying to catch our breath.

'We need to contact his next of kin – I wouldn't want to make that call,' Steph said.

'I don't think he planned to do it. He thought the officer would come back sooner but he mistimed it. He has been brought back so many times and his luck just ran out,' Chris added thoughtfully.

'See you all in coroner's court,' I murmured miserably.

All deaths in custody are considered to be unusual and are automatically referred to the coroner. Whoever has documented in the patient's notes will be called to give evidence in the coroner's court. No one wants to go to that court. We know hostile lawyers will treat us as if we are either criminally negligent or Shipmanesque murderers.

'You write good notes, you'll be fine,' Brian said.

'That's not the point,' I replied. 'There will be a jury who have no idea what goes on inside a prison. They'll think all deaths are avoidable and people only come to harm because we don't care. They don't know how hard we work and how dedicated we all are.'

We ensured the site was left undisturbed for the forensic investigators. We avoided touching Mr Mercury's body. We couldn't even close his eyes. The ligature he had used to hang himself had to be left where the officer had dropped it after cutting it loose. I looked at

Mr Mercury's collage of photographs on the wall and the soap sculptures he had taken so much pride in.

'What a bloody waste!' I said.

The house block was ominously quiet as it always was after a death.

'Is he dead?' a prisoner called.

I hung my head. He didn't need to ask again.

I bumped into Jamie Lovell on the walkways. He handed me another poem he had written. I really didn't want to read it, not right then. But he was so enthusiastic I couldn't disappoint him. I read it carefully before handing it back. I was glad I had taken the time.

'Reading your poem is the best thing that has happened today. I'm really proud of you, Jamie, keep up the good work,' I told him.

'Thank you, Dr Y,' Jamie said with a grin.

My colleagues and I headed to the boardroom for the team debriefing. The governors and officers had been assembled along with the healthcare managers. The young officer who was supposed to have been monitoring Mr Mercury was crying now and being comforted by his colleagues. He was commended for cutting Mr Mercury down, starting resuscitation and calling for help. There were words of comfort for those involved, but we were all lost in our own failures. I sat in the boardroom for a long while after the others had left. Dr Emily came and joined me.

'We couldn't have done anything more for him,' Emily said.

'Then why do I feel so shit?' I asked.

'Because as doctors we want to save lives and

someone dying, especially by suicide, feels like we've failed them,' Emily said.

'We *have* failed him. I failed him. The IPP system failed him. His shitty upbringing failed him. The medications failed him. That young officer's lack of training failed him. Being chronically understaffed failed him. The prison and healthcare systems are collapsing around us and all we are doing is propping them up. Doctors are leaving this country in droves and no one seems to be asking why. Prison healthcare is a circus and we can't retain good staff. We run from one disaster to another. We don't have significant event meetings and that failed him. We don't even discuss deaths in custody after the initial debrief – this is the only conversation we'll have – and that failed him. No one listens to the doctors and that failed him and it failed us too. We do Reception clinics in a toilet – should I continue?' I asked.

'It has been difficult to organize any meetings because all the doctors work on different days. The logistics are complex. There's currently no Medical Director to send out alerts and keep us all updated. More GPs will be recruited to work here and things will get better. Don't get disheartened. You are a great doctor and go above and beyond, anyone can see that,' Emily said, in an attempt to reassure me.

'I really don't think medical school prepares us for the actual job of being a doctor. We learn every cellular structure and about diseases and their treatment. But there's almost nothing on what the job actually entails. I didn't even know that offender healthcare was a speciality. All of this stuff that we have to deal with. The complex scenarios, decision-fatigue, unusual working environments – none of it is ever discussed. The lived experience comes as quite a shock. They shouldn't call it general practice – there's nothing *general* about it!' I said angrily.

She began to laugh and eventually I smiled too.

'I wish they'd taught us management-speak and the politics of saying nothing in hundreds of words. Now *that* is a skill,' Emily said. 'The politicians, governors and managers talk about "restructuring and change", but they actually mean cutting costs and it's endangering lives. Who are we going to complain to? Who's going to listen? You have to remember we've both only been here for a few months,' she reminded me.

Emily and I were both on a steep learning curve. She was hopeful that things would get better the more experience we got under our belts. I wasn't feeling so sure.

'When this goes to coroner's court, they're going to say I kicked him out of the Inpatient unit and the very next day he killed himself,' I said.

'He had harmed himself for years and we can't blame anyone else for that,' she replied.

'A man in his thirties has lost his life. I feel like I could have done more for him but I don't even know what else I could have done.' I slumped back in my chair.

'They're going to be organizing courtroom skills training for us,' Emily said.

'We're going to need it,' I said.

12

Who, When, Where, How?

It goes without saying but it's worth repeating. Healthcare and officers don't want the people in their care to die. We cut the noose from their necks figuratively and sometimes literally. The nurses and officers in prison carry safety knives known as 'fish knives' because hangings are not uncommon. The fish knives are so named because they are indeed shaped like a fish and all but a couple of centimetres, or the inner mouth, are covered in a thick lip of plastic. They are akin to safety scissors and can't be used as a weapon. The edge isn't serrated and cutting through a ligature takes effort. To have to do this while in shock from having found someone hanging takes some nerve.

I can't think of many things worse than peering through an observation panel and finding someone's feet dangling. Chris discovered a man hanging when she was doing nights. The cell lights were turned off and all the cell doors were locked. She was performing her rounds for hourly checks on a man on an ACCT and peered through his hatch with her torch. She saw his bare feet suspended in mid-air and called for urgent help. When the man was cut down he was beyond being revived. He'd killed himself the night before he was due in court. He had written a letter proclaiming his innocence. He had also laid out a suit he asked to be buried in. It was an image that remained with her for many years.

Sometimes when we resuscitate someone they're grateful and will say it was a moment of madness or a cry for help. One man who survived has a keloid, or thickened scar, on the back of his neck where the ligature knot had dug into his skin. It's a permanent reminder of his darkest time and whenever he feels low he touches it. He reminds himself that he is now in a better place. However, there are occasions where we save someone who doesn't want to be saved. The tears are angry and they resent us. They promise to do a better job next time. We try to ensure a next time never materializes, but that's difficult, particularly in a prison. For that reason I ask each and every patient I see if they have any thoughts of harming themselves or of suicide. Even if they come to see me about a cough or a cold I ask about their mood. If I can connect with them, perhaps they'll tell me something that needs to be heard.

Prison is an extremely gruelling experience. Many prisoners can't cope. It's a national scandal that every four days someone dies in prison in the UK. According to the Ministry of Justice there were 61,461 self-harm incidents in 2019, which is more than the rate in 2014. There's a mental-health crisis in prisons which we can't ignore. If not actively trying to kill themselves, prisoners certainly gamble with their lives by harming themselves and using drugs. Before I shake hands at the end of every consultation, I advise against drugs such as spice. Sadly, many of the deaths I witness have been complicated by drugs. Even if the death is due to hanging, if the toxicology results show illicit substances it is recorded as a contributing factor. This doesn't include the many near misses by individuals revived by people like Steph and our heroic nurses and paramedics.

A coroner's investigation is triggered if there is reasonable cause to suspect that the deceased has died a violent or unnatural death, if the cause of death is uncertain, or if they die in custody or state detention. By definition all deaths in custody, or DICs, are reported to the coroner. They decide whether to hold an inquest. The coroner is an independent lawyer, or sometimes a doctor, of at least five years' training, appointed to conduct inquests.

In the case of Mr Freddie Mercury, lawyers from the firm that represented healthcare provided a one-day inquest-training workshop. We discussed inquests, giving evidence, writing witness statements and, most importantly, how to present ourselves to the court. My perception of lawyers had already been coloured by working in prisons. Prisoners often felt disgruntled with their legal representation and would frequently add it to their list of ills when they came to see me. There were also the many inflammatory letters we

received from the legal firms acting on behalf of prisoners who had accused us of medical negligence.

The healthcare barrister's father was a doctor and she
understood our misgivings towards her profession. She
was able to allay our fears with good humour. I felt
lighter after talking to her. I was joined by all of the staff
who would be expected to attend the coroner's court
for Mr Freddie Mercury: Kitch, Graham, Chris, Dr
Emily, Steph, Dean and Brian.

'There are four questions the coroner will ask,' the
barrister told us. 'Who died? When did they die? Where
did they die? How did they die? The circumstances
form the main thrust of the inquest. You are required
to help answer these questions in the first instance by
providing a witness statement.'

I looked over my witness statement. It was over
twenty pages long. It began with my name and professional qualifications and then went on to detail every
interaction I had had with Mr Freddie Mercury. I wrote
about how he was clearly troubled and, to me, his distress was palpable on the page; it hummed in the words
I'd written. I noted that he had been discussed in the
MDT and had been informed his medications would
be cut down slowly. I documented he was discharged
from the Inpatient unit because there was someone
who needed a bed and there were no other available
spaces. He had killed himself within twenty-four hours
of this notification. I knew the opposing barrister
would make a direct correlation between my actions
and the death. On the other hand, if the other man
with spina bifida had been deprived of care and had
died as a result, I would be answerable for that too. This

was a lose-lose-lose scenario. The most important fact was that a man had died. Nothing else mattered. I fully expected my relative inexperience as a prison doctor, my professional reputation and my career to be scrutinized, and all of it used against me.

'The witness statement is a reflection on your professional standing,' the barrister said. 'It is a professional obligation according to the General Medical Council. It's a contemporaneous statement of what happened. Set out the evidence and explain usual practices. Refer to the patient by title and surname. Explain all medical terminology. Write abbreviations in full the first time they are used. Please remember the statement may be read out and will form the basis of your evidence. It is important to be truthful. If you cannot remember, say so. An inquest can take place months or years after a death and lapses in memory are understandable. When you are in the box and being cross-examined you do not want to be accused of lying. You can be jailed for perjury. Avoid giving conflicting stories.'

It was a lot to take in and I was making notes as the barrister spoke.

'Raise your hand if you have read the findings of the Francis report?' the barrister asked.

We all raised our hands. The Francis Inquiry report had been published in February 2013 – around the time I started working in this prison. It examined the failings in care at the Mid Staffordshire NHS Foundation Trust between 2005 and 2009. It found that one of the reasons unnecessary deaths had occurred was because of understaffing. Staff hadn't felt supported in raising their concerns. As a consequence of the report healthcare

organizations now needed to be open and honest. The
blame culture prevalent in healthcare, the prison service and the police service had to be counteracted. I
didn't feel confident the promised changes had materi-
alized. Looking around the room at the nervous
expressions on my colleagues' faces, I could see that
neither did they.

'The basic essentials of any witness statement are that
it must be legible,' the barrister continued. 'It has to be
typed. Spelling, grammar, punctuation must all be
checked. Use plain English. Be mindful of patient confidentiality. Avoid gratuitous comments. Read it out
aloud. Do not speculate or offer hearsay. This is not the
forum to criticize your employers or colleagues. Offer
sincere condolences at the end of the statement. Do
not sign it until it has been reviewed by the legal team.'

It was only now that I had to prepare a witness statement that I realized the importance of keeping good
records. Perhaps my notes were verbose and provided
too much detail, but I'd given the lawyers enough
material to cross-examine me for hours if they wanted.
I envied the healthcare staff who could record their
interactions in a couple of lines. They would be off the
stand in a matter of minutes. Due to my habit of writing detailed notes I could envisage myself up there for
hours and the thought filled me with dread.

Our barrister explained that inquests were held in
front of a jury. The prison was represented by its legal
team and the offender healthcare department had separate representation. Sometimes there might be points
of contention or even animosity between the legal rep-
resentatives of the prison and offender healthcare. The

family of the deceased would also have a lawyer. The
family were considered to be Interested Persons and
they were entitled to examine witnesses if they so
wished. I felt my heart sink when I imagined being
faced with a grieving family. I understood their rage,
unfiltered by time, and it was righteous anger. Their
family member had died in our care.

There was more.

'When in the coroner's court remember to breathe,'
the barrister continued. 'You are under oath and it's
your duty to assist the court. The coroner is addressed
as "Sir" or "Madam", not "Your Highness" – believe
me this has happened. Listen carefully to each question.
Wait for them to finish asking their question before
answering. Interruption can be interpreted as aggression. Answer the question you are being asked, no more,
no less. Do not just answer "yes" or "no", it can appear
defensive. However, don't ramble. If you do not know
the answer don't exaggerate. Address your answers to
the coroner and jury. Sometimes the family's lawyer
will read into silence and interpret it as uncertainty or
guilt. They will not respond after you have answered a
question. Let the silence sit there. Do not feel the need
to fill it. Unlike other courts the lawyers are allowed to
ask leading questions. They might make ludicrous sug-
gestions. Do not get angry. Take a sip of water before
answering every question. Water is your friend.'

All this was helpful, and yet I was filled with trepida-
tion. I knew that when I was nervous I had a tendency
to gabble. One of my worst habits was interrupting
people and not letting them speak. I felt compelled to
fill every silence as if it was a gaping hole with its own

gravitational pull. I also believed in justice. I wasn't prepared to cover up my own failings or the failings of the
system I was a part of. I assumed the lawyers would
have access to all the significant incident reports in
which we had raised our concerns about understaffing
and a lack of process, lack of significant event meetings,
lack of training, lack of support, and poor practice that
had been left to develop unchallenged. I wanted all
these issues to be addressed.

'The jury is the rogue element,' the barrister went
on. 'On a previous inquest a jury member was reprimanded for being unduly harsh towards witnesses.
Another jury member was reprimanded for falling
asleep. Always expect the unexpected when faced with
a panel of your peers.'

She informed us that most inquests were held in
public and the press attended. Journalists were easy to
spot; they were generally scruffily dressed, arrived late
and left early, slamming the doors as they went. They
wanted salacious and sensational details. We were
advised against speaking to them. We should instead
refer them to the prison communications team. If the
inquest revealed anything that indicated a risk of future
deaths, the coroner had to report the matter to Prevent
Future Deaths, known as a PFD. It was seen as a sys-
tematic failing of the prison, the healthcare department
and its staff. It would have direct consequences for us as
a team.

The inquest process was usually very slow. A significant delay in the system meant it could often take well
over twelve months from the death to the case being
heard in court, a long process which caused huge stress

for staff and for the families of the deceased alike. We were surprised to learn, then, that Mr Freddie Mercury's inquest had been listed for a few months' time. That it was happening with such speed was equally alarming. The coroner's court and inquests were the central topic of conversation amongst staff over the entire Christmas period. It cast a dark shadow over the usual seasonal festivities.

We were told that the inquest was not for determining blame or civil or criminal liability. The inquest was solely to ascertain who, when, where and how. And yet, when we were summoned to any inquest we all shared a sense of unease. This unease could give way to paranoia, especially in the closed environment of a prison. Many members of staff felt unable to concentrate on their work and the sickness rate soared.

The inquest loomed over me. I began visualizing nightmarish scenarios which I embellished with personal insecurities. I imagined being asked questions I couldn't answer and feeling inadequate and overwhelmed. I stopped eating, which is what I always did when I was stressed, and began to lose weight. My nights were not restful. I was permanently tired. The pressure at work continued to mount. My patients were as complex as ever and, with the increasing sickness rates around me, my clinic list and workload increased exponentially.

The managers reassured me that new doctors were being recruited and would soon join me. But it was a slow process. There were many days when I was working alone and doing the work of two doctors. To make matters worse, I became much more cautious and spent longer in my consultations. I wanted to cover all signs and symptoms and exclude anything at all that might bring harm to my patients. The prison officers became frustrated with me because I put many more patients on ACCTs than before. I began reading and rereading through my increasingly thorough notes to ensure they were correct.

Mr Freddie Mercury was in my thoughts constantly. Something as simple as washing my hands with soap reminded me of Mr Mercury with his skill for carving. I wondered if I should have accepted the skull-shaped carving he had offered me on Halloween. These thoughts and others tortured me. What if ...? If only ...? I'd replay every scenario. When I closed my eyes, his face, his body, his cell were there, filling me with sadness.

I had always thought I could switch off between my work life and home. But now I found myself taking the prison with me wherever I went. I tried to keep myself busy. I was working harder than ever – making sure every task was completed. I felt like a stressed-out medical student again. I was running on empty and hurtling towards a breakdown. If I had been my own patient I would have been much kinder to myself and advised some coping mechanisms and some time away.

The only thing I could think of was that the date of the coroner's court was rushing towards me. We were informed that due to the amount of evidence and the complexity of the case the inquest would take place over ten days. This was unusually long; most inquests took place in a couple of days. I would be called to give evidence on the second day – Valentine's Day – along with a few of my colleagues. The date was marked in my diary with a thick black outline, just like the thick black outlines I had drawn on my student wall planner around the dates of my finals exams.

Eventually the day came. I arrived early and met with our barrister in the briefing room. She knew how stressful this was for all of us and made sure to provide words of comfort and reassurance. She advised me to leave the court straight after I had given my evidence and put it behind me and do something nice with the rest of my day. She informed us that the first day had not gone well. They had discovered that Mr Mercury's bell in his new cell hadn't been working. Even if he had called for help he wouldn't have been heard. This was a major failing on the part of the prison. The prison officer who found Mr Mercury, whose job it had been to keep a close eye on him, had resigned with immediate effect due to the trauma of the event.

Dr Emily, Brian, Steph, Dean and Chris had given their evidence on the first day and had performed well, I learned. Unfortunately, someone who was no longer an employee had also been present on the first day. They had aired their grievances with the healthcare department and with the prison and said they hadn't felt supported by the managers or governors. They felt healthcare staff were overworked and understaffed. They said there was poor morale, a culture of blame, and a fear of speaking out. The other side used it as evidence that the level of care provided to Mr Mercury was substandard from the top down. One step forwards, two steps back.

In the courtroom I sat between Kitch and Graham. We wore suits and stood when the coroner entered the room. I recognized some of Mr Mercury's family because they shared a strong family resemblance. They were dressed in black and sat solemnly and held each other's hands. This must have been hell for them. I glanced at the members of the jury and was disconcerted to find they were staring at us. What did they think of us? If I put myself in their shoes, wouldn't I assume that we were incompetent, uncaring, negligent and to blame? They would have the opportunity to question us. Our goal was to give them a picture of life behind bars, the victories and the disasters. Would they be able to see our world through our eyes and walk in our shoes? It was going to be difficult to express ourselves when we were nervous and under pressure.

'How goes it, Kitch?' I whispered.

'I'm good, thanks. Is it your first coroner's court?' he asked.

I nodded.

'I've been to coroner's court nineteen times,' Kitch said. 'I was in the coroner's court last week about a bloke who burned to death. That happened before you were here. Almost eighteen months ago. I didn't even know it had gone to coroner's. I got an email from the family's barrister on the Thursday night saying, as you are aware, you're in coroner's court on Monday. This was at seven o'clock at night. I replied, this is the first I've ever heard of it. Then the healthcare barrister contacted me and said I had to attend. So I prepared my statement and went to court. They asked me to give evidence in front of everybody. The family's barrister

kept asking why I didn't open an ACCT on this individual. I said risk is assessed on an individual basis and,
at that time, he wasn't expressing any suicidal ideas. The
coroner said thank you very much and off I went,'
Kitch said calmly. I could tell he wasn't as perturbed by
being in the coroner's court as I was.

Kitch had seen Mr Mercury every time he had gone
to and come back from hospital and was called first to
give evidence. He was sworn in and he sat at a small
table, surrounded by a mound of lever arch folders that
contained all the witness statements and medical notes,
including my own copious contribution. Kitch rested
his hand on his chin, which I knew was his nervous
habit. It undercut his bravado. No one ever got used to
being called to coroner's court.

The family's barrister stood up and he was a tiny
man, no taller than Little Chris. He was wearing very
tight trousers. Graham whispered in my ear that we
could see far too much of his anatomy through his
pants and he curled his mouth with displeasure. To calm
nerves in an interview you're advised to picture your
interviewer naked. In this case we didn't have to use
too much imagination.

'He's a knob,' Graham whispered. I could tell he was
trying to make me feel better. It was gallows humour
and it was what we always fell back on. I was lucky to
have him beside me.

'This man was suicidal and you closed his ACCT
document, thereby cutting off his support system. Why
would any rational person act in this manner?'

The family's barrister had come blasting straight out
of the blocks.

He had a higher than expected voice. He circled the floor, swimming around Kitch like a shark in a suit.

'Did I? When?' Kitch asked.

He was advised to refer to one of the evidence bundles next to him on the table. Kitch read it for a few minutes in silence and then looked up at the barrister quizzically.

'That was eight months ago,' he pointed out. 'Mr Mercury died while he was on an ACCT. He was known to the In-reach mental-health team. He had access to healthcare every day. He had more healthcare input in prison than he would have had in the community.'

'But you closed the ACCT on a seriously disturbed and vulnerable individual,' the barrister persisted.

'I closed an ACCT eight months ago. It was reopened soon after. How is that relevant to the circumstances of his death?' Kitch asked.

'I think it shows the level of "care" that was available to this gentleman. We already know that his cell bell didn't work. He didn't have access to a telephone in his cell. He was a very distressed and troubled man. He was further isolated by your decision to cut off the support of an ACCT. It was obligatory for him to remain on an ACCT if he exhibited even the slightest signs of low mood or self-harm!' the barrister announced.

'That's not true. We're not going to open an ACCT on every single person who seems unhappy. No one is happy in prison but that doesn't mean they're going to self-harm. Each case is assessed on its merits. No one stays on an ACCT permanently, that is not what they are for. They are reviewed regularly and sometimes they are closed and reopened, if required,' Kitch said evenly.

The barrister questioned Kitch for two hours. He was belligerent in his manner. I would never speak to my patients or indeed to anybody in the brutal and condescending way in which he interrogated Kitch. The coroner intervened on a couple of occasions and informed the barrister that this was not a criminal case. A coroner's court was a fact-finding investigation. But the barrister continued to hector Kitch. He wanted him to admit that closing an ACCT months ago had led to Mr Mercury's death. This was despite the fact that Mr Mercury had been on an ACCT when he died. It seemed like a pointless line of questioning.

Finally, Kitch grabbed the microphone in front of him and spoke into it urgently.

'I am going to tell you and the court only once more because I have told you several times now. He was not suicidal when I saw him eight months ago. I can't answer any of those hindsight questions. You are trying to lead me down a path and are asking me a question within a question within a question. I am not clever enough to understand it. Isn't he supposed to ask me one question at a time?' Kitch asked, turning towards the coroner.

'That is correct, Mr Kitchen,' the coroner said and admonished the barrister a final time.

There were clearly some advantages to having been to coroner's court nineteen times.

We broke for a lunch break and talked about the proceedings. It was appalling, I thought. The family's barrister was looking for someone to blame. The prison service's barrister was exempting them from liability and pointing out the failings of the healthcare department – literally pointing the finger at us. The healthcare barrister deflected back to the prison service. There were no questions from the family, which was a relief to me. The jury asked a couple of questions about how prisons operated and it was clear they had very little idea of life behind those walls. I realized this process would not bring any comfort to Mr Mercury's family.

I was called to give evidence after lunch. The coroner asked me to state my name and qualifications. He asked how long I had been working in the prison. The family's barrister began circling me. He asked me to read out my statement. He picked faults with it. He nipped and nibbled at me to draw blood, but I knew the big bite was yet to come.

'We have established that Mr Mercury was a complicated gentleman. He had many health conditions and complex needs. Why would you then, a relatively inexperienced prison doctor, take it upon yourself to take him off his vital medications and eject him from the security of the Inpatient unit, the hospital department? He was moved to a cell in the prison without a cell bell. Reading through your own notes this appears to have been because he was rude to some of the nurses. A man as distressed as he was should be forgiven for dropping his Ps and Qs. You punished him by kicking him out of the prison hospital. From that point his death was inevitable. He was on an ACCT and everyone on an ACCT should be cared for on the Inpatient unit. Would you agree that you are *directly* to blame for this man's death?'

I had known this was coming and I had prepared answers but, in the moment, they all flew out of my head. I didn't want to absolve myself of guilt if I had intentionally done wrong. But that was not the case.

'That's not true,' I whispered.

'What?' the barrister snapped.

Then something extraordinary happened. If I hadn't witnessed it I wouldn't have believed it. The barrister put his foot on a chair for effect, I imagine. There was the sound of fabric tearing. He had split his trousers all the way round underneath. Some of the members of the jury covered their mouths with their hands, struggling to contain their laughter. Mr Mercury's family were shocked at first and then began to smile too. The barrister blushed, but only slightly. With his underwear clearly on show, he carried on as if nothing had happened. The only change was that he channelled any embarrassment he was feeling into rage and directed it towards me. I could imagine Graham and Kitch recounting the story later and commenting on how they could literally see he was an arse. This event would become one of those stories we would recount for years to come. Eventually no one would know whether it was true or not, one of the many urban legends that formed part of a prison's history.

I was not intimidated by him now. I sat up in the chair and leaned forward towards the microphone as Kitch had done.

'There are over fifty people in the prison on ACCTs,' I said. 'We only have twenty spaces in the Inpatient unit. We can't house everyone on an ACCT in the Inpatient unit and that is not its purpose. Not every

prison has an Inpatient unit. So where are they supposed to manage patients on ACCTs? Patients, that is
what they are to us, not prisoners, patients. The Inpatient unit is designed to be used for a short stay only
and then people relocate to the rest of the prison. We
are a healthcare department within a prison. We treat
everyone with respect and dignity. No doctor or nurse
or officer wants anyone to die. That is what is in my
statement. If you read through all of my lengthy notes
you will find that message, that ethos, again and again.'

He questioned me repeatedly. I was on the stand for
over an hour. Learning to say no politely and repeatedly was a skill I'd acquired since starting work in the
prison, but I'd never needed it as much as I did now on
the stand. There were more questions from the jury
about how offender healthcare worked. I took my time
and tried to show them my world. I wanted them to be
able to walk with us through a routine day in an uncon-
ventional environment. I told them how it looked and
more importantly how it felt to be practising medicine
behind bars. I spoke about my wonderful colleagues,
how hard we worked to safeguard those in our care.
Finally, there was a question from Mr Mercury's mother.
She had the same turquoise eyes flecked with gold.

'I didn't catch your name. Are you Dr Y?' she asked
in a hoarse whisper.

Hesitantly I said yes.

'He mentioned you. You were kind to him, thank
you,' she said quietly.

I would like to say I didn't cry. It was the surprise of
it. The graciousness of a mother who had lost her son
reaching out to offer comfort to another. It seemed like

the sort of thing my own parents would do. I wanted to jump over the desk and hug her. I wanted to say over and over again that I was sorry for her loss. I wanted to say how much a thank you could mean. How when we are travelling through darkness it is the little things, always the little things, that become our guiding lights.

13

Release

Valentine's Day marked my one-year anniversary of working in the prison and I had spent it in the coroner's court. In the evening I bought myself some chocolates to celebrate the end of a horrendous day, but I didn't have the stomach for them. I left them in the coffee room a few days later and they were gone in minutes. I was still recovering from the ordeal of the coroner's court. A man had died. I was wracked by guilt that I should have done more. The dead man still haunted my dreams. I saw him tearing off his flesh and offering it to me. I had nightmares about all the different horrific situations I had been in over the past year. It was a cacophony of autocannibals, paedophile puppeteers, using a toilet as a clinic room, being locked in rooms with sex offenders, piles of forbidden sweets, and stitching up swastikas. Every encounter seemed so implausible that even I doubted my recollections.

There was no point going to bed because I just lay there staring at the ceiling. I moved my pillow and duvet to the living room sofa and watched box sets of DVDs all night. When I did sleep I woke up in a cold sweat. I wandered around in an exhausted fog. I wasn't eating or exercising and I ached all over. Paracetamol and ibuprofen gave me heartburn, so I glugged antacids until my mouth was coated in chalk.

There was chronic understaffing in all offender healthcare departments and the workload was unmanageable. The lack of staffing compromised clinical standards and patient safety. Staff were asked to do extra hours on a regular basis. I was working from nine until nine and I was often the only doctor on site. There was always a backlog of tasks, blood results and letters. I emailed the managers and stated this wasn't safe, and underlined my words. Maybe I should have followed the example of so many excellent colleagues and left. Why would any GP, including myself, choose offender healthcare with all the additional risks and dangers? You had to be passionate about the work. But there also had to be glimmers of hope to navigate by.

I was reminded why I do the job when I went to buy a burger one weekend from a fast-food place I hadn't been to before. Nadeem, the pharmacy tech, and I often compared notes about the best places to get food and this was his tip. The fact that I had the freedom to choose my own meal – something denied to many prisoners – was something I did not take for granted. I placed my order and began to scroll through social media absent-mindedly while it was being prepared. The man behind the counter told me my meal was ready.

'How much?' I asked.

'It's on the house,' he replied.

'I don't understand,' I said, shaking my head.

'I'm not going to take your money,' he replied.

Then I recognized him – it was Mr E, the South Asian gentleman I had met in Segregation during Ramadan. He must have been released and found a job. Good for him.

We nodded at each other awkwardly and I left with my burger and fries.

I was informed second or third hand – through the healthcare rumour mill – that a consortium of external GPs wanted to take over the offender healthcare contract from the NHS Trust. The staff anxiety went into overdrive because 'someone had heard from someone' that the consortium was looking to replace all the staff, including me, with their own doctors and nurses. This was my work family – we had pulled together through so many victories, near misses and disasters. I couldn't lose them.

I was asked to meet with the consortium GPs and answer any questions they might have about offender healthcare. I felt acutely the paradox that by helping the new doctors settle in I was possibly making myself redundant. But it wasn't in my nature to do anything other than my best. My own training had been disorganized. I had more or less turned up, rolled up my sleeves and got on with it. I wanted a smoother transition for my new colleagues. Whatever my misgivings, I had to ensure they were safe, and that my patients were safe too.

I went to their community GP practice to meet them before they came to the prison. I was hardly the poster boy for a working life behind bars. My skin was sallow. I usually kept my hair short but over the past year I'd neglected it; it hung down well below my ears. Despite my appearance, all three of the doctors seemed enthusiastic if not a little apprehensive, which was only to be expected. I used the words 'interesting' and 'challenging' a lot. Working in a prison is not an act of altruism or tourism. It is hard graft and it can be dangerous physically and psychologically. I felt obliged to give them some sense of that.

I created a welcome pack and talked them through de-escalation techniques when confronted by hostile and aggressive patients. I provided them with handouts on heroin and alcohol management, which was not something community GPs dealt with because the Community Drug Team normally handled it. I explained how the Reception process worked and the various services we had in offender healthcare such as the In-reach mental-health team and IDTS drug team, the roles of Listeners, Insiders and chaplaincy. I talked them through the ACCT process and also mentioned some prison terms I had learned, such as 'prison pocket', 'plugging', 'spooning', 'sugar-water', 'cutting up', 'dirty protests', 'Canteen', 'black-eye Fridays'. I said they were welcome to sit in on my clinics to start with until they felt comfortable seeing patients on their own. I would ensure they had fifteen-minute appointment slots to start with so they didn't feel overwhelmed. They could come to me if they had any questions.

Dr S was a septuagenarian GP of Sikh heritage who

was born in Iran and trained in India. When I first met him he was sporting a bright yellow turban that matched his Daffy Duck tie. He had many passions, one of which was that he was an accredited gemologist who could identify, grade and appraise gemstones. When we were seated around the table he pointed at the jade necklace one of the other GPs was wearing and remarked on its excellent quality.

Dr W, the bearer of the jade necklace, had been gifted the necklace by close friends on a visit to Hong Kong. She had the straight back and good posture of a keen sportsperson, although she said her lacrosse days were long behind her. She and her wife preferred whiskey and gardening now. Her questions were particularly insightful. She was worried that seeming 'posh' to the prisoners might be a barrier to them trusting her. I directed her towards resources on vice slang.

Dr C didn't say much at first and had a habit of widening his eyes and raising his eyebrows when he was actively listening. Dr C was the lead in the Clinical Commissioning Group for his practice. This meant he had learned a lot about organizing and funding services. I thought he would be a great asset to us in the prison. I thought they all would be. If they did replace me once they found their feet, the prison would be in safe hands.

'How do you feel about working in the prison?' I asked Dr C.

'I feel quite excited. I like the sense of not knowing what's coming, the sense of expectation. It's going to be out of the ordinary,' he replied.

It was a good answer.

When they arrived at the prison I met them at the gate so they weren't made to feel unwanted – as I had on my first day here. I walked Dr C around the site. I took him to the Inpatient unit and Seg and introduced him to the staff. Later he shadowed me as I did my clinic.

'What are your first impressions?' I asked him when we were out of earshot of the others.

'The smell. The Inpatient unit smells awful. With a hospital you expect it to smell really nice and clean. It smells not of death but definitely like decay. And it's so noisy here. There is a constant banging of doors and jangling of keys, people screaming and shouting,' Dr C observed.

'You get used to it.'

'Overall it's not what I was expecting from offender healthcare,' Dr C said. 'It's chaotic. None of the patients arrive at their appointments on time and only half the people turn up. Outside, if a patient is five minutes late for their appointment, it's cancelled. Once you get over that and you've seen a couple of patients I suppose you could be anywhere. You've gone through a few things which have been helpful. However, the introduction has been ad hoc. I thought there would be a proper induction with patient cases.'

I resisted the temptation to say I'd had to find my own feet from the first week. I'd had little security training, conflict resolution training or even 'breakaway training', which was supposedly mandatory and demonstrated what to do if a prisoner tried to take you hostage. I'd been dropped in at the deep end and had been paddling away furiously ever since. But I couldn't argue with him because he was right. I hadn't felt prepared by my own induction process but, with a lack of time and resources, I wasn't able to offer too much more.

The new doctors took it in turns to sit behind me when I did my clinics. In between seeing patients they asked questions. I found it an intimidating process. I tried not to feel apprehensive when they took notes. They were all significantly more experienced as GPs than I was. Dr S had been a GP for longer than I had been alive. The expert manner in which they pinpointed the issues felt uncomfortably like I was being interrogated in the dock at the coroner's court at times – which was particularly true in Dr S's case because, amongst his various talents, he was also a trained barrister.

I wondered if the rumours were true and that I would be sidelined and then out on my ear. Most of all, I didn't want them to think I was practising poor medicine. I had tried to make changes, but it was difficult when we were always grossly understaffed and it was almost impossible to finish the day's work on time. They weren't excuses, they were realities. My colleagues and I were doing the best we could in very difficult circumstances. But having the new doctors on site was helping me to see things with fresh eyes. I could better pick out the flaws in how things were done. I could see that once we were fully staffed we could avoid firefighting and organize the healthcare department more efficiently.

★

On a morning that Dr C was shadowing me none of my patients arrived until over an hour into the clinic. Instead, I worked through the duty doctor tasks and dealt with queries from the nurses. I was hoping for interesting cases to discuss with Dr C. I wanted to show how interesting and diverse offender healthcare could be, because there are so many complex scenarios: haemophiliacs who were injecting drugs, unusual psychiatric diagnoses, new drugs and terminology we had never heard of.

Then my first three patients arrived at the same time. The first man was a forty-year-old bodybuilder who 'on the out' went to the gym every day. He told me he had a bad back and wanted a sick note. I explained a sick note would mean he was exempted from work and would also be unable to attend the prison gym – they were the rules for sick notes. He began to argue and said no power on earth could keep him from the gym. I believed him. He wanted me to request extra portions of protein for him from the Canteen, but there was no medical rationale for this. He snorted with irritation.

'This is ridiculous. It's like a game of snakes and ladders. You find a reason not to give me what I want. Just because I'm in prison doesn't mean I should get lesser care. It should be the same in here as it is out there,' he said with a raised voice, gesturing towards the huge white wall.

I understood his irritation and sympathized with him. 'I'm sorry.'

'What good is your being sorry to me? I don't even know why they have healthcare in prisons if you're not going to help people,' he snapped.

'If I prescribe you extra portions of protein the kitchens will veto it. If I could help you, I would. I'm not going to lie to you just to get you out of my room. I don't want to give you false hope,' I said with some irritation seeping into my voice.

A silence settled between us. Learning from my time in the coroner's court I let the silence linger. Finally he stood up and offered his hand for me to shake.

'I respect you,' he said unexpectedly and left the room.

The second patient was a VP who had arrived recently. She stated she was a transgender woman and wished to be referred to as Joanne. Joanne wanted to wear female clothing and didn't think she should be in a male prison because she was taking female hormones and in the process of transitioning. We had two other transgender women in the prison and three people who identified as gender-fluid. Being transgender was a protected characteristic under the 2010 Equality Act. We had a duty to protect them from prejudice and bullying. The decision about where transgender men and women were located, in either male or female prisons, was made by the HM Prison and Probation Service Complex Case Board. I said I would contact Joanne's community GP for details of her medications so there would be no break in her treatment. In the meantime the prison would initiate the case review process. The prison would provide Joanne with a Canteen sheet appropriate for females so she could order clothing and make-up, should she wish, in due course. She adjusted her wig and asked how she looked. I smiled politely. I wished her well – some of the prisoners could be very hostile to transgender women in male prisons. She would need to be safeguarded from assault – I would discuss her at the GP MDT so that all staff were aware of her.

The third patient was angry and wanted to have an argument with me. He was rude and demanding and the situation could easily have tipped over into violence. I sat quietly and used the de-escalation techniques I had already briefed Dr C about.

'I'd advise you speak to the senior officer, the SO, on your wing. He might be able to help you,' I said finally.

'He told me to come and see you,' the prisoner said with exasperation.

'I'm sorry, I can't ask the officers to leave your cell door open because you suffer from claustrophobia,' I replied.

'Your name is Dr Y. That probably stands for "Why Are You Even A Doctor" cos you're fucking useless. Who do you think you are anyway? You're just a fucking doctor. Do you know what I do? I rob drug dens. I have a heat gun and find houses that are hot for growing cannabis. I break in and throw acid in the faces of everyone I find. I blind 'em. Then I rob 'em. I make twenty or thirty thousand pounds a week. I could buy you ten times over!' he shouted.

I was shocked for a moment.

'Yes, but you're in prison,' I quietly pointed out.

'That doesn't matter! I've sent my money to Spain. My partner and kids are out there. In five years, I'll be living a luxury lifestyle and you'll still be sitting here in this shithole. You need to question your life choices, mate!' He banged his hand on the desk like a physical exclamation mark.

He stormed out and slammed the door.

'Tricky customer,' Dr C observed thoughtfully.

The slow drip of patients became a flood. Ten arrived at the same time. It was a blur of back pain, nerve pain, pins and needles. Low mood, poor sleep. There were also the usual requests for zopiclone, codeine, diazepam, pregabalin, mirtazapine and other sedating medications.

Since the coroner's court I was particularly careful to safety-net each patient. I always asked about their mood and highlighted the help that was available to them if they wanted to speak to someone. Prisons are stressful environments. Underfunding has vastly increased the pressures on staff and prisoners. This is hell for all of us. It seems like a marginal difference that staff can leave at the end of the day.

In between patients my colleagues appeared at my door. We talked about the horrendous coroner's court, which still hung over us all months after it had concluded, and they asked how I was.

'Living the dream,' I replied. I didn't want to say too much in front of Dr C in case it put him off.

'Coroner's court?' Dr C asked when they'd left.

Dr C hadn't been to coroner's court before. Working in prisons made it almost inevitable that he would. I gave him a brief description of the case and how it had been presented in court and a summary of my own testimony. He listened attentively. I explained how difficult I had found it. I didn't say how difficult I was still finding it.

★

During my lunch break, while Dr C went to see the Segregation unit with Chris and Brian, I sat in the car park with Graham and Marie. It was a beautifully sunny day. Maybe it was the Goth in me but I had a special skill in being able to populate any clear sky with heavy clouds.

'You look so tired, Dr Y,' Graham remarked. 'Me and Marie have been talking about taking you on holiday with us. We're going to go to the Amalfi coast. We'll drive through Italy and stop off at all the cities and towns, in honour of your father,' Graham said kindly.

Graham and Marie were my prison mum and dad, as I've said, and inevitably I'd told them about my real parents. I had explained that in the early sixties my father had worked for an Italian engineering firm in Karachi, Pakistan. He had moved to Italy in 1962. Italian food and culture were his first encounter with Europeans, and he'd developed an abiding admiration for pasta, cheese and Sophia Loren. Later he moved to England because his English was more fluent than his Italian. He and I had always planned to travel together to the places he had been to as a young man.

'I'd like that,' I said. 'And I'll have plenty of time on my hands if these new doctors take my job.'

Dr C joined me for my afternoon clinic. I asked him how the visit to the Segregation unit had been. He was still in shock and described the disgust of witnessing a dirty protest. He had never seen anything like it. He was also angry that so many people who were clearly mentally unwell were festering in prison. There weren't enough mental-health beds in the community,

I explained, although he already knew this – he later confided that his wife was a psychiatrist.

'If the NHS and Prison Service were people,' I said, 'they would have been described as the victims of actual bodily harm under Section 18 of the Offences Against the Persons Act. The politicians who perpetrated these assaults should serve life sentences.'

Dr C was not as chatty as Dr S and Dr W. They had both divulged a lot of information about themselves quite quickly, but Dr C was holding back. It was important to me to try to identify with people – to see similarities rather than differences. I noted Dr C had a London accent like my friend Matthew. He said 'noo' in one hard syllable rather than 'ne-yew'. They also shared blond hair and blue eyes. Dr C was taller than Matthew and me, and he walked as tall people often do – as if they are trying to kick off their shoes. I tried to visualize Matthew as I spoke to Dr C and I asked him if he wanted a cup of tea.

'I hate tea!' Dr C said with such vehemence that I found it comical. His anger at witnessing Seg was still palpable.

'Well, that was the final piece of the jigsaw. What sort of person hates tea? You're clearly a wrong 'un,' I replied, trying to make light of the situation.

There was a flash of a smile and then he laughed. We started talking. It was the easiest thing in the world – just two people chatting. Working in prisons had taught me to come straight to the point. I asked him if the rumours were true and the consortium he worked for was only going to employ its own doctors. He told me that my fears about being replaced were baseless. I relaxed and confessed what I really thought about working in the prison – how it was both the most exhilarating thing I'd ever done, and the most exhausting. But it was the anxiety of running from one catastrophe to another which threatened to spill over. I felt burdened by a pervasive sense that something bad was going to happen – I was always on high alert.

'I think there's a level of anxiety that comes with our line of work,' Dr C said. 'You have to talk yourself out of that. All those thoughts, when they come in, you have to deal with them. Otherwise, it's easy to become overwhelmed. Anxiety is often faceless, isn't it? It's more of a self-generated feeling. Once you face the specific anxiety it's dispelled. The more you avoid it, the more anxious you get. So, you have to challenge yourself by saying you've been in a similar tough situation before and you've managed to cope. If you survived that you can survive anything.'

I recalled Dr Emily had survived being locked in a cell with a murderer. And I had survived my father's sudden death, medical finals, the coroner's court. I had been working in prisons for just over a year and I had survived that too. No – I had flourished. I had no reason to feel such crushing self-doubt. Immediately I started to feel a little better.

Dr C was keen to work in the prison to help people who really needed it. He thought he might also like to work in a homeless practice. He, like me, had always felt an affinity for people who were marginalized and didn't have a voice in society for whatever reason, whether it was drugs or their background.

'Increasingly I've become convinced that as doctors

we can make things happen. Some people will bang on doors and still be ignored. More often than not, they'll open for us. The problem for people who are poor is not actually poverty, it's powerlessness and voicelessness,' Dr C said, and I agreed with him. I explained how I had played a small part in helping Jamie Lovell to express himself over the past year. During the afternoon session Dr C and I went to see him.

There was a time when I'd been afraid of Jamie. We were constantly at loggerheads. He was what GPs sometimes describe as a 'heart sink' patient who will not let you help them. With a lot of work from various agencies, especially the Shannon Trust charity, he had learned to read and write. Now he was a health champion and worked with Chris. He assisted the new prisoners with their literacy skills. The change in him over twelve months had been remarkable and inspiring – another victory. The officer unlocked the door and we asked permission to enter his cell. Jamie greeted us with a smile.

'I'm glad you've come to see me. I was writing you a letter, Dr Y. I wanted to say goodbye,' Jamie said. 'I'm out in two weeks' time. They're sorting out my accommodation. I've got something for you. I know you can't accept gifts, but this is different.'

Jamie handed me some poems he had written. I read them and smiled at the depth of the emotion and the clever rhymes. He refused to take them back.

'I want you to have this to remember me by,' Jamie said. 'I don't want you to think of me as that person you first met. I always thought I was stupid. It was just another thing to be ashamed of. But then I learned to read, and to write poetry, and I've discovered feelings I didn't know I had. There was all of this stuff inside of me that I was carrying around and it was weighing me down and when I wrote it down it disappeared. When I write a line I'm happy with it's better than doing coke. My writing gives me a lot of pride and enjoyment. You and the other staff kept encouraging me to write and I thought, what are they on about, but I get it now. Thank you.'

We smiled at each other.

'Are you still writing?' Jamie added.

'Sometimes I write short stories and longer things, nothing anyone would want to read,' I replied.

'I'd like to read what you write,' said Jamie.

It would have been unkind to mock his sincerity. So, rather than laugh at myself, I thanked him. His poems were very good, I told him. I said he should try to get them published, that I would love to read them in a book one day.

'When I publish my book I'll send you a signed copy,' Jamie said.

'That will be a good day,' I replied and shook his hand. We both knew we were unlikely to meet again unless he came back to prison. Neither of us wanted that.

'That's the sort of change I want to be part of,' Jonathan said as we walked away.

Epilogue: Truth is Stranger than Fiction

I read Jamie's poems repeatedly. I was captivated by his ability to write about prison life and weave a tapestry of gold from the razor wire that surrounded us. The words leapt off the page and demanded to be read with a sense of urgency. I couldn't ignore Jamie Lovell, neither when he was looming over me threateningly, nor now when he revealed his soulfulness in poetry. He inspired me to want to start writing again. I applied for a flash-fiction masterclass in London, to hone my short-story writing skills. Very short stories, in fact, but still offering plot and character development. I enjoyed this kind of writing. It was like a vignette – with its own ideas, concerns and expectations. Offender healthcare had taught me the value of freedom and having choices. I was choosing once again to do something I loved.

It was too late to book a cheap train ticket to London, so I drove down. I anticipated it would take two hours to reach Clerkenwell from Birmingham. I left early so I would have time to browse bookshops, have a coffee, and walk around without any walls or locked gates to worry about. I cursed my luck that the traffic on the M1 was unexpectedly heavy. There were extensive roadworks. I thought about turning around and heading home but I persisted. It took almost four hours to reach London.

'I'm sorry, I'm twenty minutes late,' I said as I signed in at the back of the seminar room.

'Don't worry, our speaker was late too, her train from Birmingham broke down. She had to take a replacement bus service,' the organizer said. She handed me a name badge. I almost wrote Dr Y out of habit, as if it was one of the many prescriptions I signed daily. I smiled to myself and wrote Shahed.

Some of the attendees turned to look at me as I walked in. They were irritated by the disruption I had caused. They were all much older than I was and looked rather well-to-do, a bit posh, as I imagined my patients thought I did when I first started working in the prison. A year ago, I'd been sheepish, apologetic, scared of offending people. Now I was a different person – I held their gaze and they looked away quickly. Offender healthcare had helped me to find new reserves of strength and compassion. I was hardened but not cynical. I replayed my mantra in my head; if I can survive prison for a year I can survive anything, including a room full of mildly disgruntled writers.

The award-winning writer Kit de Waal was leading the event. I knew her by reputation and had read a lot of her work. I had loved her novel *My Name is Leon* in which she had created a world as seen through the eyes of a boy whose family has been split up. This wasn't an act of ventriloquism – she seemed to inhabit her characters and that was awe-inspiring for me. What I hadn't expected was her deep Brummie accent and a penchant for swearing. Good-natured warmth seemed to wrap around her like the chunky cardigan she was wearing. She reminded me of my friends who worked in the prison. I was surprised to learn she was from the same part of Birmingham as me. When she spoke I felt as if we were walking through our streets together.

We all had a chance to write and then read out our pieces. Mine wasn't particularly good; I was out of practice. It was sinister and comical, like a clown with a bloody nose instead of an amusing painted one. At the coffee break Kit was surrounded by writers. Would she read their work in progress? Could she recommend them to her literary agent? They reminded me of the prisoners on D Block when they surrounded me and demanded to have their methadone doses increased. It was the same desperation but here it was expensively clothed in cashmere. Kit was polite but forthright – just like I was with my patients. But still they trailed after her.

I stayed in my chair and doodled a stethoscope that coiled into a heart and then a hissing snake. I was thinking about my time in the prison. The role of a doctor involves asking questions and providing answers. We are rarely candid about our own feelings or opinions. In a prison setting in particular, we are advised against giving prisoners any personal information in case they try to compromise or 'groom' us. It means that in offender healthcare a doctor is seen as a detached being who may or may not seem to care. We wear our doctor's face like a mask to hide any personal feelings and try to remain outwardly calm and reassuring. We are expected to be cerebral and dispassionate beings who can withstand huge pressures while remaining unscathed. This belief promotes resilience at the expense of our vulnerability and deprives us of our humanity. Prisoners, by the nature of their offence, can be stigmatized and also denied their sense of self. In order to care, and make meaningful changes, we need to see each other as people first and foremost, with all our strengths and weakness.

During the second session Kit used visual cues to prompt short stories. She asked if anyone recognized the famous black-and-white film from a clip she played. There was a resounding silence that surprised me. I lived in a bubble, behind locked doors and high walls, and even I knew this film – I put my hand up to name *Brief Encounter*. She said it was one of her favourites. She also talked about her love of malted milk biscuits and tea. I needed no further proof that she was a good person.

At the end of the session, she was again surrounded by people who wanted advice and guidance. They were overly courteous and complimentary – just like the VPs. I shivered as the VP clinic flashed into my mind, with its small mound of forbidden sweets and stained windows. I wondered how Mikey was doing. Had his split lip healed well? Would he, like Persephone, be marked by his descent into the underworld? I thanked the organizers and made to leave. That was another symptom of offender healthcare – itchy feet. Needing to be close to a door I could bolt out of if I felt uncomfortable. Then I overheard that they were urgently trying to arrange transport for Kit. Her train back to

Birmingham had been cancelled and there were no others.

'I'm driving back to Birmingham. I can give you a lift if you want?' I offered.

I didn't expect Kit would accept. With the roadworks on the motorway it was likely to be an interminable journey. I hated long car journeys. I would need to play music really loud to stay awake. I wouldn't be good company.

Kit looked me up and down to see if I could be trusted. I could have told her that most psychopaths are able to mimic superficial charm. First impressions are useless. Having worked with the VPs, I could have advised her against getting into a car with a stranger – even if I knew I could of course be trusted. I immediately chastised myself for being sarcastic. There was plenty of goodness in this world if you looked for it.

'I live in Birmingham. I can drop you wherever you need to go. It's no bother,' I said, softening my tone and attempting a smile.

'Great, thank you,' she said.

I could tell she was still unsure if I was a potential criminal. Maybe she could smell the prison on me. But she was weary and wanted to get home.

'So, what are you writing at the moment?' she asked me, twenty minutes into our journey.

'I've been working on a novel for years. It's set in the UK and South Asia. It has time travel and jinns, magic, that sort of thing,' I said.

'Hmm,' Kit replied, clearly unimpressed with my endeavours.

I took a moment to reassess them myself. I let the silence sit between us.

'What do you do, job-wise?' Kit asked a few minutes later.

'I'm a doctor, a GP,' I said.

'Oh, that's interesting. I don't suppose you know any prison doctors?'

I turned to her. I felt as if I had been shanked in the side with a sharp object. She drew back, perhaps thinking prison was my trigger word for turning into a monster. She had her hand in her coat pocket, possibly clutching her keys like a weapon or holding a small bottle of pepper spray. I didn't say anything for a few moments, and then I cleared my throat.

'I work in offender healthcare – I'm a prison GP,' I said.

She shook her head in disbelief.

'I'm working on something about a prison doctor,' Kit said. 'Maybe you would have some insights? It's about this prisoner who's illiterate and violent. He develops a bond with a doctor who loves literature. The doctor's a shy, introverted sort of person to start with, but he teaches the prisoner to read. They both grow from their unlikely bond.'

I was silent for a long while and then I blurted out everything. What were the chances of Kit and I meeting like this? I decided to come to London on a whim and her train had broken down. She was looking for a prison doctor and I offered to drive her home. It would seem like an improbable coincidence if it hadn't actually happened. During the three hours it took to drive back to Birmingham I told her my story and it was immensely cathartic. She listened at times with her hand over her mouth.

'It's shocking and electrifying and full of the most amazing anecdotes. It's unforgettable. You must write your account as a book,' Kit enthused.

'No one would believe it. Even I don't believe some of what I've witnessed,' I said.

'Leave that to the reader,' Kit replied.

References

Introduction

1 I was at medical school ... the inverse care law: https://www.thelancet.com/journals/lancet/article/ PIIS0140-6736(71)92410-X/fulltext

1 I was at medical school ... the least likely to receive it: https://www.researchgate.net/publication/279747864_ Inequalities_in_Health_The_Black_Report

2 Many have substance-misuse issues ... 'snowballing' or 'speedballing': https://www.drugabuse.gov/publications/ drugfacts/heroin

3 Long-term studies ... treatment works: https://pubmed. ncbi.nlm.nih.gov/26042569

3 Long-term studies ... stabilized on opioid substitution therapies: https://www.gov.uk/government/publications/ summary-of-key-findings-from-the-drug-treatment- outcomes-research-study-dtors

3 Our service works ... Terrence Higgins Trust: https:// swishservices.co.uk/sex-workers-service

3 They also work ... human trafficking: https://www. yorsexualhealth.org.uk/information-for-sex-workers

4 The homeless practice ... Special Allocation Scheme: https://www.bma.org.uk/advice-and-support/gp- practices/managing-your-practice-list/

removing-violent-patients-and-the-special-allocation-scheme

4   I didn't know . . . and GP services: https://www.rcgp.
    org.uk/clinical-and-research/resources/a-to-z-clinical-
    resources/prison-health.aspx

5   Over the past ten years . . . the 120 mark: https://data.
    justice.gov.uk/prisons

5   That's over 88,000 men . . . a variety of prisons: https://
    commonslibrary.parliament.uk/research-briefings/
    sn04334

5   Prisons in the UK . . . within a few months: https://prison
    jobs.blog.gov.uk/your-a-d-guide-on-prison-categories

5   Remand prisons . . . have been sentenced: https://www.
    gov.uk/charged-crime/remand

5   Deprivation of liberty . . . on our well-being: https://
    www.nature.com/articles/s41598-020-75026-4

6   During lockdown . . . twenty-four hours a day: https://
    www.bbc.co.uk/news/uk-55957048

6   There has been limited time . . . contact loved ones:
    https://www.gov.uk/guidance/coronavirus-covid-19-
    and-prisons

6   The impact of this . . . years to come: https://www.bmj.
    com/content/374/bmj.n2016

7   Her Majesty's Prison and Probation Service . . . by the
    courts: https://www.gov.uk/government/organisations/
    her-majestys-prison-and-probation-service

7   The justice secretary . . . responsibility: https://www.gov.
    uk/government/ministers/secretary-of-state-for-justice

7   When Liz Truss . . . 'serious and sustained pressure':
    https://www.bbc.co.uk/news/uk-38596034

7   The prison population . . . past thirty years: https://
    assets.publishing.service.gov.uk/government/uploads/
    system/uploads/attachment_data/file/541667/prison-
    population-story-1993-2016.pdf

7   Scotland, England and Wales . . . prison system in
    decades: https://www.ft.com/content/462c4a0e-e3cd-
    11e6-9645-c9357a75844a

7 Many people . . . think prisons are 'too soft': https://
www.thetimes.co.uk/article/most-people-think-prison-
system-is-too-soft-q36l3tz90

7 When he was justice secretary . . . like holiday camps:
https://www.dailymail.co.uk/news/article-2205824/Ill-
stop-jails-like-holiday-camps-says-new-minister-justice.
html

8 However, if you systematically brutalize people . . .
rehabilitate them: https://assets.publishing.service.gov.uk/
government/uploads/system/uploads/attachment_data/
file/737956/understanding-prison-violence.pdf

8 Prisons are a breeding ground . . . suicide and murder:
https://www.unodc.org/unodc/en/frontpage/towards-
more-humane-prison-systems.html

8 The prison population . . . designed for one: https://
metro.co.uk/2017/06/19/sharing-cells-open-showers-and-
masturbation-what-privacy-in-prison-is-really-like-6647837

8 The risk assessment . . . healthcare workers: https://
www.justice.gov.uk/downloads/offenders/psipso/psi-
2015/PSI_20_2015_Cell_sharing.pdf

8 Zahid Mubarek . . . in March 2000: https://thezmt.org

8 A delayed public inquiry . . . eighty-eight recommendations: https://assets.publishing.service.gov.uk/government/
uploads/system/uploads/attachment_data/file/231789/
1082.pdf

8 It costs the taxpayer . . . per prisoner: https://www.
statista.com/statistics/1202172/cost-per-prisoner-england-
and-wales

9 But the reoffending rate . . . twelve months of release:
http://www.prisonreformtrust.org.uk/Portals/0/Docu
ments/Bromley%20Briefings/Prison%20the%20facts%20
Summer%202019.pdf

9 The economic and social cost . . . £15 billion a year:
https://www.gov.uk/government/speeches/prison-reform

9 By comparison . . . just over £5 billion: https://www.
statista.com/statistics/298654/united-kingdom-uk-
public-sector-expenditure-prisons

9 Despite sending more people . . . every year since 2013: https://www.statista.com/statistics/283069/crimes-in-england-and-wales

9 We could compare . . . in the long run: https://www.economist.com/international/2017/05/27/too-many-prisons-make-bad-people-worse-there-is-a-better-way?fsrc=scn%2Ftw%2Fte%2Fbl%2Fed%2Fprisonstoomanyprisonsmakebadpeopleworsethereisabetterway

9 Building more prisons . . . short-sighted solutions: https://www.bbc.co.uk/news/uk-49309112

9 We should review . . . sensibly and safely: http://www.prisonreformtrust.org.uk/Portals/0/Documents/Bromley%20Briefings/Prison%20the%20facts%20Summer%202019.pdf

9 Locking people behind their cell doors . . . likelihood of reoffending: https://www.gov.scot/publications/works-reduce-reoffending-summary-evidence/pages/3

9–10 There is worrying evidence . . . become prisoners themselves: https://www.nicco.org.uk/userfiles/downloads/5c90a6395f6d8-children-of-prisoners-full-report-web-version.pdf

10 The start of my career . . . prison budget by a quarter: https://www.independent.co.uk/news/uk/home-news/prisons-uk-jails-crisis-cuts-conservatives-david-gauke-phil-wheatley-a8318806.html

10 Over the course of five years . . . the full-time staff: https://www.theguardian.com/society/datablog/2016/nov/18/fewer-prison-officers-and-more-assaults-how-uk-prison-staffing-has-changed

10 Moreover, a policy known as 'benchmarking' . . . voluntary redundancy: https://www.theguardian.com/society/2014/aug/19/grayling-denies-prison-crisis-inmate-numbers

10 New prison officers . . . a predominant issue: https://www.nicco.org.uk/userfiles/downloads/5c90a6395f6d8-children-of-prisoners-full-report-web-version.pdf

10 **After discussions ... in 2016 and 2018:** https://www.independent.co.uk/news/uk/home-news/thousands-prison-officers-just-decided-go-strike-a7418016.html

10 **After discussions ... levels of violence:** https://www.ft.com/content/55faf4d0-b801-11e8-b3ef-799c8613f4a1

10 **The disputes ... in 2016:** https://www.theguardian.com/society/2016/apr/21/uk-junior-doctors-may-follow-april-strikes-indefinite-walkout

10 **Front-line staff ... action by policymakers:** https://www.thesun.co.uk/news/2189367/justice-secretary-liz-truss-slams-prison-officers-for-strike-action-that-halted-jo-cox-murder-trial-saying-it-will-only-make-jails-more-dangerous

10–11 **Black and ethnic minority men ... than white men:** https://assets.publishing.service.gov.uk/government/uploads/system/uploads/attachment_data/file/849200/statistics-on-race-and-the-cjs-2018.pdf

11 **Approximately 10 per cent ... go to court:** http://www.prisonreformtrust.org.uk/Portals/0/Documents/Bromley%20Briefings/Prison%20the%20facts%20Summer%202019.pdf

11 **Almost 70 per cent ... possessing drugs:** http://www.prisonreformtrust.org.uk/Portals/0/Documents/Bromley%20Briefings/Prison%20the%20facts%20Summer%202019.pdf

11 **Yet in 2009 ... alcohol and tobacco:** https://www.nature.com/articles/nm1209-1337.pdf?origin=ppub

11 **Indeed, approximately 40 per cent ... influence of alcohol:** https://www.alcoholrehabguide.org/alcohol/crimes

11 **In 2014 ... prison crisis:** https://www.bbc.co.uk/news/uk-27847007

11 **Another former Chief Inspector of Prisons ... 'complex organisations':** https://d3n8a8pro7vhmx.cloudfront.net/taxpayersalliance/pages/234/attachments/original/1427899116/the_failure_of_the_prison_service_in_the_uk.pdf?1427899116

12 The illiteracy rates . . . less than an eleven-year-old's:
https://www.theguardian.com/inequality/2017/jun/15/
reading-for-freedom-life-changing-scheme-dreamt-up-
by-prison-pen-pals-shannon-trust-action-for-equity-
award#:~:text=Inside%20the%20Shannon%20Trust,
well%20short%20of%20that%20mark

12 Chris Grayling . . . the writing community: https://
howardleague.org/news/booksforprisonerslegalaction

12 We know . . . literacy and numeracy: http://www.
prisonreformtrust.org.uk/Portals/0/Documents/Time_
to_LearnBook.pdf

12 The excellent Shannon Trust . . . no government
funding: https://www.theguardian.com/society/2016/jan/
05/jail-reading-scheme-letter-tom-shannon-trust

12 For example . . . further sex crimes: https://www.daily
mail.co.uk/news/article-4635876/Scandal-100million-
sex-crime-cure-hubs.html

12 What does cut reoffending rates . . . employment and
stable accommodation: https://premieradvisory.co.uk/
education-housing-and-employment-three-key-factors-
for-reducing-reoffending

Chapter 1

17 This quick turnover . . . there have been eight: https://
www.gov.uk/government/ministers/secretary-of-state-
for-justice

20 Many of the prisoners . . . are very unwell: https://
www.nhs.uk/mental-health/social-care-and-your-
rights/mental-health-and-the-law/mental-health-act

20 They're awaiting beds . . . surge in requirements: https://
www.independent.co.uk/news/health/mental-health-
nhs-hospital-beds-shortage-depression-a9185581.html

27 Their criminal records . . . a username or password for:
https://www.justice.gov.uk/downloads/offenders/psipso/
psi-2014/psi-23-2014-prison-nomis.pdf

32 Senior officers . . . the outside hospital: https://www.
    theguardian.com/society/2018/oct/27/prisoners-dying-
    poor-care-services-prisons-mental-health-care-quality-
    commission-report

33 The patient . . . a hospital bed: https://www.justice.
    gov.uk/downloads/offenders/psipso/psi-2015/psi-33-
    2015-external-prisoner-movement.pdf

33 But the officers . . . fourth emergency service: https://
    forensicpsychologyuk.com/the-forgotten-service-%E2%
    80%93-how-do-prison-staff-cope

33 In the corner . . . high clinical standards: https://www.
    cqc.org.uk

Chapter 2

40 If he had been . . . to support him: https://www.appro
    priateadult.org.uk/information/what-is-an-appropriate-
    adult

40 'Anything . . . in evidence': https://www.gov.uk/arrested-
    your-rights

43 Mr R had to sit . . . a BOSS chair: http://news.bbc.co.
    uk/1/hi/magazine/7152744.stm

44 He was issued . . . a lighter: https://publichealthmatters.
    blog.gov.uk/2018/07/18/successfully-delivering-
    smokefree-prisons-across-england-and-wales

44 He was provided . . . if available: https://www.theguard-
    ian.com/uk/2006/mar/09/ukcrime.prisonsandprobation

44–5 To help soften . . . become Listeners: https://www.
    samaritans.org/how-we-can-help/prisons/listener-scheme

47 Mr R was assessed . . . first-night screening: https://
    www.justice.gov.uk/downloads/offenders/psipso/psi-
    2015/psi-07-2015-pi-06-2015-early-days-custody.pdf

48 The healthcare computer system . . . community GP
    systems: https://insidetime.org/prison-healthcare

52 It was in contravention . . . General Medical
    Council guidelines: https://www.gmc-uk.org/-/media/

documents/good-medical-practice---english-20200128_
pdf-51527435.pdf

54 'Code Blue' . . . illicit drug use: https://www.justice.
gov.uk/downloads/offenders/psipso/psi-2013/psi-03-
2013-medical-emergency-response-codes.doc

54 As soon as was possible . . . oxygen cylinder: https://
www.intersurgical.com/info/igel

55 'A flat line' . . . than I felt: https://patient.info/doctor/
defibrillation-and-cardioversion

56 It can be sprayed . . . appear normal: https://www.tele
graph.co.uk/news/2017/09/22/letters-sent-prison-
photocopied-amid-fears-soaked-drugs

56 Spice has many names . . . black mamba: https://cdn.
catch-22.org.uk/wp-content/uploads/2018/11/edited_
Catch22-Spice-and-NPS-A-Prison-Pracitioners-Guide-
1.pdf

56 And, although people . . . mind-altering effects: https://
www.thescottishsun.co.uk/news/1875688/hmp-grampian-
lags-getting-high-on-spice-like-fish-sedatives-in-their-
mail

56 One brand is called . . . comatose the user: https://
www.independent.co.uk/arts-entertainment/tv/news/
ross-kemp-spice-cannabis-vape-hmp-belmarsh-prison-
documentary-itv-a9276276.html

57 Deemed not fit . . . criminalized in 2016: https://www.
theguardian.com/cities/2019/oct/29/spice-so-called-
zombie-drug-uk-poorest-communities

Chapter 3

61 He had been prescribed . . . known side effect: https://
www.nhs.uk/mental-health/talking-therapies-medicine-
treatments/medicines-and-psychiatry/antidepressants/
side-effects

61–2 Before we could stop him . . . first offence: https://
www.sentencingcouncil.org.uk/outlines/assault

63 'The only good thing . . . the same crime': https://www.
cps.gov.uk/legal-guidance/joint-enterprise-charging-
decisions-principal-secondary-and-inchoate-liability

64 He was fluent in English . . . telephone translation
service: https://www.languageline.com/uk

64 Graham showed me . . . or IDTS: https://www.justice.
gov.uk/downloads/offenders/psipso/psi-2010/psi_2010_
45_IDTS.doc

65 The BNF . . . prescribed in the UK: https://www.bnf.org

66 it is something . . . to prescribe: https://bnf.nice.org.
uk/drug/pregabalin.html#indicationsAndDoses

70 The Assessment, Care in Custody . . . from harming
himself: https://www.gov.uk/government/publications/
the-assessment-care-in-custody-and-teamwork-process-
in-prison-findings-from-qualitative-research

76 'Now they have to . . . "at height"': https://www.man
chestereveningnews.co.uk/news/hostage-dramas-
barricades-stints-roof-16808273

78 Graham explained . . . in Mr Lovell's P-NOMIS: http://
www.prisonreformtrust.org.uk/ForPrisonersFamilies/Pris-
onerInformationPages/IncentivesandEarnedPrivileges

Chapter 4

80 The governor proclaimed . . . at 18 degrees: https://
www.hseni.gov.uk/articles/temperatures-workplace

81 'I got what is known . . . twelve-year tariff': https://
www.sentencingcouncil.org.uk/sentencing-and-the-
council/types-of-sentence/life-sentences

85 This is . . . system: https://practiceplusgroup.com/news/
patient-engagement-work-with-prisoners-is-highly-
commended-by-national-awards

86-7 'I'll contact . . . literacy charity': https://www.shan
nontrust.org.uk

87 The prison black market . . . Double Bubble: https://
latcharity.org.uk/resources/prison-rules-jargon

90 On the day I saw . . . workplace temperatures: https://
www.hse.gov.uk/temperature/index.htm

90 On the day I saw . . . housing temperatures: https://
www.unison.org.uk/content/uploads/2014/08/Toweb
Temperature-at-Work-Information-Sheet-Aug14-
update2.pdf

Chapter 5

99 This is seen . . . therapeutic relationship: https://www.
kingsfund.org.uk/projects/gp-inquiry/therapeutic-
relationship

101 The simple fact . . . basic schooling: https://www.the
guardian.com/inequality/2017/jun/15/reading-for-
freedom-life-changing-scheme-dreamt-up-by-prison-
pen-pals-shannon-trust-action-for-equity-award

102 The key . . . vent their emotions: https://www.racgp.
org.au/download/documents/AFP/2011/November/
201111sim.pdf

102 Difficult patients . . . difficult lives: https://ijmhs.
biomedcentral.com/articles/10.1186/s13033-020-00392-5

104 This appeared . . . inappropriate transfer: https://www.
prisonersfamilies.org/transfers

105 This was correct . . . could lead to death: https://
www.rcgp.org.uk/-/media/Files/Policy/2019/RCGP-
safer-prescribing-in-prisons-guidance-jan-2019.
ashx?la=en

105 I explained to him . . . epileptic seizures: https://www.
epilepsy.com/learn/professionals/diagnosis-treatment/
drugs-their-contribution-seizures/opioids-and-cns

112 Dean was correct . . . oculogyric crisis: https://n.
neurology.org/epearls/20200421

113 There was also a poster . . . Prochaska and DiClemente:
https://www.rcn.org.uk/clinical-topics/supporting-
behaviour-change/understanding-behaviour-change

114 Toni explained ... a number of compacts: https://www. justice.gov.uk/downloads/offenders/psipso/psi-2010/ psi_2010_28_custody_compacts_for_use_in_custody. doc#:~:text=The%20aim%20of%20the%20compact, respect%20between%20prisoners%20and%20staff

Chapter 6

122 She is nicknamed ... opioid overdoses: https://www. drugabuse.gov/publications/drugfacts/naloxone
123 Code Reds ... blood is involved: https://assets.pub lishing.service.gov.uk/government/uploads/system/ uploads/attachment_data/file/375853/DSO_Medical_ Emergency_Response_Codes.pdf
125 In 2011 alone ... a positive inferno: https://www.fia. uk.com/news/fire-safety-in-prisons.html
126 Officers ... noxious fumes: https://prisons.org.uk/ firesafety-hotels/psi-11-2015-fire-safety-prison.pdf
128 It was during a time ... opioid fentanyl: https://www. nationalcrimeagency.gov.uk/who-we-are/publications/ 7-recent-deaths-possibly-linked-to-fentanyl/file
132 He said he had explored ... high death rate: https:// www.bbc.co.uk/news/magazine-27203322

Chapter 7

156 'I read somewhere ... the death rate': https://www. qcc.cuny.edu/socialsciences/ppecorino/medical_ethics_ text/Chapter_3_Moral_Climate_of_Health_Care/ Reading-Death-Rate-Doctor-Strike.htm
158 His knuckles had receded ... boxer's fractures: https:// www.webmd.com/a-to-z-guides/boxers-fracture
162 Every detail ... rectal cancer: https://www.nice.org.uk/ guidance/ng151

Chapter 8

165 Fridays are Canteen day . . . the previous week: https://
www.doingtime.co.uk/how-prisons-work/how-do-
prisons-actually-work/canteen-and-money

Chapter 9

177 These are usually short stays . . . every fourteen days:
http://www.prisonreformtrust.org.uk/ForPrisoners
Families/PrisonerInformationPages/Segregation

177 There is a crisis . . . in the community: https://blogs.
bmj.com/bmj/2021/03/05/mental-health-beds-are-full-
leaving-patients-without-treatment-and-clinicians-with-
difficult-choices

177–8 The number of community . . . need for them:
https://www.theguardian.com/society/2021/jul/05/
number-of-nhs-mental-health-beds-down-by-25-since-
2010-analysis-shows

178 The United Nations called . . . banned in 2011: https://
news.un.org/en/story/2011/10/392012-solitary-
confinement-should-be-banned-most-cases-un-expert-
says

178 The psychological harm . . . well documented: http://
safealternativestosegregation.vera.org/wp-content/
uploads/2018/07/The-Psychological-Effects-of-
Solitary-Confinement-A-Systematic-Critique.pdf

178 The psychological harm . . . mental illness: https://www.
medicalnewstoday.com/articles/solitary-confinement-
effects#mental-health-effects

178 It lists . . . Segregation population: https://www.justice.
gov.uk/downloads/offenders/psipso/psi-17-2006.doc

178 The World Health Organization . . . Human Rights:
https://elearning.icrc.org/detention/en/story_content/
external_files/Principles%20of%20Medical%20Ethics%
20(1982).pdf

178 The World Health Organization . . . solitary confinement: https://www.euro.who.int/__data/assets/pdf_file/0009/99018/E90174.pdf

186 Many of them . . . becomes available: https://www.mind.org.uk/information-support/legal-rights/courts-and-mental-health/section-47

186 The officers informed me . . . the Troubles: http://news.bbc.co.uk/hi/english/static/northern_ireland/understanding/events/dirty_protest.stm

193 'He can give you . . . colouring books and crayons': https://www.uos.ac.uk/news/criminology-students-create-distraction-packs-prisoners-during-coronavirus-pandemic

195 This is compassionate . . . parole hearing: https://insidetime.org/executive-release

195 The psychiatrist reviewed him . . . personality disorder: https://www.nhs.uk/mental-health/conditions/antisocial-personality-disorder

195 The psychiatrist reviewed him . . . schizoaffective disorder: https://www.mind.org.uk/information-support/types-of-mental-health-problems/schizoaffective-disorder/about-schizoaffective-disorder

195–6 The next step . . . if he was released: https://www.gov.uk/government/publications/multi-agency-public-protection-arrangements-mappa-guidance

196 His rectal cancer marker . . . a promising sign: https://www.nhs.uk/conditions/cea-test/#:~:text=A%20carcinoembryonic%20antigen%20(CEA)%20test,antibodies%20to%20help%20fight%20them

Chapter 10

206 Staff in other prisons . . . convicted rapists: https://www.thesun.co.uk/news/1726529/nurse-sexually-assaulted-at-private-jail-holding-some-of-uks-worst-sex-offenders

208 **There had been ... as much as Mikey did:** https://
www.bbc.co.uk/news/uk-38931580

211 **Not long before ... physically sick:** https://www.science
direct.com/topics/medicine-and-dentistry/psychoneuro
immunology#:~:text=Psychoneuroimmunology%
20is%20the%20study%20of%20the%20interaction%20
between%20the%20mind,may%20impact%20the%20
immune%20system

218 **'I think once ... the VP wing':** https://metro.co.uk/
2018/04/30/sex-offenders-food-spiked-with-poo-urine-
and-pieces-of-metal-by-fellow-inmates-7510849

Chapter 11

221 **Imprisonment ... introduced in 2005:** http://www.
justice.gov.uk/downloads/legislation/bills-acts/legal-aid-
sentencing/ipp-factsheet.pdf

221 **They were intended ... a life sentence:** http://www.
prisonreformtrust.org.uk/WhatWeDo/Projectsresearch/
IPPsentences

221 **They had been abolished ... human rights violation:**
https://www.theguardian.com/law/2012/sep/18/
strasbourg-judges-indeterminate-sentences-unlawful

222 **'He cuts off ... toes and ears':** https://www.healthline.
com/health/autocannibalism

222 **'It's a psychiatric ... pica,' I said:** https://www.national
eatingdisorders.org/learn/by-eating-disorder/other/
pica#:~:text=Pica%20is%20an%20eating%20disorder,%
2C%20dirt%2C%20and%20paint%20chips.&text=
There%20are%20no%20laboratory%20tests,clinical%20
history%20of%20the%20patient

222 **'Just eating ... Rapunzel syndrome':** https://www.
health.com/condition/digestive-health/what-is-
rapunzel-syndrome

222 'Undigested material . . . a bezoar': https://www.mayo clinic.org/diseases-conditions/gastroparesis/expert-answers/bezoars/faq-20058050

229–30 He had been prescribed ... drug resistance: https://www.nhs.uk/conditions/antibiotics/antibiotic-antimicrobial-resistance

230 The psychiatrists . . . personality disorder: https://patient.info/doctor/emotionally-unstable-personality-disorder

241 All deaths in custody ... referred to the coroner: https://www.cps.gov.uk/sites/default/files/documents/publications/death_in_custody_guidance_2017.pdf

Chapter 12

245 The nurses . . . not uncommon: https://www.theguard ian.com/uk/2006/dec/27/ukcrime.prisonsandprobation

246 It's a national scandal ... in the UK: https://www.inquest.org.uk/deaths-in-prison

246–7 According to the Ministry of Justice . . . the rate in 2014: https://www.inquest.org.uk/safety-in-custody-jan2020

247 There's a mental-health crisis ... we can't ignore: https://www.thelancet.com/journals/lanpsy/article/PIIS2215-0366(17)30446-7/fulltext

247 Even if the death ... a contributing factor: https://www.theguardian.com/society/2016/may/09/number-of-prison-deaths-linked-to-legal-highs-rises-steeply

247 The coroner ... conduct inquests: https://www.cps.gov.uk/legal-guidance/coroners

249 'It is a professional obligation ... General Medical Council': https://www.gmc-uk.org/ethical-guidance/ethical-guidance-for-doctors/acting-as-a-witness/acting-as-a-witness-in-legal-proceedings

249 It examined ... between 2005 and 2009: https://www.bbc.co.uk/news/uk-england-stoke-staffordshire-50836324

251 The family . . . if they so wished: https://coronerscourts
     supportservice.org.uk/wp-content/uploads/2018/11/
     CCSS-EL_Inquest_Factsheet_Final29317221_3.pdf
252 If the inquest . . . known as a PFD: https://www.judi
     ciary.uk/related-offices-and-bodies/office-chief-coroner/
     https-www-judiciary-uk-subject-community-health-
     care-and-emergency-services-related-deaths

Chapter 13

268 Dr C was the lead . . . for his practice: https://www.
     england.nhs.uk/ccgs
272 The decision . . . Complex Case Board: https://assets.
     publishing.service.gov.uk/government/uploads/system/
     uploads/attachment_data/file/863610/transgender-pf.pdf
276 'If the NHS . . . Offences Against the Persons Act':
     https://www.cps.gov.uk/legal-guidance/offences-
     against-person-incorporating-charging-standard

Acknowledgements

I feel deep gratitude towards everyone I have met behind bars – staff and inmates. I continue to learn and grow from every encounter. I hope I help in whatever small way I can. There are incredible staff in offender healthcare and in the prison, who work in staggeringly difficult circumstances and do so while maintaining their sense of humour – however dark it is at times.

My family have given me unwavering love and support. Especially my wonderful parents Mohammed Yousaf and Bilqeas Begum and my sister Shahzadi Farrah Yousaf. I would also like to thank my agent Simon Trewin for the confidence boosts and the great people at Penguin Random House for their guidance, especially my wonderful editors Andrea Henry and Sharika Teelwah, and my eagle-eyed copy-editor Richard Mason. A big sweary thank you to Kit de Waal for all the work she does to support emerging voices – this book would not have been possible without you. Thank you to my Middle Way Mentoring writing family for helping me to find my writer's voice and to the Writing West Midlands Room 204 programme. My family and friends are my guiding lights who have illuminated my path with kindness, humour and hope. Ideally I would like to thank everyone who has ever held out a helping hand – if there are any notable omissions please forgive me in advance. I would like to thank the following:

Louise Abel, Melanie Abrahams, Lin Addy, Olusola Adeyemo, Amdad Ahmed, Shanaz and Riaz Hussain, Nicola Alfieri, Imran Arshad, Brian Atack, Victoria Baldwin, Neeta Bhadauria, Susmita Bhattacharya, Anees Bhayat, Antoinette Boucher, Kari Breecher, Helen Brookes, Gerard Browne, Gaynor Bryan, Michele Byrne, Jo Campbell, Nandani Campbell, Richard Canter, Yvonne Carter, Heather Catherwood, Karen Caves, Laura Ceaser-Kennedy, Mandy Chainey, Emma Chaplin, Mubeen Chaudhry, Mohammed Chothia, Purti Choudhary, Jo Clarke, Tracy Colbourne, Jonathan Coleman, Gilly Cooper, Emily Craven, Adam Cross, Raj Das, Sue Davies, Rich Day, Joyce Dormer, Simon Drakely, Patricia Duxbury, Dean Earl, Sadat Edroos, Dave Farmer, Adil Farraz, Ben Fletcher, Desiree Ford, Joy Francis, Simon Franks, Andy Galbraith, Steve Gilson, Susannah Goswell, Lorraine Hague, Charlie Halford, Sam Halls, Ros Hatfield, Caroline Hawche, Dave Hayward, Alice Heward, Deborah Hill, Ross James, Sarah M. Jasat, Rebecca Jayne, Amanda Jones, Kalbinder Kaur, Olivia Kimber, Asha Krishna, Laura Lane, Ian Langley, Kassia Lowe, Stephanie Lucas, Colin Macdougall, Mumtaz and Nawaz Malik, Stevie Marsden, Jill Matthews, Dennis Maxwell, Helen McCarthy, Victoria Mee, Saima Mir, Claire and Chris Morris,

Laurene Morris, Bonnie and Alan Murphy, Rich Nelson, Alex Ogilby, Ade Okunade, Steven Owen, Helen Pilbeam, Sharon Prescott, Adam Pritchard, Emma Pugh, Rachel Pullinger, Graham Reed, Lisa Riddell, Marie Robinson, Charlie Rogers, Nicola Ruth, Harcharan Sahni, Farhana Shaikh, Nadeem Sheikh, Anne-Marie Sherridan, Jass Sidhu, Surinder Singh, Tom Skelding, Gwyneth and Brian Sommerlad, Matthew Sommerlad, David Spademan, Christine Streeter, Holly Sutch, Yvonne Sutch, Ali Tarrant, Paul Taylor, Stephanie Taylor, Lisa Thompson, Kelly Tyrrell, Jo Unwin, Jignesh Vaidya, Nazira Vania, Avi Kaur Virdee, Claudia Walker, Rachael Walker, James Wall, Mateusz Waskiewicz, Robert Watkins, Caroline Watson, Katie Watson, Sean Watts, Tim Welsh, Garry Weston, Penny and Scott Wheeler, Nikki Whittingham, Shane Williams, John Willis, Emily Winters, Warren Wood, Sally Wright, Sophie Yeomans and Madonna Yousaf.

About the Author

Dr Shahed Yousaf is a GP who works in prisons and with the homeless community, with a focus on substance misuse. He was shortlisted for the Bath Flash Fiction Prize 2016 and commended for the Faber & Faber FAB Prize 2017. He won a place on the Writing West Midlands Room 204 Mentoring Scheme and the Middle Way Mentoring Project in 2019.